NASHVILLE DAY
Tennessee Centennial
SEPT 11ᵗʰ 1897

Nashville

A Pictorial History

Nashville

A PICTORIAL HISTORY

by George Rollie Adams
and
Ralph Jerry Christian

Design by
Jamie Backus Raynor
Donning Company/Publishers
Virginia Beach

Revised Edition 1988

The Donning Company/Publishers
5659 Virginia Beach Boulevard
Norfolk, Virginia 23502

Library of Congress Cataloging-in-Publication Data:

Adams, George Rollie
   Nashville.

   Includes index.
   1. Nashville—History. 2. Nashville—Description.
I. Christian, Ralph J., joint author. II. Title.
F444.N257A3   976.8′55   80-20196
ISBN 0-89865-013-5

T. V. Peticolas del

VIEW OF

to the memory of
Maggie Jones Adams
(1872-1965)
and to
Victoria Gabrys Christian

Contents

Foreword

History, as defined by many professional and lay historians, is the collected, analyzed, interpreted, and written memory of a people, whether local, regional, national, or international. In recent decades historians have often focused on national and international history to the exclusion of local history. However, in the last few years the bicentennial celebration of American Independence, the phenomenal national reaction to the writings of Alex Haley and Eliot Wigginton (of *Roots* and *Foxfire* fame), and the increased momentum and success of the historic preservation movement have stimulated interest across the land in the history of families, neighborhoods, communities, counties or parishes, and states. It is here that the American people can be seen in all of their great character and diversity. It is here, in our own historical backyards, that we can come to feel a sense of time, place and belonging.

The Donning Company has responded to this trend by publishing a "Portraits of American Cities" series, encompassing over twenty communities at this writing, of which this volume on Nashville is the most recent. The authors, George Rollie Adams and Ralph Jerry Christian, are superbly qualified for the task they undertook in assembling this excellent history of Nashville. Adams currently serves as director of the education division of the American Association for State and Local History, while Christian coordinates its National Historic Landmarks project.

As Nashville area residents, both bring an appreciation and understanding of the Nashville community and its development that is difficult for an outsider to sense and communicate. However, since they are not natives of Nashville or Tennessee, Adams and Christian also bring an important element of balance and perspective. Finally, the professional experiences of these two historians bring also a feeling for a national context that few writers can achieve.

Nashville: A Pictorial History should appeal to a broad audience even outside of Tennessee: local history enthusiasts, historic preservationists, Civil War buffs, architectural historians, country music lovers, and the hundreds of thousands of Americans who have Tennesseans and Nashvillians in their family trees. It should go without saying that all Nashville residents who want to better understand the past, present, and future of their hometown should make this book a must for their home libraries.

This volume will offer something new as well as much that is familiar to most, but all should be fascinated by the rich diversity of materials located by the authors in their quest to assemble a visual documentation of two centuries of a community that began as a "frontier crossroads" and became later both the "Athens of the South" and "Music City U.S.A."

And if this volume will stimulate readers to ransack their attics for letters, diaries, journals, postcards, prints, maps, and photographs about the history of this community or others, then the volume will have also served another great need.

James K. Huhta
Professor of History,
Middle Tennessee State University

Three interstate highways converge on downtown Nashville. This section of I-40 West, at the Fessler's Lane on-ramp, is one of the busiest in the city. More than 100,000 cars and trucks travel it each day.
Photograph by Jimmy Ellis; Courtesy of The Tennessean.

Nashville is an important crossroads. Every day automobiles and trucks carry people and goods through the city on interstate highways that converge from three directions. Barges loaded with coal and other commodities ply the Cumberland River between Middle Tennessee and the Ohio and Mississippi valleys. Freight and passenger trains rumble past on steel rails that connect the growing South with markets and factories in the North. And dozens of jet aircraft come and go from the Metropolitan Nashville Airport.

In one way or another, the Nashville area has been a crossroads for thousands of years. Prehistoric Indians ranged north from the Gulf coast to hunt in future Middle Tennessee as early as 8000 B.C. Later, others settled in the region, and some carried on trade in marine shells from the Gulf of Mexico and copper from near the Great Lakes. The last Indians to live here were the Shawnees. They migrated south from the Ohio River at the beginning of the historic age and remained until early in the eighteenth century, when Cherokees from East Tennessee and Chickasaws from West Tennessee came and forced them to leave. The Cherokees and Chickasaws did not live here, but their hunters returned periodically to kill game.

The first white men to pass through the area were French traders. Some traveled up the Mississippi Valley from Louisiana, while others journeyed south from Canada. About 1710 one of them, a man named Charleville, established a temporary trading post on salty Lick Branch near the Cumberland River, just north of what is now Nashville's downtown business district. Englishmen, who traded regularly with Overhill Cherokees east of the Cumberland plateau, ventured into Middle Tennessee from the Carolinas about this same time. The excursions of these Europeans were more than random wanderings by hardy frontiersmen. France and England had been vying for dominance in Europe, Asia, and North America since the mid 1600s, and their agents competed for both territory and the loyalty of Indian tribes throughout the Trans-Appalachian West. This rivalry culminated in the outbreak of the French and Indian War in 1754. When the war ended in 1763 France ceded

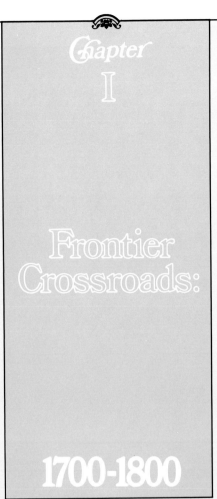

Chapter I

Frontier Crossroads:

1700-1800

Canada and the eastern portion of the Mississippi Valley, including Middle Tennessee, to Great Britain.

By this time backwoodsmen and adventurers from the Carolinas and Virginia had explored much of Middle Tennessee. As early as 1750 Thomas Walker of Virginia had crossed the mountains through the Cumberland Gap, which he discovered and named. Others followed. They were known as "long hunters" because they remained in the wilderness for months and even years at a time. Henry Scaggs penetrated into the vicinity of present metropolitan Nashville in 1763-65. Daniel Boone and Kasper Mansker came in 1770-71 as agents of Judge Richard Henderson, a North Carolina land speculator who in 1775 organized the ill-fated Transylvania Company to plant a proprietary colony in Kentucky. The colony survived, but Henderson lost control of it to Virginia, whose territorial claims extended from the Atlantic to the Mississippi.

Henderson's failure in Kentucky led to the founding of Nashville in territory claimed by North Carolina. Early in 1779 Henderson engaged James Robertson, who earlier had helped establish a settlement on the Watauga River in East Tennessee, to lead pioneer families to the French salt lick on the Cumberland River. After taking a small advance party to explore the site and to plant corn, Robertson returned to Watauga and divided the emigrants into two groups. In October he set out overland with the first party. Following hunters' paths and animal trails, they trudged three hundred miles through the wilderness before reaching the Cumberland in late December. They found the river frozen, and so settlers, horses, cattle, hogs, and sheep crossed on ice to the future site of Nashville.

Meanwhile John Donelson led the second Watauga party in a flotilla of thirty-three boats down the Holston River, down the Tennessee, up the Ohio, and up the Cumberland. They reached French Lick on April 24, 1780, after a journey of one thousand miles. Robertson's party had already begun felling trees and building cabins on the bluff overlooking the river. They had also named the site Nashborough after General Francis Nash of North Carolina.

Shawnees, Chickasaws, Cherokees, and other Indians once hunted buffalo, deer, bear, turkey, and other game where Nashville now stands.
Drawing from McGee,
A History of Tennessee.

The arrival of Donelson's party swelled the population to more than three hundred, most of whom were of Scotch-Irish descent. Some among this number settled beyond Robertson's site, and soon eight stations, or clusters of cabins, stood along the Cumberland. Because of their remoteness from established government, some 250 men of the settlements met on May 13, 1780, and signed the Cumberland Compact. Written by Henderson, who probably received help from Robertson and Donelson, this document formed the first civil government in Middle Tennessee.

If the Cumberland Compact enhanced the Nashborough settlers' sense of security, the effect was short-lived, for they had trekked westward almost in the middle of the American Revolution. Like many others who crossed the Appalachians in 1778-79, they thought that fighting had ended in the West, but it had not. In 1780 British agents used presents and oratory to inflame the Cherokees and other tribes against the "land-hungry rebels" once again. For the next two years Nashborough and other frontier settlements from Georgia to Canada stood on the brink of destruction. Indians threatened all the Cumberland stations. On January 15, 1781, Cherokees attacked Freeland's Station, at what is now 1400 Eighth Avenue North, and Rains' Station, a short distance north of the present state fairgrounds. Some of the surviving settlers fled to Kentucky. Others moved into Fort Nashborough and successfully defended it on April 2 in the Battle of the Bluff. When that fight ended, only seventy original settlers remained in Nashborough. How-

ever, under James Robertson's strong leadership, they hung on until the war ended in 1783.

The next year the North Carolina legislature created Davidson County and chartered the Nashborough settlement as the town of Nashville. The lawmakers also set aside a reserve of land for Revolutionary War veterans, opened the rest of Tennessee to settlers, and directed that two hundred acres in Nashville be surveyed into one-acre town lots and sold to buyers who promised to erect brick or stone houses at least sixteen feet square. In the years that followed, both Nashville and Tennessee grew steadily. Newcomers to Nashville included Thomas B. Craighead, a Presbyterian minister who arrived in 1785 to head Davidson Academy; Dr. John Sappington, who became the community's first physician that same year; Lardner Clark, who opened the city's first dry goods store on Market Street (Second Avenue) in 1786; John Overton, an attorney who arrived in 1789 and became a prominent lawmaker and judge; and Andrew Jackson, who came in 1788 and eventually represented Nashville and the nation in the White House.

In 1796 Tennessee became the sixteenth state in the Union. By this time Nashville was fast becoming a strategic point in overland travel to Natchez and the lower Mississippi. Thus the community remained a frontier crossroads, but one which by 1797, according to English traveler Francis Baily, was beginning to take on "a spirit of refinement."

"Long hunters," adventurers who stayed in the wilderness for months and years at a time, explored much of Middle Tennessee in the 1760s and 1770s. One of them, Thomas Sharpe Spencer, is shown cooking bear meat over an open fire. He spent the winter of 1778-79 in Sumner County near present Nashville.
Drawing from McGee,
A History of Tennessee.

James Robertson led the first white settlers to the future site of Nashville in 1779. Born in North Carolina in 1742, Robertson settled on the Watauga River in present East Tennessee in 1770. He soon became a respected political leader and skilled Indian negotiator, and in 1779 land speculator Richard Henderson selected him to lead settlers into what is now Middle Tennessee. The choice proved wise, for Robertson, more than any other person, kept Nashborough going during its difficult early years. He served as colonel of the militia, represented the community in the North Carolina Assembly, and acted as a trustee of Davidson Academy. Later he represented Davidson County in the Tennessee Constitutional Convention of 1796 and sat in the Tennessee Senate. In subsequent years Robertson was United States agent to the Chickasaw Indians in West Tennessee, where he died in 1814.
Engraving by E.G. Williams & Brothers;
From Wooldridge, History of Nashville.

This sketch map shows the routes that James Robertson and John Donelson followed to Middle Tennessee in 1779-80. Robertson and a party of men traveled overland with livestock, while Donelson and a group made up mostly of women and children traveled in flatboats along a water route. Because his boats were not completed on time, Donelson did not set out until mid-winter, and ice jams delayed him several weeks. Near the end of the journey spring floods proved troublesome. Robertson and his group had been at Nashborough about five months when the Donelson party finally arrived in April 1780.

Sketch map by George Rollie Adams.

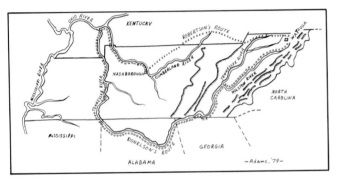

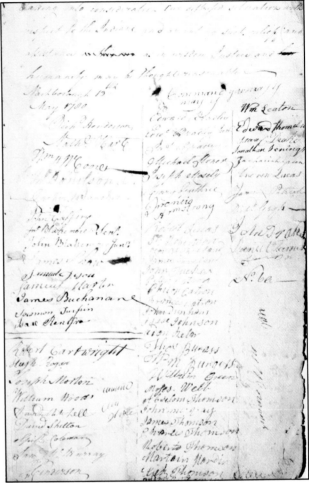

Because hundreds of miles separated them from established legal authority, Nashborough men gathered on May 13, 1780, and signed the Cumberland Compact, one page of which is shown here. It provided for a civil government to last until North Carolina could protect the settlers. One article of the compact contained the first known provision in the United States for recalling public officials. The original document is preserved in the Tennessee State Library and Archives.

Photograph courtesy of National Archives

Historians disagree about when Robertson's party reached the Cumberland, but the most popularly accepted date is December 25, 1779. This romanticized drawing, done years later by an unidentified artist, suggests the isolation that the first settlers probably felt, whatever the date.

Drawing courtesy of Tennessee State Library and Archives.

Indians menaced Nashborough often during its early years. On April 2, 1781, Cherokees attacked the fort and drew some of the defenders outside. Hand-to-hand fighting ensued in the Battle of the Bluff along what is now lower Broadway. Some of the Indians managed to get between the settlers and the stockade and threatened to storm it. At that moment someone inside the fort—legend credits Mrs. James Robertson—unleashed the settlers' dogs on the Indians, and in the confusion that followed, the attack was repulsed.

Drawing from McGee,
A History of Tennessee.

This house, situated off Old Buena Vista Pike north of downtown, is one of the oldest residences in metropolitan Nashville. Constructed sometime before 1797, it consists of a pair of two-story log cabins connected by an enclosed dogtrot or breezeway. Its builder, Frederick Stump, was one of the original Nashborough settlers and a signer of the Cumberland Compact.

Photograph courtesy of
Historical Commssion of Metropolitan
Nashville—Davidson County.

Fort Nashborough was built on the west bank of the Cumberland River in 1780. This sketch of the fort is based on a crude drawing by Andrew Castleman, who apparently lived there. According to his notes the stockade was 247 feet long by 123 feet wide, and the log cabins were about 15 feet square. James Robertson lived in a cabin near the center of the west (left) side. Today a replica of the fort stands along the river on First Avenue North between Church Street and Broadway.

Drawing by William Ziegler
and James Young;
courtesy of Fort Nashborough.

James Barton Longacre painted this portrait of Andrew Jackson during the presidential campaign of 1828. A frontier lawyer and dashing military hero, Jackson defeated incumbent John Quincy Adams and became the first president from west of the Appalachian Mountains. Few others knew Jackson's views on political issues, but most admired his reputation and forceful personality.
Photograph of painting courtesy of National Portrait Gallery, Smithsonian Institution.

During the first half of the nineteenth century, Nashville grew from a frontier crossroads into a western metropolis known throughout the nation. No one influenced this development more than Andrew Jackson. Almost from the moment he arrived in 1788 until he died in 1845, Jackson, who could behave like a Saturday-night roughneck or a polished gentleman, strode center stage while the city matured. First as a military hero and later as president of the United States, Jackson brought Nashville fame and gave the community far-reaching influence in national politics. To a large extent that fame and influence have endured to the present day.

The Nashville that greeted Jackson when he rode into town on October 26, 1788, was singularly unimpressive, consisting only of a courthouse, two taverns, a distillery, and a scattering of tents, cabins, and crude houses. The twenty-one-year-old Jackson, who brought with him little more than a limited understanding of the law and an appointment as prosecuting attorney, became a boarder in the home of John Donelson's widow. There he met and fell in love with the widow's daughter, Rachel, who was recently estranged from her husband, Lewis Robards. In 1791, believing Robards had obtained a divorce, Andrew and Rachel married. Two years later they discovered, to their horror, that no divorce had been granted. Although Jackson and his bride repeated their vows for a second time early in 1794, their marriage became grist for gossip which grew worse when he became a national figure.

Jackson's name is often associated with the period of American history, roughly 1820 to 1850, that some historians call the "Age of the Common Man." However, during his early career in Nashville, Jackson showed a decided bias toward wealthier citizens. And to a large extent he was their savior. At the time of his arrival the city's debtors had banded together, refusing to pay their debts and daring the authorities to act against them. Jackson responded to this crisis by obtaining writs against seventy of the delinquents. Shortly afterward, one irate debtor approached the young prosecutor on the street and stomped on his foot. Jackson, who was rarely outdone, calmly picked up a large stick and knocked

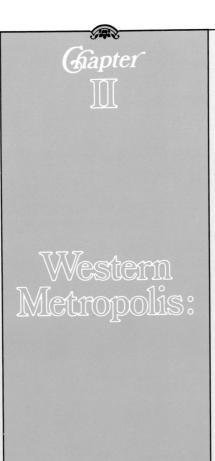

Chapter
II

Western
Metropolis:

1800-1845

his attacker out cold. Despite such shenanigans, or perhaps partly because of them, Jackson soon developed a flourishing law practice. For many years afterward he argued up to one-half of all the law cases heard in Davidson County. Often taking his fees in land grants, he rapidly became one of the city's wealthiest men, and despite local gossip, his marriage ties to the Donelson family gave him social prestige as well.

The law-and-order tactics of Jackson and others helped inspire confidence in Nashville's future and contributed to the city's early development. By 1802 the population had passed the thousand mark, and the town boasted a new market house on the Public Square at the north end of Market Street (Second Avenue). Businesses in the community now included several mercantile houses; a tannery; factories that made cotton gins, cloth, and nails; and small shops where coppersmiths, tinsmiths, cabinetmakers, shoemakers, tailors, blacksmiths, saddlers, and silversmiths offered their wares. In 1806 the legislature incorporated the growing community as a city, and Nashvillians elected Joseph Coleman as their first mayor.

As Nashville grew, it took on more and more aspects of a settled city. By 1810 it had nearly two thousand inhabitants, most of whom lived north of the Public Square on Water (First Avenue), Market (Second Avenue), College (Third Avenue), and Cherry (Fourth Avenue) streets. A number of people still occupied log houses, but these had begun to give way to frame and brick dwellings. Due largely to the efforts of Thomas G. Bradford, the community also enjoyed several local publications: the *Clarion and Tennessee Gazette*, a newspaper; the *Tennessee Almanac*, first issued in 1808; the *Museum*, a magazine established in 1809; and *Tennessee Justice*, a book by attorney John Haywood.

Due to its relatively easy access to the Mississippi River via the Cumberland, Nashville soon became an important trading center. Each spring barges and keelboats left Nashville for New Orleans laden with flour, pork, tobacco, hemp, iron and other products. At first Nashville entrepreneurs simply sold these products in the Crescent City and returned overland on the Natchez Trace. However, in 1806 James Stewart and James Gordon man-

Rachel Donelson was thirteen when she accompanied her father to Nashborough in 1780. On the Tennessee frontier she became an expert horsewoman, sprightly dancer, and charming storyteller. In 1785 she traveled to Kentucky, where she met and married Lewis Robards. An intensely jealous man, Robards made Rachel's life miserable, and in 1788 she returned to Tennessee. Her subsequent divorce from Robards and marriage to Andrew Jackson caused considerable gossip, especially during the presidential campaigns of 1824 and 1828. Rachel died on December 22, 1828, before Jackson was inaugurated as president.

Portrait attributed to Ralph E.W. Earl; photograph courtesy of Ladies Hermitage Association.

This early map of Nashville is based on notes made by a resident in 1804. It shows Lick Branch, right, north of town, the Public Square, center, at the north end of Market Street, and Cedar Knob, now Capitol Hill, top, west of town. Structure number ten, second from right on the west side of Market Street, is the store of Timothy Demonbreun, a Frenchman who traded with Indians in Middle Tennessee several years before the first settlers arrived.

Map from Clayton, History of Davidson County.

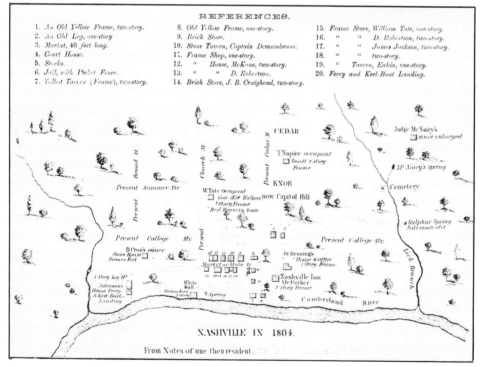

REFERENCES.

1. An Old Yellow Frame, two-story.
2. An Old Log, one-story.
3. Market, 40 feet long.
4. Court House.
5. Stocks.
6. Jail, with Picket Fence.
7. Talbot Tavern (Frame), two-story.
8. Old Yellow Frame, one-story.
9. Brick Store.
10. Stone Tavern, Captain Demumbrane.
11. Frame Shop, one-story.
12. " House, McKane, two-story.
13. " " D. Robertson.
14. Brick Store, J. B. Craighead, two-story.
15. Frame Store, William Tate, one-story.
16. " " D. Robertson, two-story.
17. " " James Jackson, two-story.
18. " " two-story.
19. " Tavern, Eakin, one-story.
20. Ferry and Keel-Boat Landing.

NASHVILLE IN 1804.

From Notes of one then resident.

The Nashville Inn, depicted here about 1840, was built sometime in the 1780s. It stood on the north side of the Public Square and was a popular community gathering place. Andrew Jackson often brought his prize roosters here for cockfights, and in 1813, after his famous brawl with Jesse and Thomas Hart Benton, he lived here while recovering from near-fatal wounds. President James Monroe stayed in the inn during his visit to Nashville in 1819, and in May 1825 it was the scene of a banquet for the Marquis de Lafayette. The famous hostelry burned in 1856.
Lithograph by T. Sinclair; courtesy of Tennessee State Library and Archives.

aged to bring a barge upriver with sugar, coffee, and other groceries purchased in Louisiana. By 1814 barges were operating regularly between the two cities.

Because Nashville depended upon New Orleans as a trade outlet and was situated near the Texas and Florida frontiers where the British and Spanish were engaged in international intrigue, most Nashvillians were highly nationalistic. They favored direct measures in relations with other countries. In 1805 former vice-president Aaron Burr won considerable support in Nashville for a proposed expedition against the Spanish in Texas, and in 1812 Nashvillian Felix Grundy played a leading role in persuading Congress to declare war on Great Britain.

While Grundy's role as a "war hawk" brought him a measure of fame, the war itself made Jackson an American folk hero. He led American troops to impressive victories over the Creek Indians in 1813 and 1814 and over the British in 1815. These accomplishments, together with subsequent forays into Spanish Florida, catapulted him into contention for the presidency in 1824.

Nashville served as the nerve center of Jackson's campaign. The "Nashville Junto," a group made up of Judge John Overton, U.S. Senator John H. Eaton, Major William B. Lewis, Congressman Sam Houston, and Felix Grundy, directed the Jackson effort through a nationwide network of committees of correspondence. Although Jackson lost to John Quincy Adams in an extremely close race, the Junto never stopped campaigning. As a result, in 1828 Jackson not only won the White House but transformed the nation's political system as well. Through conventions, barbecues, parades, propaganda, and published polls, the Junto aroused tremendous national support for Jackson. The modern Democratic party believes that its roots lie in the Jackson movement. If so, then Nashville deserves consideration as that party's birthplace.

Jackson's occupancy of the White House kept Nashville in the national limelight. While president, he made several trips back to the city and received numerous distinguished guests at the Hermitage, his beautiful residence east of town. Some of these visitors were other Nashvillians who rose to

Keelboats, such as the one shown here, helped link Nashville with New Orleans. Long, narrow, and light of draft, they were built for speed. Each vessel's shallow hold was covered with a cargo cabin and walkways for men who propelled the craft through low water by pushing poles against the river bottom. In deep water oars and sails drove the boats, and in turbulent water crews walked along the shore and towed them.
Drawing courtesy of
U.S. Army Corps of Engineers.

prominence on Jackson's coattails. John Eaton was now secretary of war, Felix Grundy had succeeded Eaton in the U.S. Senate, and William B. Lewis had moved into the White House to serve as a presidential advisor. Others included John Bell, who won election as Speaker of the House of Representatives in 1834, and James K. Polk, who wrested that position from him in 1835.

Despite Jackson's prestige, Nashvillians did not follow him blindly. Bell in particular grew restive in the Democratic camp. In 1834, when Jackson decided to support Martin Van Buren of New York as his successor, Bell, who favored Knoxvillian Hugh Lawson White, left the Jackson fold and became a major fixture in the national Whig party. A majority of the city's voters followed Bell's lead, and Nashville remained reliably Whig until that party disintegrated in the 1850s.

After leaving office in 1837, Jackson spent his remaining years supervising affairs at the Hermitage and counseling other Democrats. Virtually every important Democrat in the country either corresponded with Jackson or made a pilgrimage to the Hermitage to see him. In 1844 he worked quietly for his protégé James K. Polk, who won the democratic presidential nomination in a deadlocked convention and became the first successful "dark horse" candidate to reach the White House. Touted as "Young Hickory," Polk went on to conduct one of the most successful administrations in the nation's history. Meanwhile, Jackson died at the Hermitage on June 8, 1845. His passing marked the end of an era in which Nashville, a frontier metropolis, importantly influenced the course of the nation's history.

John Coffee, a land surveyor and speculator, was one of Andrew Jackson's closest friends during his early days in Nashville. In 1804 they joined John Hutchings in opening a general store at Clover Bottom, the site of a race course near the Hermitage. During the War of 1812 Coffee commanded Tennessee cavalrymen in Jackson's famous victories at Horseshoe Bend, Alabama, and New Orleans, Louisiana.

Engraving courtesy of Tennessee State Library and Archives.

When Thomas Hart Benton posed for this portrait in 1837, he was Jackson's chief spokesman in the United States Senate. Twenty-four years earlier, however, Benton and his brother Jesse had almost killed Jackson in a brawl on Nashville's Public Square. The fight, which grew out of an argument over Jackson's role as second in a duel, involved pistols, knives, and clubs. The Bentons shot Jackson twice, and one of the bullets shattered his shoulder, almost causing him to bleed to dath. To escape reprisals by Jackson's friends, Thomas Hart Benton fled to Missouri, where in 1820 he was elected to the Senate.

Lithograph by Charles Fenderich; photograph courtesy of National Portrait Gallery, Smithsonian Institution.

Felix Grundy was a member of the "Nashville Junto," which managed Jackson's successful quest for the presidency in 1828. Grundy came to Tennessee from Kentucky in 1807 and earned a reputation as the best criminal lawyer in the Southwest. Within four years he had won election to Congress, where he advocated going to war with Great Britain to settle maritime and territorial disputes. After the War of 1812 he supported the political aspirations of its greatest hero, Jackson. In 1829 Grundy succeeded John H. Eaton in the United States Senate and served there until 1838, when he resigned to become attorney general under President Martin Van Buren.

Engraving by T.B. Welch from a painting by W.B. Cooper

Jackson's triumph over the British in 1815 confirmed America's independence and made him a national hero. Within weeks after the Battle of New Orleans a popular tune called "Jackson is the Boy" swept the country and proclaimed "He's still for action." This idealized portrait shows Jackson in resplendent uniform with drawn sword.

Lithograph by E.B. and E.C. Kellogg; courtesy of Tennessee State Library and Archives.

Bank president, lawyer, and possibly the wealthiest man in Tennessee in the 1820s, Judge John Overton was the most influential member of the "Nashville Junto." He moved to Nashville only a few months after Jackson and, like him, boarded with Mrs. John Donelson. In later years Overton and Jackson became partners in numerous land deals, one of which led to the founding of Memphis in 1819. Today Nashvillians remember Overton as the builder of Traveller's Rest, a National Historic Place restored by the National Society of the Colonial Dames of America in Tennessee.

Engraving by Samuel Sartain; from Clayton, History of Davidson County.

Sam Houston, shown here in 1857, was the junior member of the "Nashville Junto." He won Jackson's attention first at the Battle of Horseshoe Bend in 1814 and later as district attorney for Nashville. In 1823 city voters sent Houston to Congress, and in 1827 Tennessee voters elected him governor. Following a brief marriage that ended in a shroud of mystery in 1829, Houston resigned from office and went to live in Indian Territory. From there he moved to Texas and helped it win independence from Mexico in 1836.

Engraving by E.C. Kellogg; courtesy of Tennessee State Library and Archives.

Jean Marie Leroux did this engraving of the Marquis de Lafayette in 1824, one year before Lafayette visited Nashville. The sixty-seven year old hero of the American and French revolutions spent two days in the city in May 1825. While here he maintained a pace that would have exhausted most younger men. On the first day he attended welcoming ceremonies in the Public Square, greeted Revolutionary War veterans, gave a reception for the city's women, and went to a banquet in his honor at the Nashville Inn. On the second day he reviewed the Tennessee militia, toured Nashville Female Academy and Cumberland College, visited Jackson at the Hermitage, had tea with Mayor Robert Currey, and attended a grand ball at the Masonic Hall. At the last function Lafayette reportedly danced with almost every woman present.

Photograph of engraving courtesy of National Portrait Gallery, Smithsonian Institution.

Andrew Jackson was a hard-money man who distrusted commercial banking. He waged one of his most famous political battles against the Second Bank of the United States. Hoping to defuse Jackson's opposition to that institution, its president, Nicholas Biddle, approved the establishment of a branch in Nashville in 1827. That office, shown here, stood at the corner of College (Third Avenue) and Union streets. Although Jackson's financial advisor, Josiah Nichol, headed the branch and several friends served as directors, Biddle's ploy failed. Jackson remained opposed to the Second Bank, and in 1832 he vetoed a bill to recharter it. The Nashville branch closed in 1836, and the building was later demolished.
Drawing courtesy of Public Library of Metropolitan Nashville-Davidson County.

This view of Nashville from the south is from a survey by Matthew Rhea. It depicts the city about 1830 when its population was around 5,500. The houses, stores, and other buildings show the influence of federal and classical styles prevalent at that time.
Drawing by W.E. Tucker; courtesy of Tennessee State Library and Archives.

VIEW of NASHVILLE

SOME ACCOUNT OF SOME OF THE BLOODY DEEDS OF
GENERAL JACKSON.

The 1828 presidential campaign stands out as one of the most sordid in the nation's history. Jackson supporters accused President John Quincy Adams of living with his wife before marriage, pimping for the czar of Russia, using public money to buy gambling equipment for the White House, and breaking the Sabbath by riding around the countryside in a jockey's costume. Adams supporters accused Jackson of adultery, seduction, murder, theft, and treason, and criticized him for dueling, cockfighting, horseracing, and swearing. The Adams camp also used "Coffin Handbills" or broadsides such as this one to portray Jackson as a tyrant and bloodthirsty killer because he had ordered six convicted militia deserters shot in September 1814.

Broadside courtesy of Tennessee State Library and Archives.

Andrew Jackson erected the Hermitage in 1819 as a gift to his wife, Rachel Donelson. Originally it was a simple, square, brick house devoid of pretension. In 1831 Jackson remodeled it for his daughter-in-law, Sarah York Jackson, and added wings and front and rear porticos. Fire damaged much of the house in 1834, but Jackson rebuilt it by 1837. This view, taken in 1972, shows the front facade standing almost apart from the original structure.

Photograph by Jack E. Boucher; courtesy of Historic American Buildings Survey.

Nashvillian John Bell, shown here about 1860, also commanded considerable national political attention in the antebellum years. He represented the city in Congress from 1827 to 1841 and served as Speaker of the House in 1834. Although originally a Jackson man, he broke with Old Hickory over the national bank issue and Jackson's support of Martin Van Buren for the 1836 Democratic presidential nomination. By 1840 Bell was a prominent leader in the new Whig party, and when it won the White House that year, President William Henry Harrison appointed him secretary of war. Later Bell served twelve years in the United States Senate, where he was a leading Southern moderate. In 1860 the Constitutional Union party nominated him for president, and he carried three states.

Photograph by Mathew Brady; courtesy of National Archives.

Although Andrew Jackson's friends often hailed him as the champion of the common man, and his opponents frequently pictured him as an uncouth frontiersman, these original furnishings in the Hermitage dining room indicate that he was a man of aristocratic tastes.

Photograph by Jack E. Boucher; courtesy of Historic American Buildings Survey.

In the 1820s and 1830s cartoons became popular forms of political commentary both in Nashville and throughout the country. This anti-Jackson piece was inspired by his war on the Second Bank of the United States, particularly his decision in 1833 to transfer government funds from branches of the B.U.S. to state banks. In the cartoon Jackson (the jackass) is trampling branch banks (baby chicks) to the applause of pro-Jackson newspapers (the hounds).

Drawing courtesy of Tennessee State Library and Archives.

James K. Polk, the second Tennessean to win the presidency, maintained a close connection with Nashville all his life. He first resided in the city in the mid-1820s while studying law with Felix Grundy and serving in the state legislature. He next lived in Nashville in 1839-41 while governor. In 1844 Polk captured the Democratic nomination for president and narrowly defeated Whig candidate Henry Clay for the nation's highest office. After enjoying one of the most successful presidential administrations ever, Polk returned to Nashville in 1849. Until his death on June 15 of that year, he resided in Felix Grundy's former house, now demolished, on the corner of Union and Vine (Seventh Avenue).
        Lithograph by Charles Fenderich (1838); courtesy of National Portrait Gallery, Smithsonian Institution

Andrew Jackson died at the Hermitage on June 8, 1845. This Nathaniel Currier lithograph of the scene at his deathbed depicts both the end of an era in Nashville's history and the sense of personal loss that many Americans felt upon learning that Jackson had expired.
        Lithograph courtesy of Tennessee State Library and Archives.

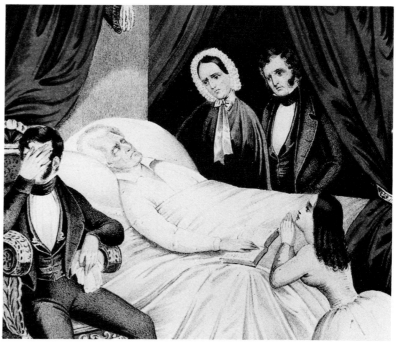

In 1845 William Strickland estimated that construction of Tennessee's Greek revival-style capitol would take three years and cost a quarter of a million dollars. Due to shortages of materials and skilled workers, the job eventually required fourteen years and about one million dollars. For foundations and walls Strickland used huge blocks of fossilized limestone quarried by state penitentiary inmates less than a mile from Capitol Hill. Expert stonecutters and masons cut and fitted the blocks so closely that mortar joints averaged less than three-sixteenths of an inch. Within twenty years, however, the limestone began showing excessive deterioration. In 1953 the legislature voted funds for restoration, and today the revitalized building is a National Historic Landmark. Engraving by H. Bosse; from Nashville City and Business Directory for 1860-61.

On October 7, 1843, the Tennessee General Assembly selected Nashville as the state's permanent capital. This action ended almost fifty years of controversy during which the lawmakers had met first in Knoxville and then in Kingston, Nashville, and Murfreesboro. In 1844 the legislature authorized a commission of five Nashville businessmen to choose an architect for a capitol. They picked William F. Strickland of Philadelphia. Having served an apprenticeship with national Capitol architect Benjamin Latrobe and having designed a number of prominent structures in Philadelphia, Strickland was the country's foremost authority on Greek revival style. He completed plans for a Tennessee capitol in 1845, and on July 4 of that same year Nashvillians gathered under a blistering sun on dust-covered Cedar Knob, now Capitol Hill, to watch dignitaries lay the cornerstone. The ceremonies marked an acceleration of economic growth, cultural development, and architectural achievement in the capital city.

Central to Nashville's progress was a network of turnpike, river, and railroad transportation that linked the city to the rest of the nation. Turnpike building had commenced the previous decade with the Franklin (1831), Murfreesboro (1838), and Gallatin (1839) pikes. In the 1840s workers opened the Nolensville (1841), Charlotte (1842), Lebanon (1842), and White's Creek (1845) turnpikes. Others were completed in the fifties, and together they extended out from the city like the spokes of a wheel. Over these usually rough, dusty toll roads—which today remain major Nashville traffic arteries—passenger stages, freight wagons, and farm carts bounced to and from the city. Pedestrians, horseback and mule riders, and herds of cattle and hogs traversed them, too. Travelers who entered Nashville from the north and east crossed the Cumberland River on a covered toll bridge erected in 1823. After mid-century they used the city's first suspension bridge, engineered by prominent Nashville architect Adolphus W. Heiman.

Steamboats began plying the Cumberland River in 1819, and by the mid-1830s the smoke-belching monsters had nearly replaced slower barges and keelboats. In the forties steamboating on the Cumberland entered a "golden age." Nash-

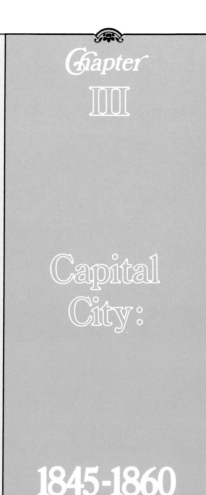

Chapter III

Capital City:

1845-1860

villians could travel to New Orleans and back in fifteen days on sleek, 260-foot-long packets that could accommodate thirty or more passengers in stately cabins while carrying several hundred tons of cargo. Bearing names like *America*, *Susquehanna*, *Talleyrand*, and *Red Rover*, these vessels hauled cotton, tobacco, corn, flour, and other products to New Orleans and returned with molasses, coffee, sugar, clothing, and other necessities. Some packet operators entertained passengers with music, dances, liquor, and games of chance and made riverboat travel seem glamorous. Actually it was dangerous. Sparks and embers from the wood-burning vessels' smokestacks could ignite roofs and decks in seconds, and snags in the river could rip open hulls just as quickly. Despite these hazards, Nashvillians relied heavily on steamboat transportation for much of the nineteenth century.

By the mid-1840s steamboats were docking in Nashville at the rate of forty to fifty each year. To tie this booming river trade to other markets in the middle South, the city's merchants began calling for the construction of railroads. Chief among those advocates was Vernon K. Stevenson. In 1847 he canvassed the entire city to stir public sentiment for railroad building. Early the next year he founded the Nashville and Chattanooga Railroad, which he completed in 1854. By then he had already begun a second line, the Nashville and Northwestern, which he planned to extend to Hickman, Kentucky. He managed to lay only about thirty miles of track from Nashville, however, before the onset of the Civil War. A third line, the Louisville and Nashville, chartered by the Kentucky legislature in 1850, reached south to Nashville in 1859 and linked the city by land to the Ohio River.

Nashville's transportation facilities served a variety of commercial and industrial enterprises and helped the city increase its importance as a regional trade center. For example, in 1854 thirteen packet lines operated out of Nashville. Some worked the upper Cumberland, bringing back corn and tobacco from Gallatin, hogs and cedar lumber from Lebanon, and poultry and hides from Celina. Others worked the lower Cumberland and brought back nails, chains, horseshoes, and other foundry

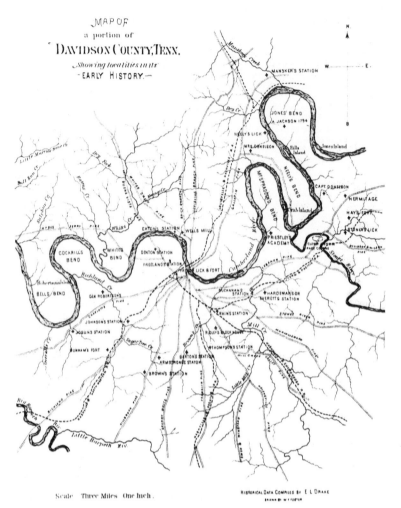

MAP OF
a portion of
DAVIDSON COUNTY, TENN.
Showing localities in its
— EARLY HISTORY —

Scale   Three Miles   One Inch.

HISTORICAL DATA COMPILED BY E L DRAKE
DRAWN BY W F FOSTER

This early map of Davidson County shows sites of some of the first settlements and routes of the turnpikes built in the 1830s and 1840s. The pikes radiate from Nashville like spokes from the hub of a wheel. Most of them are still major traffic arteries.

Map by W.F. Foster and E.L. Drake; from Clayton, History of Davidson County.

By the time he was named architect of the Tennessee State Capitol in 1845, William Strickland had already designed a number of nationally known buildings. They included the Second Bank of the United States (1824), the United States Mint (1829), and the Merchants Exchange in Philadelphia (1834) and the United States Branch Mint in New Orleans (1835). Although Strickland encountered many difficulties in constructing the capitol and died in 1854 before completing it, he liked Nashville and found time to design several other structures in the city. Among those were Saint Mary's Catholic Church (1845) and the First Presbyterian Church (1849), now the Downtown Presbyterian Church. Both Strickland and businessman Samuel D. Morgan, who accepted chief responsibility for finishing the capitol after Strickland died, are buried in its walls. This portrait of Strickland, by an unknown artist in the 1840s, hangs in the capitol today.

Photograph courtesy of Public Library of Metropolitan Nashville-Davidson County.

products from iron works near Ashland City and Clarksville. Hardware, general mercantile, and commission merchants prospered in Nashville by distributing these and other goods to customers throughout Middle Tennessee. Wholesale dry good and grocery concerns fared even better. They extended their markets into western Kentucky and northern Alabama and Georgia.

The success of these enterprises in turn stimulated more growth and development. By 1860 Nashville had nearly seventeen thousand people and boasted several foundries, four millwork and furniture plants, one steamboat yard, a carriage factory, a boot and shoe manufactory, a brickyard, three patent medicine firms, a facility for producing artificial limbs, four insurance companies, two tobacco factories, three breweries, and several banks and hotels. An analysis of the census for that year shows that the city also had sixty-nine houses of prostitution, situated mostly along Front,

Although photographed after the Civil War, this scene is typical of activity on the Nashville Wharf as early as the 1840s. Merchants, clerks, draymen, roustabouts, and boat crewmen conduct their business amid gangplanks, boat lines, piles of freight, and clusters of curious townspeople. The wharf, built in 1828, was little more than a stretch of river bank graded to a gentle slope so that the shallow-drafted steamboats could draw close enough for their gangplanks to reach ashore.

Photograph by Calvert Brothers; courtesy of Tennessee State Library and Archives.

In 1853 a new suspension bridge, designed by Adolphus W. Heiman, linked Nashville, right, with Edgefield. When the bridge was proposed, some citizens wanted to put it at the foot of Broad Street. Others favored a location near the Public Square. The latter site was chosen, but not before Felix Zollicoffer, editor of the Republican Banner and proponent of the Broad Street location, fought a gun battle with John L. Marlin, editor of the Nashville Union and advocate of the other site. Note the Nashville Wharf and the Water Street (First Avenue) commercial buildings in the background of this unsigned view.

Drawing courtesy of Tennessee State Library and Archives.

In the 1840s reciprocal agreements among the larger steamboat lines improved passenger schedules and aided transfer of freight from one line to another. By 1845 Nashvillians could travel by steamboat to New Orleans and back in fifteen days. They could make a round trip to Memphis or Saint Louis in ten days and to Pittsburgh in twelve. And with the help of "forwarding merchants" such as H.H. Harrison and Son they could ship manufactured goods and agricultural products almost anywhere in the country.

Advertisement from Nashville City and Business Directory *for 1860-61.*

Like the wharf, the Public Square was a beehive of commerce in the 1840s and 1850s. Much of the activity centered around the City Hall and Market House, left foreground. Built in 1828 and enlarged and remodeled in the 1850s, it was 270 feet long and more than 60 feet wide. At each end a two-story wing held government and other offices, while in the center a covered market housed one hundred stalls for merchants and farmers. Sometimes trading overflowed into the streets, as in this photograph taken about 1860. The City Hall and Market House continued in use until the 1930s, when it was torn down to make room for the new Davidson County Courthouse.

Photograph courtesy of Tennessee State Library and Archives.

Wholesale and commission merchants occupied many of the offices and warehouses around the Nashville Wharf and Public Square. The wholesalers imported groceries, liquor, cloth, hardware, machinery, and other goods and sold them to retailers in Tennessee, Kentucky, Georgia, and Alabama. The commission merchants marketed cotton, tobacco, wheat, corn, bacon, and other local commodities throughout the nation. By 1860 Nashville had more than sixty of these firms. One of the largest was S.D. Morgan and Company, a wholesale dry goods operation owned by Samuel D. Morgan. He had this Italianate structure built on the north side of the Public Square in 1856. Known in recent years as the Morgan-Reeves Building, it was demolished in 1975.

Engraving by H. Bosse; from Nashville City and Business Directory for 1860-61

This sketch shows the Davidson County Courthouse in 1856, shortly before fire destroyed it and numerous surrounding buildings. The stately structure, which stood on the east side of the Public Square opposite the City Hall and Market House, had burned twice before, in 1832 and 1848, and in each instance the county had rebuilt it. This time the county leveled the site and erected a new building designed by Francis Strickland, son of the capitol architect.

Drawing by William Eichbaum; courtesy of Tennessee State Library and Archives.

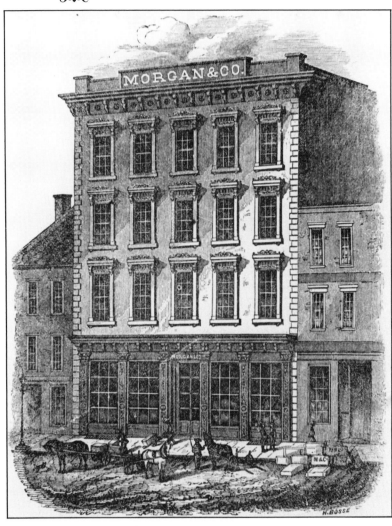

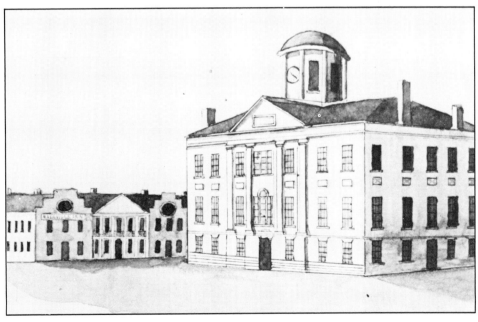

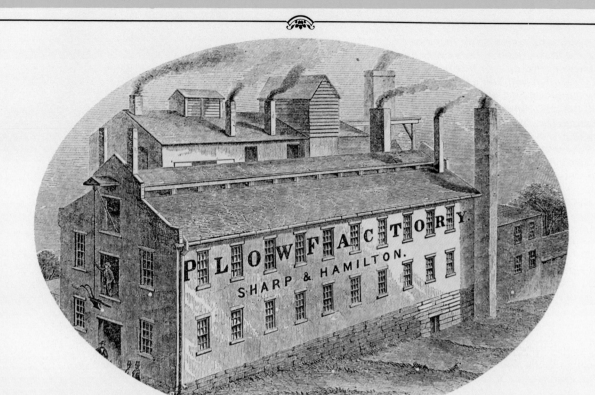

Market, College, and Cherry streets (First, Second, Third, and Fourth avenues) south of Spring (Church) Street.

With its capitol building under construction, its streets jammed with freight wagons and two-horse hacks, and its wharves snarled with gang-planks, lines, crates, sweating roustabouts, and noisy livestock, Nashville in the 1850s may have seemed merely a rowdy boom town to some visitors. Closer inspection would have revealed, however, that Nashville was also a city of newspapers, schools, churches, and fine architecture.

As in almost any thriving young community with frequently shifting political currents, news-papers came and went. During the 1840s and 1850s the *Republican Banner* was the favorite of most Nashvillians, but they also read the *Nashville True Whig*, the *Nashville Gazette*, the *Nashville Union*, and others. All reported the actions of Tennessean James K. Polk in the White House, carried news of Nashvillians fighting in the war with Mexico, and, later, editorialized about the nation's growing crisis over slavery.

Nashville also offered its citizens variety in education and religion. In 1824 Cumberland College, formerly Davidson Academy, became the University of Nashville, and before its literary department succumbed to financial problems in 1850, it graduated 432 students. Its reputation for excellent teaching was equaled, if not surpassed, by that of the Nashville Female Academy. Founded in 1816, it became the largest girls' school in the South by the 1850s. Other notable Nashville educational institutions included the Tennessee School for the Blind (1846), the medical department of the University of Nashville (1851), and Hume School (1855), the first public school in the city.

By 1840 Nashvillians could choose among a number of religious denominations, including Presbyterian, Methodist, Baptist, Episcopal, and Catholic. Several churches established near mid-century survive, as do three church buildings: St. Mary's Roman Catholic Church on Fifth Avenue North at Charlotte Avenue, the Downtown Presby-terian Church on Church Street at Fifth Avenue North, and the Holy Trinity Episcopal Church on Lafayette Street at Sixth Avenue South. All three are noteworthy architecturally. William Strickland, architect of the capitol, designed the Saint Mary's and Downtown Presbyterian churches, while New York architects Frank Wills and Henry Dudley planned the Holy Trinity Church.

The construction of outstanding buildings like these churches, together with the erection of Adolphus Heiman's Central State Hospital and University of Nashville structures and the comple-tion of a number of grand country houses, comple-mented the new state capitol and helped make Nashville the cultural as well as the political capital of Tennessee in 1860.

Nashville had several iron furnaces, rolling mills, foundries, and machine shops in the 1840s and 1850s, but apparently all suffered from competition with Northern factories. In 1860 the editor of the city directory lamented that Nashville's foundries and shops had "to contend with that restless desire and general practice which has characterized the body of Southern men when supplying themselves with any kind of machinery or implements, to purchase at the North, when, more frequently than otherwise, a better article at the same or less price may be obtained at home." A.W. Putnam built this factory in 1856 and sold it to Sharp and Hamilton in 1859. It produced steel and wrought iron plows at the rate of 150 a week.

> Drawing from Nashville City and Business Directory for 1860-61.

The Methodist Episcopal Church, South, established the Southern Methodist Publishing House in 1854, and within five years it was one of the largest publishing operations in the South. During the Civil War Federal troops used it as a military printing office. This building, which stood near the northeast corner of the Public Square, burned in 1872, but the Methodists replaced it and remained in this location until 1906, when they moved to Ninth Avenue at Broadway.

> Engraving by Van Ingen; from Nashville City and Business Directory for 1860-61.

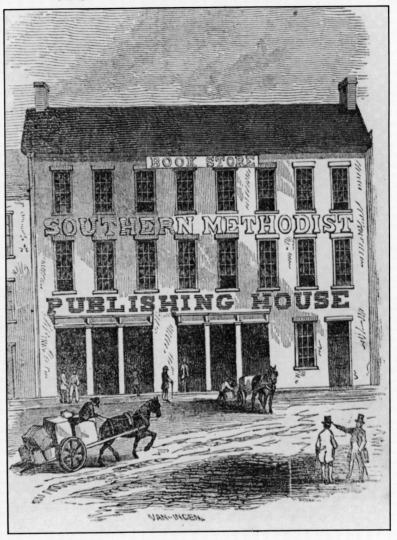

NASHVILLE & N. WESTERN

RAILROAD.

Double Daily Trains are run between

NASHVILLE AND HICKMAN,

EAST AND WEST,

Affording facilities and advantages to the traveling public worthy of special attention, it being the

CENTRAL SHORT ROUTE TO

Humboldt, Jackson, Memphis, New Orleans,

CAIRO, ST. LOUIS AND THE WEST.

Due largely to the efforts of Vernon K. Stevenson, a merchant turned railroad builder, Nashville got its first operating rail line, the Nashville and Chattanooga, in 1853. By the time that road reached all the way to Chattanooga, in 1854, Stevenson was already at work on another, the Nashville and Northwestern to Hickman, Kentucky. Nashville raised $270,000 for construction of the line, but the Civil War began before Stevenson could finish it. The federal government completed part of the road during the war, and the Nashville and Chattanooga constructed the remaining stretch later. This advertisement for the Nashville and Northwestern appeared in 1869.

> From King's City Directory.

Newspaper publishing was an unstable business in early Nashville. Between 1800 and 1840, newspapers appeared under more than two dozen mastheads, and between 1820 and 1860 there always were four or five papers competing for readers. James T. Bell's Nashville Daily Gazette *was the third newspaper to bear that name. Established in 1844, it went through fourteen changes of ownership before ceasing publication during the Civil War.*
Advertisement from Nashville City and Business Directory for 1860-61.

Built for the Louisville and Nashville and the Edgefield and Kentucky lines, the Nashville Railroad Bridge opened to traffic in 1859. It had four spans totaling seven hundred feet. The end spans were fixed, while those in the center were designed to turn for steamboats. The turn spans, each measuring 120 feet, were the longest in the country. In 1862 retreating Confederate troops tried to burn the bridge but failed. The masonry portions, now strengthened, remain in use.

Drawing from Lossing, Pictorial Field Book of the Civil War.

JAMES T. BELL,   M. V. B. HAILE

NASHVILLE
DAILY GAZETTE.

JAMES T. BELL & Co., Proprietors.

JAMES R. BRUCE, *Editor.*

The GAZETTE is independent in politics and religion, devoted to Literature, Home Interests, and the News of the day. The circulation of the daily issue in Nashville and the country immediately surrounding the city, is much greater than that of any other paper; by virtue of which fact, the GAZETTE is the medium for advertising the list of UNCALLED FOR LETTERS. It is by far the best advertising medium in the State of Tennessee.

TERMS OF SUBSCRIPTION:

Daily Gazette, $5 per annum; Tri-Weekly $4, and Weekly $2; in all instances in advance.

JOB PRINTING.

We are prepared to do Job Printing of all kinds, with neatness & dispatch

JAS. T. BELL & Co.,
Gazette Building, Corner Deaderick and Cherry Sts.

John Berrien Lindsley, son of Philip Lindsley, has been called the "Benjamin Franklin of Nashville." He was a graduate of the college of medicine at the University of Pennsylvania, a professor of chemistry, an ordained Presbyterian minister, the first president of the Nashville Board of Education, the first secretary of the Tennessee State Board of Health, a historian, and a pioneer prison reformer. In 1850 Lindsley played a leading role in founding the medical department of the University of Nashville, and from 1855 to 1870 he served as chancellor of the university.
Engraving by Samuel Sartain; from Clayton, History of Davidson County.

Philip Lindsley moved to Nashville in 1824 to assume the presidency of Cumberland College. The reason he took the job is unclear, for he enjoyed considerable distinction as a professor of languages at the College of New Jersey (later Princeton), and earlier he had declined the presidency of the University of Ohio. What is clear, however, is that he helped educate a generation of Nashvillians. Soon after his arrival the board of trustees renamed Cumberland College the University of Nashville, and Lindsley planned to make it one of the leading universities in the South. He assembled an excellent faculty but could not obtain the financial support necessary for expansion. Finally, after struggling for twenty-six years, Lindsley resigned in 1850.
Engraving by Illman Brothers; from Clayton, History of Davidson County.

The University of Nashville was situated on College Hill not far from where General Hospital now stands. In 1850 dwindling enrollment and lack of funds forced the university to close its literary department. Classes resumed in 1854, however, and the following year the literary department was merged with the Western Military Institute. This engraving shows the university campus in 1860. At right is Lindsley Hall, designed by Adolphus Heiman in 1853 for the literary department. Still standing majestically on the hilltop, the gray limestone structure today houses offices of the metropolitan government. At center is the military building, no longer extant.

Engraving by H. Bosse; from Nashville City and Business Directory for 1860-61.

In 1828 the city's Baptists split over the doctrine of Alexander Campbell, a traveling evangelist who founded the Disciples of Christ Church and preached frequently in Nashville. The few persons who remained in the Baptist fold worshipped in various homes until 1835, when they persuaded Reverend Robert Boyte C. Howell to come from Norfolk, Virginia, to pastor their church. Within six months after he arrived, Howell established the Tennessee Baptist, *the first Baptist journal in the West, and started building this church on Summer Street (Fifth Avenue North) between Deaderick and Union. The Baptists later sold the structure to a Lutheran congregation, which used it until 1951. It was later demolished.*

Engraving by J.F. Wagner; courtesy of Tennessee State Library and Archives.

Completed in 1859, Two Rivers, shown in 1970, was the last great country estate erected near Nashville before the Civil War. It was built by David H. McGavock near the junction of the Stones and Cumberland rivers. There is disagreement about who designed the house: some sources suggest William Strickland, but he died five years before work on Two Rivers began; other sources suggest McGavock, but he was not an architect. It is known, however, that slaves made brick and quarried stone for the house near the building site. Now restored, Two Rivers is owned by the city and used as a conference center.

Photograph by Jack E. Boucher; courtesy of Historic American Buildings Survey.

In 1807 John Harding bought a 250-acre tract on Richland Creek a few miles southwest of Nashville, and during the next thirty-five years, through twenty-nine separate transactions, he built it into a 3,500-acre plantation known as Belle Meade, French for "beautiful meadow." On it Harding produced corn, barley, wheat, oats, hay, and fine thoroughbred race horses. Structural evidence indicates that he began Belle Meade mansion, depicted here about 1970, sometime prior to 1840. Over the years famous visitors to the stately edifice have included five presidents: James K. Polk, Grover Cleveland, Benjamin Harrison, Theodore Roosevelt, and William Howard Taft. Today the house and remaining grounds are maintained by the Association for the Preservation of Tennessee Antiquities.
Photograph courtesy of the Association for the Preservation of Tennessee Antiquities.

When Adelicia Hayes Franklin married Colonel Joseph Alexander Smith Acklen in May 1849, she was considered by many to be the richest woman in the United States. Three years earlier her first husband, slave-trader Isaac Franklin, had died and left her an estate in Sumner County, seven plantations in Louisiana, and fifty thousand acres in Texas. To insure that she never lost any of that property, she made Acklen sign a marriage contract guaranteeing her continued ownership. The Acklens built this house, Belmont, in 1850 on land she bought before they were married. Once a splendid plantation house, the mansion is now Acklen Hall, a landmark on the campus of Belmont College. Both William Strickland and Adolphus Heiman are said to have contributed to the design of Belmont.
Photograph by Jack E. Boucher; courtesy of Historic American Buildings Survey.

William Stockell's house, at 42 South Cherry Street (Fourth Avenue), was a popular gathering place for Confederate soldiers in 1861 and early 1862. Here a "Johnny Reb" talks with family members on the stoop, while a servant poses for the camera. The house, a fine example of Italian villa architecture, suggests that Stockell's stucco and plastering business headquartered on Broad Street, was a successful enterprise.

Photograph courtesy of The Tennessean.

When Nashville clocks struck midnight on December 31, 1860, they tolled the end of a decade of growth and the beginning of a painful epoch that drastically altered the lives of many residents. In May 1861 the state legislature voted to take Tennessee out of the Federal Union and join other Southern states in the newly formed Confederacy. This action followed a long and bitter national debate over slavery; it heralded four terrible years of Civil War. During most of that time Nashville was occupied by Federal troops. A number of Nashvillians were killed or wounded in the war, and many more lost their homes, businesses, and other possessions. Those who owned slaves were forced to give them up. Those who were enslaved gained their freedom.

For years Nashvillians had been watching sectional discord grow into a bubbling cauldron. Ever since 1819-20, when a national crisis had erupted over the spread of slavery into Missouri, the city's populace had periodically debated both slave holding and the concept of the Union. Despite the fact that they owned slaves—3,211 of them in 1860—and thus had a substantial stake in the fate of the South's "peculiar institution," most Nashvillians had favored political moderation. For example, they had supported the so-called Compromise of 1850, which postponed a solution for the slavery crisis for a decade. And they had refused to endorse Southern rights resolutions adopted by political extremists at a special regional convention held in Nashville that same year.

Even heated national controversy over possible expansion of slavery into Kansas and Nebraska in 1854 and John Brown's bloody anti-slavery raid at Harper's Ferry, Virginia, in 1859 had not eroded Nashvillians' devotion to the Union. In 1860, when remnants of the Whig and American parties formed the Constitutional Union party and nominated John Bell as a middle-of-the-road candidate for president, Nashvillians supported him by better than a two-to-one margin. Bell won only three states, however, and finished a distant fourth nationwide.

As soon as Republican Abraham Lincoln was announced as the winner of the election of 1860, a number of extremist pro-slavery leaders began

Chapter IV

Occupied City:

1860-1865

clamoring for the Southern states to secede from the Union immediately. However, despite the secession of South Carolina on December 20, 1860, most Nashvillians remained steadfast. They held large pro-Union meetings in the courthouse in December 1860 and January 1861. Governor Isham G. Harris and a majority of the legislature favored secession, though, and Harris called an election on February 9, 1861, to determine whether a secession convention should be held. Like a majority of Tennesseans, Nashville voters rejected the idea.

With the exception of the *Union and Republican*, most Nashville newspapers urged maintenance of the Union. The *Republican Banner* greeted Lincoln's inauguration as a "mild and conservative" development and declared that if war came it would not be the president's fault. The *Patriot* attacked Southern secessionists so stridently that it attracted attention throughout the South. And one Nashville paper, the *Democrat*, was so vehement in its unionism that a secessionist paper in Georgia called for a ban on its circulation.

On April 12, 1861, Confederate troops in Charleston, South Carolina, fired the opening shot of the Civil War by bombarding Union-held Fort Sumter. This and President Lincoln's call on April 15 for 75,000 volunteer soldiers rallied most Nashvillians, finally, to the Confederate cause. The *Union and Republican* asked dramatically: "Are we but the bastard sons of the heroes who...won for our State the glorious...appellation of *the volunteer state?*" Many Nashville men responded by forming military companies. Within a few weeks the city boasted nearly forty of these units with colorful names like Cheatham Rifles, Hickory Guards, Cumberland Patriots, Hermitage Light Infantry, and Tennessee Rangers.

Because of its river connections, good macadamized roads, and particularly its rail lines, Nashville soon became the most important arsenal and storehouse in the western portion of the Confederacy. A local powder mill established by the Military and Financial Board of Tennessee was the largest in the South. In addition to supplying the Confederate Army of Tennessee, this mill provided gunpowder for Southern troops at the first Battle of

Bull Run and for garrisons at Mobile and New Orleans as well. By autumn 1861 Nashville's ordnance plants were producing 100,000 percussion caps a day, and its factories, shops, and foundries were turning out huge quantities of foodstuffs, uniforms, blankets, saddles, sabers, small arms, and guns.

This vital service to the Confederacy ended abruptly in February 1862. On the sixteenth of that month Union forces under General Ulysses S. Grant captured Fort Donelson on the lower Cumberland and gained control of the river all the way to Nashville. Because residents had done little to fortify the city, General Albert Sidney Johnston, commander of the Confederacy's Western Department, decided that Nashville could not be defended against the advancing Federal army; therefore, he ordered his Army of Tennessee to abandon the city. This order created panic in Nashville. Many citizens fled, while others went on a wild binge of rioting and looting. By February 23 Union troops had encamped across the river in Edgefield. The following day Nashville Mayor Richard B. Cheatham and a citizens' committee surrendered the city to General Don Carlos Buell.

Nashville became an occupied community and the principal supply base for the Union army in the West. From here Grant launched the campaigns that split the Confederacy and won him military renown. Because of the city's strategic importance, Grant and his chief lieutenant, General William T. Sherman, were determined to hold it at all costs. Between 1862 and 1864 Federal soldiers constructed nearly twenty miles of forts, breastworks, trenches, and rifle pits around the city, making it one of the most heavily fortified communities in the

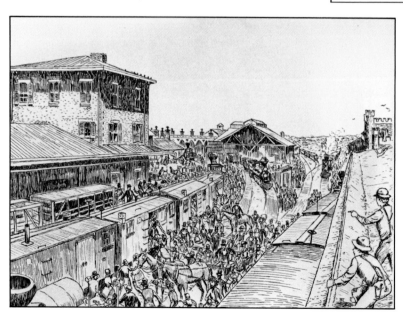

On February 16, 1862, when residents heard that Federal troops under General Ulysses S. Grant had captured Fort Donelson, on the lower Cumberland north of Nashville, and started up the river, panic gripped the city. Some citizens wandered through the streets in dismay. Others threw their belongings into wagons, carriages, and carts and fled southward on the turnpikes. Still others rushed to the Nashville and Chattanooga Railroad depot and crowded onto Southbound trains.
Drawing courtesy of The Tennessean.

Although Nashville was never a major slave-trading center, the city had its share of men like Rees W. Porter, who bought and sold other humans. This advertisement, which appeared in 1857, is a graphic reminder of the chief cause of the Civil War.
From Nashville Business
Directory for 1857.

This view from the northeast shows the suspension and railroad bridges shortly before General Albert Sidney Johnston's Confederate army withdrew from Nashville in February 1862. To slow the Union advance, the retreating Southerners set fire to both bridges, but only the suspension bridge burned.
Drawing from Lossing,
Pictorial Field Book of the Civil War.

country.

Until late 1864 Confederate military activity around Nashville was confined largely to skirmishes on the city's outskirts. In early December 1864, however, General John B. Hood and a force of 23,000 Confederates moved into position south of town. Tired, ill, and frustrated by repeated defeats near Atlanta, Hood had foolishly decided to try to capture Nashville, march north to Cincinnati, cross the Ohio, and regain a measure of glory for both himself and the South. In the subsequent Battle of Nashville on December 15 and 16, Union General George H. Thomas, who commanded nearly 55,000 men, left his fortifications, attacked Hood, and forced him to withdraw. The battle was chiefly one of maneuver, with fewer than two thousand lives lost on both sides, but Confederate troops never again threatened Nashville.

For most Nashvillians the war years proved extremely trying. Union forces seized numerous public and private buildings for use as hospitals, barracks, offices, and warehouses. They even forced some citizens to give up their residences and made others quarter soldiers. In March 1862 President Lincoln appointed Andrew Johnson military governor of Tennessee, and during the next two years Johnson made life difficult for Nashvillians who refused to take an oath of allegiance to the Union. Commonly referred to as "the Old Devil," he occasionally imprisoned city officials, ministers, and other leaders on charges of disloyalty.

Not all Nashvillians suffered during the war, however. Merchants who took the oath of allegiance prospered from Federal business, and many made substantial fortunes. Moreover, Nashville suffered little physical damage from the war and emerged from the conflict in much better condition than most other Southern cities.

This lithograph depicts the first dress parade of Union troops in Nashville following surrender of the city on February 24, 1862. The soldiers, from Ohio, drill on the Public Square, while residents watch from sidewalks, windows, and balconies. Nashville was now an occupied city under military government and would remain so until the end of the war in April 1865.

Lithograph courtesy of Public Library of Metropolitan Nashville-Davidson County.

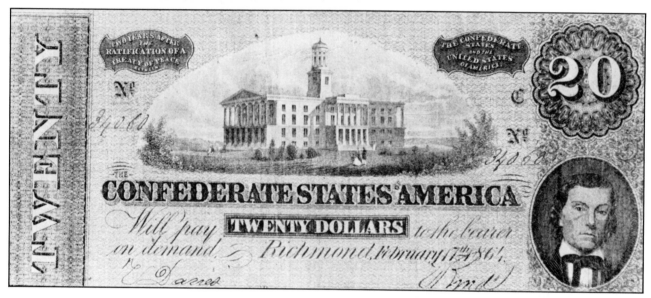

Although Nashville remained under Union control after February 1862, the Confederate Treasury department continued to depict the Tennessee capitol on its twenty dollar bills. This one is dated February 17, 1864. Pictured at right on the bill is Confederate Vice-President Alexander H. Stephens.

From the collection of Ralph Jerry Christian.

Because Tennessee's Federal military governor, Andrew Johnson, feared that the Confederates would try to recapture Nashville, he transformed the state capitol into a fortress, which the citizens derisively nicknamed "Fort Andrew Johnson." Notice the soldiers bivouaced on the grounds and the cedar stockade surrounding the building. Not visible are earthworks, barricades made of cotton bales, and fifteen heavy guns. These defenses were maintained throughout the war.

Photograph by Mathew Brady; courtesy of National Archives.

Union strategy for winning the Civil War called for splitting the Confederacy along the Mississippi River and then conquering its agricultural heartland. Nashville's rail lines and position on the Cumberland River made the city vital to the success of the Federal plan. This map, prepared by Benson J. Lossing shortly after the war, shows the city's rail connections and Union troop movements in Middle Tennessee and portions of Kentucky, Mississippi, and Alabama in 1863.

Map from Lossing, Pictorial Field Book of the Civil War.

These steamboats are docked at the Nashville Wharf in late 1862. From left to right are the Rob Boy, Belle Peoria, Irene, Revenue, Palestine, Lizzie Martin, and Mercury. Scenes such as this occurred frequently during the war, as boats shuttled back and forth between Nashville and points on the Cumberland, Tennessee, Ohio, and Mississippi rivers with supplies for Federal troops.

Photograph courtesy of Tennessee State Library and Archives.

Because Confederate cavalry forces, under commanders like Nathan Bedford Forrest, John Hunt Morgan, and "Fighting Joe" Wheeler, kept constant military pressure on rail lines leading in and out of Nashville, Union army engineers built log stockades, such as this one on the Louisville and Nashville Railroad, at intervals along all the lines.
Drawing by Frank Beard; from Harper's Weekly, February 7, 1863.

This United States Army Signal Corps photograph shows the Nashville and Chattanooga Railroad shops, freight warehouse, and passenger station a few blocks southwest of the capitol. The view is to the north from a point near present Broadway and Tenth Avenue in front of Union Station. Barrels and crates of military supplies sit on the loading platform awaiting shipment. None of these structures is extant.
Photograph courtesy of National Archives.

A closer view of the Nashville and Chattanooga Railroad depot shows sixteen locomotives ready to move freight cars around the yard and pull trainloads of supplies to distant points.
U.S. Army Signal Corps photograph; courtesy of National Archives.

To help insure that its supply trains kept rolling, the Union army took over the operation of railroads in Middle Tennessee. This building was erected in the Nashville and Chattanooga rail yard for United States Military Railroad and Quartermaster Corps offices.
U.S. Army Signal Corps photograph; courtesy of National Archives.

The Union army's Taylor Depot Commisssary Storehouse was supposedly large enough to hold fifteen million complete rations. Shown here from the south, the gigantic structure filled an entire block between present Fifth and Sixth avenues near their junction with Lafayette Street. Silhouettes of the capitol and the Downtown Presbyterian Church towers are visible in the background. The railroad tracks are those of the Nashville and Chattanooga line.
U.S. Army Signal Corps photograph; courtesy of National Archives.

During their occupation of Nashville, Federal troops built nearly twenty miles of earthworks, barricades, trenches, and other defenses. General James S. Negley, shown here, a Pennsylvanian in command of Union reserves in Nashville, began building fortifications in the city in 1862. Work continued on them for two more years at an eventual cost of slightly more than $365,000. The war department in Washington thought this sum extravagant and sent General Zealous B. Tower, superintendent of the United States Military Academy, to Nashville to investigate suspected waste. Instead of criticizing the defenses as unnecessary, Tower recommended that they be strengthened because of Nashville's strategic importance as the "great depot of the West."

Drawing from Lossing, Pictorial Field Book of the Civil War.

Officers and civilian employees of the Union Quartermaster Corps posed for this photograph by an unknown cameraman in 1864. These men were responsible for obtaining and distributing supplies to Federal troops in the field.

Photograph courtesy of Tennessee State Library and Archives.

General James Saint Clair Morton, chief Federal military engineer in Nashville, laid out the city's line of defenses and designed Fort Negley, depicted in these illustrations. Before the war this promontory was a beautifully wooded picnic area called Saint Cloud Hill. After the war it was, according to some Nashvillians, a popular hideout for thieves. Today the Cumberland Science Museum is situated on the north side of the hill and Greer Stadium on the southeast.

SOUTH WEST VIEW OF FORT NEGLEY.

This drawing, by W.H.H. Fletcher, shows Fort Negley from the southwest in 1864.
Courtesy of Library of Congress.

U.S. Army engineers' plan for Fort Negley in 1864.
Drawing courtesy of National Archives.

Eastward view from the south side of Fort Negley in 1864.
Photograph courtesy of National Archives.

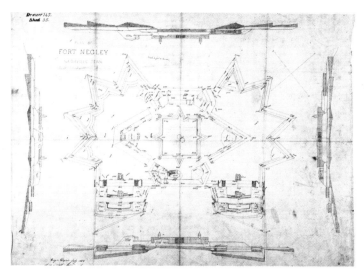

Union troops used buildings on the University of Nashville campus as barracks and hospital facilities. This photograph, taken from the roof of the Western Military Institute on College Hill, shows Lindsley Hall at left and Forts Negley and Casino in the distance. Fort Negley is on the first hill from the left; Fort Casino is on the second.

Photograph courtesy of Tennessee State Library and Archives.

Shortly after arriving in Nashville in 1862 Federal authorities seized this house at 13 High Street (Sixth Avenue) for use as official military headquarters. It was the residence of George W. Cunningham, a prominent wholesaler of hardware, guns, and cutlery. Almost every important Union officer in the western theater of operations entered the house at one time or another. While here in March 1864, Ulysses S. Grant learned of his appointment as general-in-chief of the armies of the United States and issued his first orders in that capacity. After the war the house was returned to the Cunningham family. From 1882 until well into the twentieth century it served as headquarters of the Hermitage Club. A restaurant now occupies the site.

Photograph courtesy of Public Library of Metropolitan Nashville-Davidson County.

General William Starke Rosecrans assumed command of the newly created Federal Army of the Cumberland in October 1862, when Confederate forces under General Braxton Bragg threatened Nashville. In late December Rosecrans moved out of the city, attacked Bragg at Stones River near Murfreesboro, and forced him, by January 3, 1863, to retreat southward to Shelbyville. Rosecrans returned to Nashville and remained in the city nearly six months before advancing toward Chattanooga. In September 1863 he suffered a major defeat in the Battle of Chickamauga and was relieved of command.

Oil on canvas by Samuel Price; photograph courtesy of National Portrait Gallery, Smithsonian Institution.

Andrew Johnson, Tennessee's federally appointed military governor, was the most unpopular official associated with the Union occupation. Although he had resided in the city as the elected governor from 1853 to 1857, Johnson, who came from rural East Tennessee, had never cared much for Nashville's political, financial, and social leaders. Following his election to the United States Senate in 1857, he had stood steadfast against secession and refused to surrender his seat when Tennessee left the Union in 1861. In March 1862 President Abraham Lincoln appointed Johnson military governor with the rank of brigadier-general. During the next two years Johnson put pro-Union men in most offices of city government and imprisoned many prominent citizens for suspected disloyalty. In 1864 he was elected vice-president of the United States, and early the next year he left Nashville for Washington. Following Lincoln's assassination in April 1865, Johnson succeeded to the presidency.

Photograph by Mathew Brady; courtesy of National Archives.

Following the Battle of Chickamauga, General George H. Thomas became commander of the Army of the Cumberland. On December 15-16, 1864, he successfully defended Nashville against 23,000 Confederates under General John Bell Hood. Afterward the Nashville City Council, a pro-Union body appointed by Governor Andrew Johnson, passed a resolution thanking Thomas for saving the city.

Photograph by Mathew Brady; courtesy of National Archives.

Although never headquartered in Nashville, General William Tecumseh Sherman was a frequent wartime visitor. He relied on the city for supplies during successful campaigns in Mississippi, Tennessee, and Georgia. Sherman posed for this portrait in 1866 shortly after marching and fighting his way into military annals as one of the most effective commanders in American history.

Oil on canvas by G.P.A. Healy; photograph courtesy of National Portrait Gallery, Smithsonian Institution.

Of all the military men whose careers were intertwined with Nashville, none achieved as much recognition as Ulysses S. Grant. After his seizure of Fort Donelson left Nashville defenseless and caused the Confederate troops to abandon the city, Grant recognized its potential as a supply base and resolved to hold it at all costs. He visited Nashville on numerous occasions and was here in March 1864 when President Lincoln asked him to assume command of all the Union armies. After the war Grant was twice elected president on the Republican ticket.

Photograph by Mathew Brady; courtesy of National Archives.

In addition to Andrew Johnson and Ulysses S. Grant, two other future presidents of the United States spent time in Nashville during the war. James A. Garfield, shown here in 1881, resided briefly in the city in 1863 while serving as General Rosecrans' chief of staff. Garfield was elected president as a Republican in 1880 and assassinated in July 1881.

Albumen silver print by A. Bogardus photograph courtesy of National Portrait Gallery Smithsonian Institution.

Benjamin Harrison was the fourth future president associated with wartime Nashville. As a colonel in the 70th Indiana Infantry, he helped guard the Louisville and Nashville Railroad. During the Battle of Nashville in December 1864, he commanded the 1st Brigade of General Charles Cruft's Provisional Division, which held a portion of the Union line along Granny White Pike. Harrison, a Republican, won election to the presidency in 1888.

Photograph by Notman Photograph Company; courtesy of National Archives.

In addition to serving as a vital supply base for Union armies, Nashville was also a major center for the care and treatment of wounded and ill soldiers. Federal authorities seized both public and private buildings for military hospitals, and by the summer of 1863 Nashville had twenty-five such institutions. Pictured here is the old Howard School building on College Street (Third Avenue South) as viewed from the southeast. Designated Hospital No. 1, Division 1, it had 250 beds.

U.S. Army Quartermaster Corps photograph; courtesy of National Archives.

The Nashville Female Academy, which stood on Church Street near the Nashville and Chattanooga Railroad depot, also served as a military hospital. Founded in 1816, the academy became the South's largest girls' school by the 1850s. During the panic that followed the fall of Fort Donelson in February 1862, nearly all the school's boarding students fled on Nashville and Chattanooga trains, and classes ceased. After the war, efforts to reopen the academy failed.

Drawing courtesy of Tennessee State Library and Archives.

The United States Sanitary Commission's Soldiers Home occupied the Planter's Hotel, shown here, at the corner of Summer (Fifth Avenue) and Deaderick streets adjacent to Saint Mary's Church. The Sanitary Commission was a civilian auxiliary to the Union Medical Department and functioned in the Civil War much like the Red Cross in subsequent wars. Volunteers throughout the North, especially in large cities, held fundraising "sanitary fairs" to support the organization.

U.S. Army Quartermaster Corps photograph; courtesy of National Archives.

The Watson House, a hotel at 28 North Market Street (Second Avenue), served as an annex to a larger, 450-bed hospital nearby. This view is to the south toward College Hill. The conditions in Nashville's military hospitals varied according to location and size, but all followed standard medical department procedures. For example, when a patient was admitted in movable condition he was, in order, stripped, washed, given new hospital clothing, assigned a number and a bed, and then examined by a surgeon.
U.S. Army Quartermaster Corps photograph; courtesy of National Archives.

The University of Nashville's Lindsley Hall on College Hill (Second Avenue South near present General Hospital) was also used as a medical facility and could hold three hundred patients. Notice the windows opened for ventilation.
U.S. Army Quartermaster Corps photograph; courtesy of National Archives.

The Union Medical Department maintained separate hospitals for black patients. This one stood on College Street (Third Avenue) between Broad and Spring (Commerce) streets and could accommodate 375 persons. Although military hospitals often employed black women as nurses, the number of females in this photograph suggests that this facility treated both soldiers and slaves who had fled behind Union lines.
U.S. Army Quartermaster Corps photograph; courtesy of National Archives.

John Overton, descendant of Judge John Overton, started construction on this hotel, the Maxwell House in 1859. Early in the war Confederates quartered troops in the still-incomplete structure and called it Zollicoffer Barracks in honor of General Felix K. Zollicoffer, a former Nashville newspaperman and congressman who had turned volunteer soldier. After Union forces occupied the city they used the building successively as a barracks, hospital, and prison. In September 1863 several Confederate prisoners reportedly died here when a stairway collapsed on them. Following the war, construction resumed, and the Maxwell House opened as a hotel in 1868. It stood at the corner of Cherry (Fourth Avenue) and Church streets until destroyed by fire in 1961. The Third National Bank Building occupies that corner today.

U.S. Army Quartermaster Corps photograph; courtesy of National Archives.

This sketch of the Battle of Nashville is the artist's conception of Union Colonel Sylvester G. Hill's Third Brigade charging a Confederate position between present Woodmont Boulevard and Graybar Lane east of Hillsboro Road on December 15, 1864. Hill was fatally wounded in this action.

Drawing by George H. Ellsburg; from Harper's Weekly, January 14, 1865.

On April 3, 1865, Union supporters in Nashville celebrated the fall of Richmond, Virginia, to Federal troops, and on the tenth they rejoiced over Robert E. Lee's surrender at Appomattox. A general feeling of relief seemed to pervade the entire city. Then on April 14 John Wilkes Booth fatally wounded President Lincoln at Ford's Theatre in Washington, and the mood changed dramatically. This "extra" April 15 edition of the Nashville Union is one example of the anger and confusion that Unionists in the city experienced. The paper referred to Booth and his suspected accomplices as "the rebel fiends" and reported Secretary of State William H. Seward dead when he was not.

Newspaper courtesy of Public Library of Metropolitan Nashville-Davidson County.

NASHVILLE UNION
Extra.

Saturday Morning, April 15th, 1865.

THE REBEL FIENDS AT WORK.

President Lincoln Shot.

Secretary Seward Stabbed.

The President and Mr. Seward both Dead.

Grief of Mrs. Lincoln.

Seward's Son and Attendants Attacked.

Young Seward's Skull Fractured.

Wilkes Booth the President's Assassin.

Although compared to many other Southern cities, Nashville suffered little physical damage during the Civil War, it lost some of its most talented citizens. Colonel Randel W. McGavock, a Harvard Law School graduate and former mayor of Nashville, was killed near Vicksburg, Mississippi, in May 1862. General Felix K. Zollicoffer, editor and three-term congressman from Nashville, was fatally wounded near Mill Springs, Kentucky, in January 1862. And Colonel Adolphus W. Heiman, architect of many of Nashville's finest buildings, died in a military hospital in Jackson, Mississippi, in December 1862.

Colonel Randel W. McGavock.
Engraving by E.B. Hall's Sons;
from Lindsley,
Military Annals of Tennessee.

General Felix K. Zollicoffer.
Drawing from Harper's Weekly,
February 8, 1862.

Colonel Adolphus W. Heiman.
Engraving by E.B. Hall's Sons
from Lindsley,
Military Annals of Tennessee.

As governor of Tennessee from 1865 to 1869 William G. "Parson" Brownlow presided over the state's political Reconstruction, and apparently most Nashvillians found him no more to their liking than Civil War governor Andrew Johnson. Like Johnson, Brownlow came from East Tennessee, was an ardent Unionist, and had little use for Nashville. The city, he said, had an air of disloyalty; its ministers were traitors, its women stiff-necked and proud. Probably neither the ministers, the women, nor most other residents were sorry in 1869 when the state legislature sent Brownlow to Washington to represent Tennessee in the United States Senate. If nothing else, the appointment got him out of Nashville.

Photograph by Mathew Brady; courtesy of National Archives.

When the Civil War ended, Nashville's future seemed uncertain to some residents. "Lawyers, doctors, newspaper men, merchants, etc. are today making fortunes," one wag observed, but "tomorrow they might be packing up for some other region—all but the lawyers." The truth, however, was that Nashville, along with a handful of other Southern cities, had benefited from the war. It had escaped destructive bombardment, its merchants had profited from the presence of Federal troops for three years, and its population had swelled with emigrants from both North and South. Thus in 1865 Nashville stood on the verge of another boom. During the next three decades its economic development was equaled only by the phenomenal advance of its cultural institutions. By 1880 Nashville was the leading commercial center and wholesale market below the Ohio River, and by 1890 it was the "Athens of the South."

Before it achieved these advances, Nashville, like the rest of the South, went through a period of political Reconstruction imposed by Congress. In 1867 Tennessee's Reconstruction governor, William G. Brownlow, installed Yankee carpetbagger Augustus E. Alden as Nashville's mayor. Although Alden inaugurated free public education for black Nashvillians and improved municipal welfare programs, most historians have characterized him as a freebooter because of political corruption in his administration. In June 1869 conservative leaders ousted Alden from office and placed the city government in receivership until a successor could be elected in September.

By 1870 Nashville boasted a new city government, a rejuvenated trade along the Cumberland River, and a population of 25,000. Visitors to the community could ride on horse-drawn street railway lines and stay in the Maxwell House, a new luxury hotel that soon would be known throughout the country. Still, the city faced problems. A majority of the populace continued to live, as they had from the beginning, near the waterfront, or at least within a twenty or thirty-minute walk. Merchants and shopkeepers often resided with their families in loft apartments above downtown stores and warehouses, while transient dock-

Chapter
V

Athens
of the
South:

1865-1897

workers and riverboat crews boarded along the river in vice-ridden areas known as "The Jungle" and "Black Bottom." Even wealthy lawyers and bankers lived no farther away than the eastern edge of what is now the Vanderbilt campus. Although typical of American cities in the nineteenth century, this congestion, combined with the lack of both sewers and public regulations governing slaughterhouses and tanneries, was a constant threat to health. The *Republican Banner* lamented in 1873 that Nashville "looks like a pig pen." That same year the filth led to a cholera epidemic that killed more than one thousand residents.

Financial panic also struck the city, as well as the rest of the nation, in 1873, but Nashville weathered it better than most communities, and by 1878 the smoke of industry hung more heavily than ever in the air, signaling not only recovery but also expansion. The city's factories turned out cotton, lumber, iron, machinery, furniture, flour, Tennessee whiskey, and myriad other products. Contractors could not fill all their work orders, and for more than two weeks in the summer not a single nail could be bought in Nashville. As a fitting symbol of this boom, workmen raised a massive new federal custom house on the southeast corner of Spruce (Eighth Avenue South) and Broad streets. A Gothic revival structure designed by William Appleman Porter, it was also symbolic of the end of Reconstruction. In September 1877 President Rutherford B. Hayes, compromise winner of the hotly disputed election of 1876, had traveled to Nashville to lay the building's cornerstone in a gesture of reconciliation between North and South.

Educational progress matched economic progress in post-Civil War Nashville, as a number of new colleges, universities, and academies opened their doors to students. Three of the new institutions eventually gained national prominence. Fisk School, now Fisk University, was first to do so. Founded in 1865 by representatives of the American Missionary Association and the Freedmen's Bureau, a federal agency which helped former slaves adjust to freedom, Fisk began accepting students in January 1886. It held classes in an old Union military hospital on West Church Street and offered a "broad Christian education" at both the secondary and college levels, with emphasis on training black teachers. Within a few months enrollment reached one thousand as black Nashvillians, young and old alike, took full advantage of their first opportunity to receive a formal education. To raise money to keep the school open, its outstanding chorus, the Fisk Jubilee Singers, gave performances throughout the world. Another new school for blacks was Central Tennessee College. Established in South Nashville in 1866, with aid from the Freedmen's Bureau and the Missionary Society of the Methodist Episcopal Church, this institution evolved ultimately into Meharry Medical College, America's foremost training center for black physicians, dentists, and nurses. In the 1870s Vanderbilt University offered white Nashvillians a new place of higher learning. The Methodist Episcopal Church, South, established this school with a gift of one million dollars from Commodore Cornelius Vanderbilt. Now one of the great private universities in the nation, Vanderbilt began classes in 1875 on a magnificent new campus just west of Hillsboro Pike.

While Fisk, Meharry, and Vanderbilt were getting started, the city's oldest college, the University of Nashville, underwent a series of changes that destined it for fame, too. Shortly after the Civil War the school began seeking aid from a special education fund endowed by Massachusetts philanthropist George Peabody to promote teacher training in the South. In 1875 the Peabody Fund offered assistance on condition that the university transfer all its resources to a new state normal school which the legislature had just established in Nashville. The officials obliged, and today the institution that grew out of that union, George Peabody College for Teachers, conducts classes both in Nashville and in extension centers throughout the United States and in Europe. Peabody College is now a school of Vanderbilt University, having merged with that institution in July 1979, but it retains its identification as a premier center for training teachers.

Other Nashville schools established in the postwar years include Ward's Seminary for Young Ladies (1865); Montgomery Bell Academy (1867), long a department of the University of Nashville; Saint Bernard Academy (1868), a Catholic school for girls; and Watkins Institute (1880), the city's first school for adults. Of those, all but Ward's Seminary are still operating.

An even greater number of postwar schools failed to last through the century. Nevertheless, Nashvillians of the 1890s could take pride in all of them, as well as in sundry other trappings of cultural advancement, such as dozens of professional and philanthropic organizations like the Ladies Hermitage Association (1889), a pioneer preservationist group dedicated to saving the home of Andrew Jackson; a host of new churches and the Union Gospel Tabernacle (1892), a center for evangelistic revivals, theatrical presentations, and political rallies; and a still-lively press that featured influential regional periodicals like the *Southern Lumberman* (1881) and the *Southwestern Journal of Education* (1884).

No wonder, then, that in 1897 when the state of Tennessee celebrated its centennial, a year late, with an exposition in Nashville, the citizenry joyously supported the construction of a replica of the Greek Parthenon as the main exhibition building. When completed, the structure symbolized a nickname—"Athens of the South"—that Nashvillians had used for their city since the 1820s. It seemed a sobriquet richly deserved in the nineties. ❧

During Reconstruction, citizens whose property had been seized in the Civil War could seek reimbursement from the federal government. Two Yankee soldiers, J.W. Paramore and F.S. Sowers, remained in Nashville after the war and opened an agency to help residents file claims for payment. The pair had an office on Cherry Street (Fourth Avenue North) near Broad and lived about one and one-half miles south of town on Franklin Pike.

Advertisement from
Nashville City Directory for 1867.

The Maxwell House, which had been a barracks for both Confederate and Union troops during the Civil War, opened to the public in 1868. For almost a century afterward it was a Nashville landmark and one of the South's best-known hotels. Presidents Andrew Johnson, Rutherford B. Hayes, Grover Cleveland, William McKinley, and Theodore Roosevelt visited it, as did numerous other notable Americans. And entrepreneur Joel Cheek took its name for his famous blend of coffee. These representations of the hotel's exterior and lobby are from its turn-of-the-century stationery. The photograph shows the hotel's dining room in the same period.

Stationery courtesy of
Victoria B. Christian.
Photograph by Calvert Brothers;
courtesy of Tennessee
State Library and Archives.

One of the city government's priorities after the Civil War was replacing the suspension bridge burned by retreating Confederate troops in 1862. With the help of famous bridge and railroad engineer Albert Fink, city engineer Wilbur F. Foster supervised the work. The new suspension bridge, completed in 1866, used the masonry towers of the first bridge but was designed to carry more weight. Each cable contained 2,456 wires, with a total strength of 7,368,000 pounds, enabling the bridge to accommodate a live load of up to 604,000 pounds. Construction costs were paid by the collection of tolls, including seventy-five cents for a four-horse carriage, fifteen cents for a horse and buggy, ten cents for one hundred chickens, five cents for a man on horseback, and a penny for a hog. Pedestrians crossed free, but according to the sign in this circa 1880 photograph, if they failed to keep to the right, they could be fined one dollar. The Woodland Street bridge replaced this one in 1886.
Photograph by Calvert Brothers; courtesy of Tennessee State Library and Archives.

Although taken later in the century, this photograph of Cherry Street (Fourth Avenue) shows one of three horse-drawn street railways that opened in Nashville just after the Civil War. This line, the South Nashville Street Railroad, was the first. Completed in 1866, it extended south from Cedar Street (Charlotte Avenue) along Cherry (Fourth Avenue) and College (Third Avenue) streets and covered about four and one-half miles. Nineteen men and forty-three horses kept five cars running regularly. Later, mules replaced the horses. By 1870 the McGavock and Mount Vernon Street Railroad reached north from the Public Square to Jefferson Street, and the Church and Spruce Street Railroad extended west to the outskirts of town.
Photograph courtesy of Tennessee State Library and Archives.

THE INDIAN DOCTOR'S

Chills, Fever and Ague Cures,

WILL CURE

Dumb Ague, Swamp Fever Chills,

AND IS THE BEST REMEDY FOR FLUX IN AMERICA

IT HAS CURED

CHRONIC DIARRHEA

OF THREE YEARS STANDING.

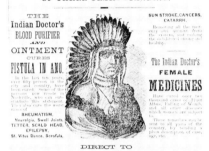

THE
Indian Doctor's
BLOOD PURIFIER
AND
OINTMENT
CURES
FISTULA IN ANO.

RHEUMATISM,
Neuralgia, Swell Joints,
TETTER, SCALD HEAD,
EPILEPSY,
St. Vitus Dance, Scrofula,

SUN STROKE, CANCERS,
CATARRH.

The Indian Doctor's
FEMALE
MEDICINES

DIRECT TO

INDIAN DOCTOR,

No. 51 South Union Street,

ONE HUNDRED YARDS FROM THE SPRUCE STREET R. R.

NASHVILLE, TENN.

Despite such signs of progress as street railways and the magnificent Maxwell House, postwar Nashville bore, according to the Republican Banner, a striking resemblance to a "pig pen." The overcrowded city had neither sewers nor laws governing waste disposal by tanneries or other industries. Such conditions increased the incidence of illness and disease in Nashville and kept both its physicians and its patent medicine peddlers busy. The manufacturer who placed this advertisement in the 1867 city directory claimed that his medicines would purify a person's blood and cure him of illnesses ranging from dumb ague and swamp fever (malaria) to diarrhea, rheumatism, and epilepsy.

Advertisement from Nashville City Directory for 1867.

This view east from the capitol shows the crowded living and working conditions that prevailed in downtown Nashville during the 1870s and 1880s. Notice the mixture of stores and residences. The Public Square, the Davidson County Courthouse, and the City Hall and Market House with its twin office wings are in the upper center of the picture.

Photograph courtesy of Tennessee State Library and Archives.

Until the 1870s Nashville had no federal building to house government offices. Congress had authorized the erection of a custom house and post office in Nashville in 1856, but work overloads in the U.S. Treasury Department's construction division, combined with the effects of the Civil War, delayed the project nearly twenty years. Work finally commenced in 1876 at the corner of Spruce (Eighth Avenue) and Broad. William Appleton Porter, supervising architect for the treasury department, drew the plans for the massive granite and limestone edifice, and work crews completed it in 1883. This photograph was snapped by an unidentified cameraman about 1900. At present the structure is undergoing renovation as a private office building.

Photograph courtesy of Historical Commission of Metropolitan Nashville-Davidson County.

In 1877 President Rutherford B. Hayes made Nashville's United States Custom House a symbol of the end of Reconstruction. After winning the presidency in an election so hotly disputed that Congress had to appoint a special electoral commission to decide the winner, Hayes, a Republican, made a goodwill tour of the South to help heal the emotional wounds of the Civil War. Accompanied by his wife and several cabinet members, the president stopped in Nashville on September 19, 1877, and helped lay the Custom House cornerstone.

Albumen silver print by unidentified artist; photograph courtesy of National Portrait Gallery, Smithsonian Institution.

Nashville grew rapidly in the late 1870s and 1880s. Among those who applauded that growth loudest was Arthur S. Colyar. A staunch Democrat and aggressive journalist, Colyar has been called "the Henry W. Grady of Nashville." Like Grady, the Atlanta Constitution *editor who earned national attention extolling a "new" industrial South, Colyar, as editor of the Nashville* American, *encouraged investors to put their money in factories and railroads rather than land and financial institutions.*

Photograph courtesy of Tennessee State Library and Archives.

Much of the lumber used during Nashville's 1878 building boom was supplied by Prewitt, Spurr, and Company, a firm established in 1866 on the east bank of the Cumberland almost opposite the Nashville Wharf. The company employed 125 men and boys in a sawmill, planing mill, bucket factory, varnish room, warehouse, and three kilns, and produced lumber, buckets, churns, and ashware. Notice the log rafts anchored to the shore. These were formed upriver, floated down the Cumberland, and left in the water until the logs could be hoisted one at a time into the mill yard.

Drawing from Clayton, History of Davidson County.

Steamboats remained an important means of transportation in Middle Tennessee after the Civil War. In fact, steamboat companies both increased and improved their service. As suggested in this 1878 advertisement, boats left the Nashville Wharf almost daily for Paducah, Evansville, Louisville, Cincinnati, and Pittsburgh on the Ohio River; for Cairo, Saint Louis, Memphis, Vicksburg, and New Orleans on the Mississippi; and for dozens of lesser ports in between. They moved both passengers and freight with greater speed and efficiency than before the war. As a result, by 1880 Cumberland steamers were carrying one million tons of freight each year.

Advertisement from Nashville City Directory for 1878.

This 1879 view of Front Street (First Avenue) north of Broad shows the continued bustle of commerce on the Nashville Wharf following the Civil War. The boats are the John Galt, built in 1857; Eddyville, constructed in 1871; and Dora Cable, completed in 1877.

Photograph by Calvert Brothers; courtesy of Tennessee State Library and Archives.

Over the years a number of steamboats bore the name Nashville. The last one, pictured here in the 1890s, operated until about 1920 and made regular runs up the Cumberland and Caney Fork rivers southeast of Carthage, Tennessee. *Photograph courtesy of Deborah Cooney.*

Many of the Cumberland packets bore the names of entrepreneurs who financed them. The boat being unloaded here, about 1890, is the H.W. Buttorff. It was named for Harry W. Buttorff, co-founder and president of the Phillips and Buttorff Company, a Nashville firm that manufactured stoves, tinware, and household furnishings and was for many years a principal shipper on the Cumberland.

Photograph by Calvert Brothers; courtesy of Tennessee State Library and Archives.

These vessels, docked at the Nashville Wharf in the early 1890s, are left to right: the Jno. W. Hart, J.J. Odil, and I.T. Rhea. The last was named for Isaac T. Rhea, son of steamboat operator Byrd S. Rhea and a major importer of midwestern grain. Although his investments in steamboats were sizeable, Isaac T. Rhea relied more on railroads than on steamboats to transport grain because the railroads gave Nashville dealers privileged rates that enabled them to unload grain, mill it, and reship it without paying additional handling charges. This helped make Nashville the South's chief grain distributor and leading flour and meal manufacturing center. It also took business away from the steamboat companies and helped speed the demise of steamboating on the Cumberland early in the twentieth century.

Photograph from Art Work of Nashville.

NASHVILLE & DECATUR

RAILWAY.

THE OLD ESTABLISHED ALL RAIL ROUTE TO

HUNTSVILLE, MEMPHIS, NEW ORLEANS,

MOBILE, SELMA,

AND ALL INTERMEDIATE POINTS.

Connects at Decatur with Memphis & Charleston Railroad for
Memphis, Selma, Mobile, Jackson and Vicksburg, Miss.,
New Orleans, La., Huntsville and all
intermediate points.

In 1872, three years after this advertisement appeared in the Nashville city directory, the Louisville and Nashville Railroad leased the Nashville and Decatur line for thirty years. A few months later the L & N acquired controlling interest in the South and North Alabama Railroad and linked Nashville with Montgomery. These lines, combined with the L & N's Louisville-to-Nashville and Bowling Green-to-Memphis routes, gave that firm 780 miles of track and made it one of the South's largest corporations. The success of the L & N, along with the progress of the Nashville, Chattanooga, and Saint Louis Railroad, helped make Nashville a major rail center.

*Advertisement from
Nashville City Directory for 1869.*

Edmund W. Cole, one of postwar Nashville's leading railroad men, was almost penniless when he arrived in the city in 1845. Although only eighteen and straight off a Giles County farm, Cole managed to get a job as clerk in a clothing store. During the next few years he held a variety of similar positions, selling suits, books, and shoes. In all those jobs he demonstrated an ability to work with figures, and in 1849 he landed the bookkeeper's position at the Nashville post office. A few years later he transferred to a similar job with the Nashville and Chattanooga Railroad. In 1857 he was elected superintendent, and in 1868 he became president of the line. Cole added the Nashville and Northwestern, McMinnville and Manchester, Winchester and Alabama, and Tennessee Pacific roads to the Nashville and Chattanooga, and in 1872 it became the Nashville, Chattanooga, and Saint Louis Railroad, or N, C & St. L. In 1880, after the L & N bought Vernon K. Stevenson's interest in the N, C & St. L, Cole resigned. He remained in Nashville, though, and in 1883 he established the American National Bank, now the First American National Bank.

*Engraving by A.H. Ritchie;
photograph from Clayton,
History of Davidson County.*

By 1890 the Nashville, Chattanooga, and Saint Louis Railroad operated 92 locomotives and more than 2,500 freight, passenger, and other cars over 650 miles of track. This photograph of the N, C & St. L depot north of present Union Station shows an N, C & St. L passenger train being prepared for departure, while an L & N freight car sits on a siding, left. The view is to the southeast; the tower in the left background is that of the U.S. Custom House.

Photograph from
The 400: American Society Journal
of Travel (April 1897).

These buildings on Broad Street, south of the Nashville, Chattanooga, and Saint Louis Depot, housed the railroad's administrative headquarters at the turn of the century. The company built the main structure, on the left, and converted the other from a residence. Standing at the entrance of the principal building are John W. Thomas, president of the line, and William L. Danley, general passenger agent. Neither structure is extant. Their places are occupied today by a bookstore, parking lot, and hotel.

Photograph from
The 400: American Society Journal
of Travel (April 1897).

This 1875 map illustrates Nashville's postwar growth. Notice the L & N depot (at "2") north of the City Hall and Market, and the N, C & St. L depot (left of "10") near Church and McLemore streets. At the upper right (near "6") is South Nashville, consolidated with the city of Nashville before the Civil War.

Map compiled by Wilbur F. Foster, city engineer; courtesy of Public Library of Metropolitan Nashville-Davidson County.

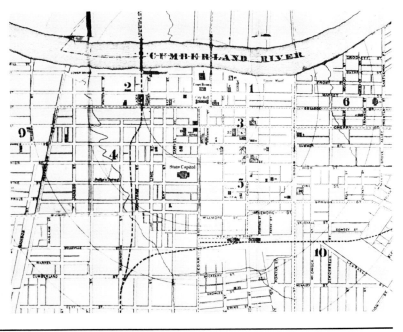

An electric trolley makes its run along West End Avenue in the 1890s. In the years since this photograph was taken, these stately houses have given way to the wrecking ball, and West End has become one of the busiest commercial streets in the city.

Photograph courtesy of Historical Commission of Metropolitan Nashville-Davidson County.

Nashville was one of the first cities in the South to have electric streetcars. In 1888 the McGavock and Mount Vernon Street Railroad began switching from horse-drawn to electric cars, and within a year it was operating the new conveyances over seventeen miles of track from Cherry Street (Fourth Avenue) east to McNairy Street (Twelfth Avenue) and from Broad Street north to Jefferson and Monroe streets. By 1890 the South Nashville Street Railroad had converted its lines to electricity, the City Electric Railway had been incorporated to serve the Market Street and Wharf areas, and electric lines had been extended over streetcar tracks in Edgefield and East Nashville. With more than fifty miles of lines electrified, the various companies merged in February 1890 as the United Electric Railway. In this April 1889 photograph Governor Robert Taylor and city officials are gathered with family members to inaugurate electric trolley service on Broad Street. Notice the horse-drawn trolley at left. The buildings in the background are the First Baptist Church and the U.S. Custom House.

Photograph courtesy of The Tennessean.

Fisk University was the first of several notable educational institutions established in Nashville after the Civil War. It was named in honor of General Clinton B. Fisk, assistant commissioner of the Freedmen's Bureau for Tennessee and Kentucky. As agent for a federal program charged with helping former slaves adjust to freedom, Fisk was impressed by the efforts of Erastus M. Cravath and Edward P. Smith, representatives of the American Missionary Association, to found a black university in Nashville. He helped them secure a campus for the school and then continued to support it after returning home to New York and becoming a prosperous banker. In later years General Fisk, shown here, served on the federal Board of Indian Commissioners and ran for president on the Prohibitionist ticket.

Engraving by A.H. Ritchie; photograph from Clayton, History of Davidson County.

These Union army hospital barracks served as the first campus of Fisk University. They were situated on West Church Street between Knowles and McCrary streets, near where Church now intersects Interstate 40. Classes began here in January 1866, and during the first year nearly one thousand men, women, and children showed up every day for classes in elementary subjects. In 1867, after the city began offering classes for black youths, Fisk established academic and normal departments. Some whites opposed the school, and on March 5, 1868, members of the Ku Klux Klan rode along Church Street to frighten the students. Fisk's trustees persisted, however, in keeping the school open, and by 1869 they were planning a new campus.

Photograph courtesy of National Archives.

The Jubilee Singers raised most of the money needed for Fisk University's new campus and buildings. Music instructor George L. White founded the Jubilee Singers in 1867, and in 1870, after they won enthusiastic praise at a National Teachers' Association convention in Nashville, he decided to take the group on a fundraising tour. In 1871-72 they traveled twice through the North and East and returned home each time with twenty thousand dollars. The singers later toured the entire United States and much of Europe, but the funds from the first two trips proved sufficient to buy a new twenty-five-acre campus and to begin excavations for a new building. Members of the first touring Jubilee Singers were, left to right: Minnie Tate, Green Evans, Isaac Dickerson, Jennie Jackson, Massie Porter, Ella Sheppard, Thomas Rutling, Benjamin M. Holmes, and Eliza Walker.

Photograph courtesy of National Archives.

Workers began moving earth for the foundations of Fisk University's first permanent building on January 1, 1873. Exactly three years later, on January 1, 1876, faculty members, students, and guests dedicated the completed structure. It is pictured here on the cover of a special anthem which the Jubilee Singers performed on that occasion. Appropriately named Jubilee Hall, the new building was a magnificent Victorian Gothic edifice designed by New York architect Stephen D. Hatch. It rose six stories in height, was shaped like an "L" with wings of 128 and 145 feet, and could accommodate the entire operations of the university.

Program courtesy of Fisk University Library's Special Collections.

PROF. F. A. CHASE. PROF. H. C. MORGAN.

The officers and faculty of Fisk University in 1879 included Erastus M. Cavath, president and professor of mental and moral science; Adam K. Spence, dean of faculty and professor of Greek and French; Henry S. Bennett, professor of theology and German; Frederick A. Chase, professor of natural sciences; and Helen C. Morgan, professor of Latin. Clinton B. Fisk remained president of the board of trustees.

Photograph from Clayton, History of Davidson County.

Today Jubilee Hall is the oldest permanent building in the United States for the education of blacks, and it is a National Historic Landmark. The stately edifice is situated at the north end of the Fisk University campus, near the corner of Jefferson Street and Eighteenth Avenue North.

Photograph by Jack E. Boucher, courtesy of Historic American Buildings Survey.

Methodist Bishop Holland N. McTyeire played the leading role in establishing Vanderbilt University. After the Civil War he became convinced that the Methodist Episcopal Church, South, needed better-prepared ministers. He failed to persuade the church's general conference to support a ministerial school, but in 1871-72 he acquired the backing of several state conferences for a general university with theological, literary, scientific, moral, legal, and medical departments. In 1872 commissioners from several southeastern states obtained a charter for the school, to be called Central University of the Methodist Episcopal Church, South, but until Cornelius Vanderbilt came to their aid in 1873, the commissioners lacked funds to open it. In March of that year McTyeire, whose wife was Mrs. Vanderbilt's cousin, persuaded the multimillionaire railroad magnate to give the school half a million dollars; in return the Methodists changed its name to Vanderbilt University.

Photograph by Carl G. Giers; courtesy of Vanderbilt University Photographic Archive.

Vanderbilt University opened for classes in 1875. Its campus occupied a slightly elevated seventy-five acre tract two miles west of the capitol and included about twenty brick and frame buildings. Nashville architect William C. Smith designed the Main Building, shown here, and eight campus residences. In 1905 fire gutted this Victorian Gothic structure, and J. Edwin Carpenter, a Tennessean working for a New York firm, supervised its reconstruction and gave it an Italianate facade. Now called Kirkland Hall in honor of the school's second chancellor, the building remains a campus landmark.

Photograph courtesy of Nashville Area Chamber of Commerce.

In establishing a medical department, Vanderbilt University worked out an agreement with the University of Nashville whereby Vanderbilt utilized both the faculty and facilities of the older institution. This arrangement continued until 1895, when Vanderbilt erected this building on the southeast corner of Fifth Avenue South and Elm Street. The structure stood until the 1930s, when it was torn down for the extension of Lafayette Street and U.S. Highway 41.

Photograph from Art Work of Nashville.

Astronomer Edward Emerson Barnard was among those who earned degrees from Vanderbilt University during its early years. By the time he entered the university, Barnard was almost thirty years old and fairly well known as a photographer of comets. After graduating in 1887 he worked at the Link Observatory in California and Yerkes Observatory in Wisconsin and published more than nine hundred scientific papers. In 1892 he discovered the fifth satellite of Jupiter.

Photograph by T.B. Blackshear; courtesy of Metropolitan Historical Commission of Nashville-Davidson County.

St. Bernard Academy, Nashville, Tenn.

Saint Bernard Academy was one of several girls' schools begun in Nashville after the Civil War. Established by the Sisters of Our Lady of Mercy in 1868, Saint Bernard first occupied the former residence of military governor Andrew Johnson on Cedar Street (Charlotte Avenue) across from the capitol. Near the turn of the century the sisters moved the school to a new campus on Hillsboro Pike a few blocks south of Vanderbilt University. This building, which is still in use, was designed by the Nashville architectural firm of Thompson, Gibel, and Asmus and was dedicated on Saint Patrick's Day, 1905.

Postcard courtesy of Public Library of Metropolitan Nashville-Davidson County.

Samuel Watkins gave Nashville an educational institution that today ranks among the oldest of its kind in the nation. A successful but uneducated businessman, Watkins provided, through his will, both money and a plan for establishing a self-supporting free school for adults. Watkins Institute began receiving students in 1885. Soon it will celebrate its one hundredth anniversary.

Engraving courtesy of Watkins Institute for Adults.

Another postwar Nashville girls' school was Ward's Seminary for Young Ladies. William E. Ward, a Presbyterian minister, founded the nonsectarian institution in 1865 and moved it the following year into this building on Spruce Street (Eighth Avenue) between Church and Broad. Although known for its courses in art and drama, Ward's Seminary also had one of the first girls' basketball teams in the South. This photograph, taken in October 1887, shows the student body waiting to greet President Grover Cleveland, who was visiting the city with his bride. Eventually Ward's Seminary merged with Belmont College, and this structure was demolished.
Photograph courtesy of Deborah Cooney.

This circa 1920 photograph of the Watkins Institute Building, erected in 1885 on the southwest corner of High (Sixth Avenue) and Church streets, illustrates Samuel Watkins' plan for supporting the school he conceived. While holding classes in part of the huge structure, the institute rented the remaining space to private businesses—here the Tennessee Electric Power Company, an H.G. Hill grocery store, and a Joy's floral shop—and used the rental income to pay school expenses. Today Watkins Institute charges a small fee for classes but follows a similar financial scheme. The school shares a new building on this site with an F.W. Woolworth store.
Photograph courtesy of Watkins Institute for Adults.

Nashvillians voted in 1851 to establish the city's first public school system. The next year the city council sent Alfred Hume, principal of the Nashville Female Academy, to Boston and Philadelphia to study their public schools as possible models for Nashville. Hume's report formed the basis for a Nashville system created in 1853. Within two years the city erected its first public school building, the Hume School, on Spruce Street (Eighth Avenue) just north of Broad. In 1874 high school classes were moved into a new building, Fogg School, left, which was built on the adjoining corner lot and named for Francis B. Fogg, first president of the board of education. Today Hume-Fogg High School, below, a massive Tudor Gothic building, designed by William B. Ittner and Robert S. Sharp and erected in 1912-16, occupies that site.

Photograph by Calvert Brothers; courtesy of Tennessee State Library and Archives.

Photograph by George Rollie Adams.

In the early 1890s public school enrollment in Nashville reached approximately eight thousand. These educators administered some of the city's schools in those years. Left to right, front row: Timothy W. Haley, former principal of Pearl High School and principal of Caldwell School when this photograph was taken; Emma B. Clemons, teacher at Tarbox School, which could accommodate one thousand students; Zachariah H. Brown, former Hume principal and after 1885 superintendent of schools; James F. Lipscomb, principal of Fogg High School; and John E. Bailey, supervisor of music for all public schools. Left to right, back row: William H. Ferrell, principal of Watkins Seminary; William R. Manlove, teacher at Hynes School; Richard W. Jones, principal of Elliott School; and Marcus M. Ross, principal of Trimble School.

Photograph courtesy of Public Library of Metropolitan Nashville-Davidson County.

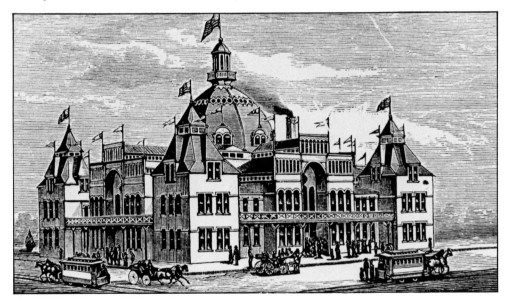

Between April 23 and May 29, 1880, Nashvillians celebrated the city's centennial with speeches, parades, fireworks, military drills, and the unveiling of an Andrew Jackson equestrian statue by noted sculptor Clark Mills. Residents also visited myriad exhibits in the specially constructed Centennial Exposition Building. Designed by William C. Smith and erected for eighteen thousand dollars by Simmons and Phillips, Contractors, the iron-ribbed edifice was situated on the southeast corner of Spruce (Eighth Avenue) and Broad streets, across from the Custom House. It fronted 189 feet along Broad and 159 along Spruce and contained nearly fifty thousand square feet of floor space. The centennial commission, which included John Berrien Lindsley, A.G. Adams, and William Stockell, filled the exposition building with historical memorabilia, works of art, and examples of the latest inventions. The U.S. Courthouse occupies this site today.

Drawing by Riches Company of Saint Louis from Clayton, History of Davidson County.

In 1897 Tennesseans celebrated the one hundredth anniversary of statehood by holding a magnificent Tennessee Centennial Exposition in what is now Centennial Park. Planning for the event began in 1893, but economic depression delayed its opening until nearly a year after the anniversary date. Because they were intended only for temporary use, the exposition buildings, shown here, were constructed of wood with stucco exteriors and plaster interiors. Despite this economy, the exposition cost more than $1.1 million. Subscriptions provided about one-half of that sum; admissions, concessions, and other receipts supplied the remainder.

Photograph by W.G. and A.J. Thuss, Photographers; from Art Album of the Tennessee Centennial and International Exposition.

On May 1, 1897, President William McKinley officially opened the Tennessee Centennial Exposition in a ceremony in Washington, D.C. He pushed a button and sent a signal along telegraph wires to start machinery on the exposition grounds. Six weeks later the president and his wife traveled to Nashville by train and spent two days visiting the buildings and exhibits. In honor of both opening day and the president, Nashvillians decorated the city with flags and bunting. This opening day photograph shows lower Broad Street westward from Market Street (Second Avenue).

Photograph by Otto B. Giers; courtesy of Tennessee State Library and Archives.

Because electricity was gaining widespread use in the mid-1890s, the Machinery Building became one of the most popular exhibits at the Tennessee Centennial Exposition. George W. Thompson and J.G. Zwicker designed the Greek revival structure, which measured 350 feet long by 100 feet wide and cost twenty thousand dollars to erect. Other specialized exhibit buildings included the Agriculture Building, Mineral and Forestry Building, Transportation Building, Commerce Building, Educational Building, United States Government Building, Women's Building, and Negro Building.

Photograph by Calvert Brothers; courtesy of Tennessee State Library and Archives.

The Tennessee Centennial Exposition also included amusements. There were donkey and boat rides, a carnival midway, dancing girls, a "Chute-the-Chute" boat ride that carried visitors down a steep slide into a pool of water, and a "Giant See-Saw" that lifted thrill-seekers two hundred feet into the air. Designed by Nashvillian Art J. Dyer, the see-saw offered riders a bird's-eye view of the exposition grounds. Some visitors thought the device dangerous, especially after its power mechanism failed one evening and left a group of riders suspended over the grounds all night.
Photograph by W.G. and A.J. Thuss, Photographers; from Art Album of the Tennessee Centennial and International Exposition.

Inside the Machinery Building visitors could view a variety of engines, boilers, and generators. Some of the machines powered other equipment on the exposition grounds.
Photograph by W.G. and A.J. Thuss, Photographers; from Art Album of the Tennessee Centennial and International Exposition.

The centerpiece of the Tennessee Centennial Exposition was an exact replica, reproduced from plans furnished by the king of Greece, of the Parthenon, a Greek temple erected in 447-432 B.C. to honor Athena, the goddess of wisdom. Major Eugene C. Lewis, director-general of the exposition, conceived the idea of replicating the renowned structure. William C. Smith drew the working plans for it, and George J. Zolnay made the models for the sculpture. Like the other exposition buildings, the Parthenon was a temporary exhibit building and housed works of art. Unlike the others, however, it remained long after the exposition closed and the grounds became a public park. In the 1920s the edifice began to crumble, and the City Parks Board had it rebuilt in concrete. This time, Nashville architect Russell E. Hart made the working drawings, the Foster and Creighton

Company handled the construction, and the Earley Studios of Washington, D.C., and Belle Kinney of Nashville cast the figures and ornaments from models rendered by several sculptors. Earley also made the columns, using a mixture of Potomac River gravel and crushed ceramic tile to obtain the proper coloration. Today the Parthenon is a popular tourist attraction and focal point for Centennial Park. The structure has provided a backdrop for public activities ranging from crafts fairs to movie filming and from park concerts to an outdoor party for the entire United Nations delegation.

Left photograph by Calvert Brothers, 1897; courtesy of Tennessee State Library and Archives.
Right photograph courtesy of Nashville Area Chamber of Commerce, 1978.

September 11, 1897, was Nashville Day at the Tennessee Centennial Exposition, and many citizens proudly wore lapel buttons, such as this one, depicting the Parthenon. The building was a fitting symbol for a city whose residents considered it the "Athens of the South."
    Button courtesy of Public Library of Metropolitan Nashville-Davidson County.

When the Tennessee Centennial Exposition concluded, the city converted the grounds into a park. Watauga Lake, named for the East Tennessee community that gave Nashville most of its first settlers, became a popular spot for Sunday afternoon boating.
    Postcard courtesy of Public Library of Metropolitan Nashville-Davidson County.

During the 1890s Nashvillians, like most other Americans, experienced a bicycle craze. Bicycling became the most popular sport in the country, and enthusiasts everywhere formed clubs to sponsor outings and races. Each year in Nashville the Capital City Cycling Club and others pedalled in a one-hundred-mile race from Nashville through Lebanon, Eagleville, Murfreesboro, and Triune, and back to Nashville. Here, cyclists from Vanderbilt University pose in front of Kirkland Hall for the school's 1892 yearbook.
    Photograph courtesy of Vanderbilt University Photographic Archive.

DUNCAN R. DORRIS...

National
...Pierce and
Gendron

BICYCLES

153 North
Spruce Street

WHEELS FOR RENT.
THE BEST REPAIR SHOP IN
THE SOUTH.

Duncan R. Dorris was one of four Nashville bicycle dealers at the turn of the century. According to this 1897 advertisement, he sold National, Pierce, and Gendron makes and offered both a repair and a rental service. Within a few years he graduated from bicycles to automobiles, and in 1903 he opened the first motor car dealership in the city. Advertisement from Souvenir Program of Fiftieth Anniversary of St. Mary's Cathedral.

Following the display of Andrew Jackson memorabilia at the Nashville Centennial Exposition in 1880, interest in artifacts associated with the nation's seventh president remained high. In February 1889 Andrew Jackson III, Mary C. Dorris, and William A. Donelson helped organize the Ladies Hermitage Association to preserve President Jackson's home and its grounds. Andrew Jackson III still lived in the Hermitage, but it had belonged to the state since 1856, when financial difficulties had forced Andrew Jackson, Jr., to sell it. In April 1889 the state turned the house and land over to the Ladies Hermitage Association, which became one of the nation's pioneer historic preservation organizations. When Andrew Jackson III moved out of the house in 1893, the association opened it to the public. Ever since that time the Ladies Hermitage Association has continued to take care of it and has improved both the property and their methods of presenting it to the public. This 1890s photograph reveals, on the wall to the right of the main stairway, a sign warning that visitors who "mutilate the wallpaper or otherwise deprecate" the premises will be arrested and fined.

Photograph by A.J. Thuss; courtesy of Andy Corn.

For a decade after the Ladies Hermitage Association opened Andrew Jackson's home to the public, "Uncle Alfred" Jackson, a former slave who had served as the late president's personal servant, acted as a guide for visitors. He poses here, at right, with a group viewing Jackson's tomb. When "Uncle Afred" died in 1901, his body lay in state in the Hermitage and later was buried near Jackson's.

Photograph by A.J. Thuss; courtesy of Andy Corn.

While the Ladies Hermitage Association preserved the residence of Andrew Jackson a few miles east of Nashville, William Hicks Jackson maintained another famous plantation home, Belle Meade, a few miles southwest of the city. A graduate of West Point and a Confederate general in the Civil War, Jackson became a planter after Appomattox. In 1868 he married Selene Harding, whose father, William Giles Harding, owned Belle Meade. That same year Jackson assumed responsibility for the plantation's nationally known thoroughbred stud farm, which Harding had operated since the late 1830s. This photograph, taken shortly before Harding's death in 1886, shows Jackson, standing at left in the first row left of the table, and Harding, seated second from right, hosting a Belle Meade picnic for Confederate veterans.

Photograph courtesy of the Association for the Preservation of Tennessee Antiquities.

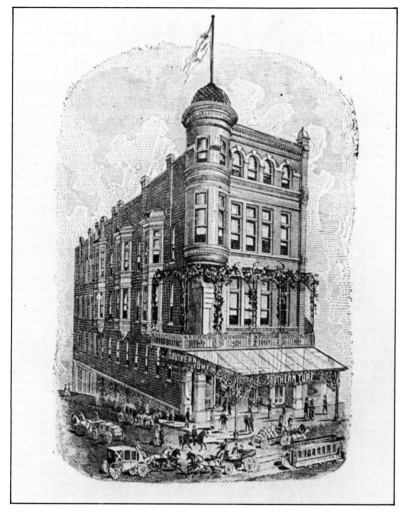

During the 1880s Nashville was known among traveling businessmen for its numerous posh saloons. This reputation grew bigger in the 1890s after entrepreneurs opened several new saloons in the area between Cherry (Fourth Avenue) and Front (First Avenue) streets. Marcus Cartwright, who, according to the American Journal of Commerce, was a nationally famous bookmaker, erected the Southern Turf in 1895 at what is now 212 Fourth Avenue North. He filled it with mirrors, bronze statues, rare paintings, and mahogany furnishings, and the manager, Ike Johnson, sold choice domestic and imported liquors and wines and top brand cigars. The Italianate structure is still standing next to two other extant "Gay Nineties" buildings, the Climax Saloon (number 210) and the Utopia Hotel (number 206). Today those edifices serve a variety of commercial uses.

Advertisement courtesy of Tennessee State Library and Archives.

Victor E. "Manny" Shwab, a German immigrant and business partner of whiskey-maker George A. Dickel, built the Silver Dollar Saloon, pictured here, about 1893. It was a popular eating and drinking place until 1910, when Tennessee adopted statewide prohibition. Designed by Nashvillian J.G. Zwicker, the building is now restored for adaptive use and houses offices of the Metropolitan Historical Commission and Historic Nashville, Inc. It is situated on the northeast corner of Second Avenue and Broad.

Photograph courtesy of Tennessee State Library and Archives.

Some Nashvillians objected to the saloons that operated in the city's waterfront district; they also objected to gambling that occurred on riverboats and to prostitutes who solicited business on Cherry Street. Thus, whenever Georgia revivalist Sam Jones, shown here, made one of his periodic visits to the city, large crowds gathered to hear him preach hellfire and damnation. Jones' most famous Nashville convert was steamboat captain Thomas G. Ryman, who, after hearing the evangelist in 1885, closed all the bars and gambling dens on his river packets.
Photograph courtesy of Tennessee State Library and Archives.

After hearing evangelist Sam Jones in 1885, riverboat captain Thomas G. Ryman, who lived in this now-demolished house at 514 South Market Street (Second Avenue), decided to build a permanent tabernacle for Jones' revivals and other religious gatherings in Nashville. Ryman gave generously of his own funds and labored ceaselessly to convince others to contribute, too.
Photograph courtesy of Public Library of Metropolitan Nashville-Davidson County.

Inspired by revivalist Sam Jones, designed by Nashville architect Hugh C. Thompson, and funded largely through the efforts of riverboat captain Thomas G. Ryman, the Union Gospel Tabernacle was constructed on North Summer Street (Fifth Avenue) near Broad between 1889 and 1892. Although erected for religious services, the building became one of the South's largest and best-known assembly halls and theaters. Jones preached in the structure in 1890, even before its roof was completed, and held revivals in it in 1894 and 1895. Dwight L. Moody followed with meetings in 1896 and 1898, but by 1900 lyceum and chautauqua lectures, theatrical perfomances, and political gatherings accounted for most uses of the building. The list of famous persons who spoke or performed in the tabernacle reads like a who's who of world political and theatrical history and includes William Jennings Bryan, Carrie Nation, Booker T. Washington, Helen Keller, Champ Clark, John Philip Sousa, Victor Herbert, Billy Sunday, Enrico Caruso, Pavlova, Sarah Bernhardt, Isadora Duncan, Charlie Chaplin, Bob Hope, and many others. Following Ryman's death in 1904, the structure became known as the Ryman Auditorium. From 1941 to 1974 it housed the Grand Ole Opry. Today it enjoys a listing on the National Register of Historic Places and a reputation as a major Nashville tourist attraction.

Photograph by Calvert Brothers, circa 1900; courtesy of Tennessee State Library and Archives.

As the nineteenth century drew to a close, the Davidson County Courthouse, designed by Francis Strickland and built by Smith, Hughes, and Sloan, Contractors in 1857, continued to serve Nashville and outlying communities. The venerable building stood in the center of the Public Square until the 1930s when it, along with the City Hall and Market House, was torn down to make room for a new county courthouse.

Photograph by Calvert Brothers; courtesy of Tennessee State Library and Archives.

At 3:30 p.m. on September 3, 1900, Engine Number Five of the Nashville, Chattanooga, and Saint Louis Railroad pulled the first train out of Nashville's new Union Station. During the next few weeks curious citizens toured the building's arched vestibule, skylighted waiting room, and spacious shed. On October 6 the city formally dedicated the structure with a parade, concert, speeches, and fireworks. August Belmont, chairman of the board of the L & N, traveled from New York to make the principal address. Photograph courtesy of The Tennessean.

Upon completing Nashville's Union Station in 1900, the builders placed the figure of Mercury—the Roman god associated with speed, change, and progress—atop the central tower. That statue both embellished the building and suggested the city's future. During the next thirty years Nashville experienced rapid physical expansion, economic growth, and social change. By enthusiastically supporting American participation in two foreign wars, taking advantage of new methods of transportation and communication, endorsing numerous social and political reforms, and having several local businessmen gain nationwide success, Nashville threw off the cloak of Southern provincialism that it had worn since the Civil War and moved back into the national mainstream.

On April 19, 1898, less than six months after the Tennessee Centennial Exposition closed its doors on Nashville's western outskirts, the United States went to war with Spain. Nashvillians, like most Americans, had read sensationalized newspaper accounts of Spanish atrocities in Cuba, and so they greeted the declaration with a burst of patriotism. On April 21 residents flocked to railroad crossings to cheer troop trains passing en route to the Gulf of Mexico, and on the twenty-second they rejoiced at news that the gunboat *Nashville* had fired the first shots of the war and captured a Spanish ship off Key West. A number of Nashvillians volunteered for military service. Most of those went into the First Tennessee Regiment and served in the Philippines. Their unit was the only one from Tennessee to see combat.

The Spanish-American War lasted only a few months, and on October 9, 1900, many Nashvillians celebrated the beginning of the twentieth century by dedicating Union Station. Some citizens refused to revel in the pomp and gaiety of that event, however. They believed that the Louisville and Nashville Railroad and the Nashville, Chattanooga, and Saint Louis Railroad, which had jointly financed the station, were charging exorbitant rates, restricting competition, and hurting the city's economic growth. As a result, in 1901 city voters approved municipal financial support for attorney Jere Baxter's new Tennessee Central Railroad, which linked Nashville with the Illinois

Chapter VI

City on the Move:

1897-1929

Central at Hopkinsville, Kentucky, and with the Southern at Harriman, Tennessee. This gave Nashville additional rail connections and started an intense transportation rivalry that lasted half a century.

Meanwhile, Nashville grew both physically and economically. In 1900 the city covered 10 square miles and had 140 miles of improved streets, 59 miles of sewers, 72 miles of streetcar lines, and a population of 80,865. The latter figure was misleading, however; it did not include the suburbs, which had expanded rapidly after 1890 when the advent of electric streetcars had freed working people of the need to live within walking distance of their jobs or near one of the relatively short horse-drawn lines.

Because installation of electric streetcars coincided with the breakup of large country estates like Rokeby and Belmont and the formation of realty firms such as the Belmont Land Company and the Nashville Land Improvement Company, Nashvillians flocked in ever-increasing numbers to "streetcar suburbs" like West Nashville, Belmont Heights, Waverly Place, Sylvan Park, Lockeland, and Eastland. The city annexed most of these in 1906, and by 1910 Nashville's population stood at 110,364. Subsequent annexations brought in additional land and people, and by 1930 the city covered twenty square miles and boasted a population of more than 150,000.

Commerce and industry expanded along with area and population. In 1900 Nashville led Tennessee in manufacturing and accounted for nearly one-fifth of the state's total industrial output. In printing, milling, and boot and shoe manufacturing, the city led the entire South. Nashville remained a lumbering center, too, and by 1906 it was turning out more hardwood than any other city in the world. Nashville also continued to serve as a major distributor of wholesale groceries and became, as a result, an important site for roasting and grinding coffee. H.G. Hill produced "Fit for a King" Coffee, and the Cheek-Neal Coffee Company gained national attention with its Maxwell House blend. Demand for the latter became so great that the company opened branch plants in New York, Florida, Texas, and Virginia. And in 1902 and 1903

These photographs show Union Station in various stages of construction. Financed jointly by the Louisville and Nashville and Nashville, Chattanooga, and Saint Louis Railroads, the 150-foot-square Richardsonian Romanesque head house was designed by Richard Monfort, chief engineer of the L & N, and was constructed of Bowling Green gray stone and Tennessee marble for $350,000. The shed cost an additional $100,000. Today the station is a National Historic Landmark and is undergoing restoration and conversion into a federal office complex.

In this April 1899 view, workmen are raising the station walls with wooden cranes. Most of the houses in the background, southwest of the station, have now given way to Interstate 40.
Photograph by Robert S. Patterson; courtesy of Joe B. Sills.

Nashville took its first steps toward becoming an insurance center, as C.A. Craig helped organize the National Life and Accident Insurance Company and A.M. Burton founded the Life and Casualty Insurance Company of Tennessee.

Politically, Nashvillians took part in the "progressive" reform movement that swept the country in the early twentieth century. Between 1900 and 1903, under the leadership of Mayor James M. Head, the city brought streetcar lines under closer public supervision, obtained an option to purchase the gas company, constructed a municipal power plant, established a parks board, and tried to get all telephone, telegraph, and electric lines placed underground. Two national reforms caught the imagination of Nashvillians, too, and many citizens advocated prohibition and woman's suffrage. In November 1914 the National American Woman Suffrage Association held its national convention in Nashville, and in July and August 1920, Carrie Chapman Catt and other leading suffragettes came to Nashville to urge the Tennessee legislature to approve the nineteenth amendment, which it did on August 18.

Nashvillians' affinity for reform showed also in their zealous support of America's entry into the First World War in April 1917. To help make the world "safe for democracy," they volunteered for military service, worked in war industries, conducted bond drives, and saved food, fuel, and other resources. And for the first time in history they sent their daughters as well as their sons to war: on May 1, 1917, Will Allen Dromgoole, literary editor of the Nashville *Banner*, enlisted in the Navy, and other women followed. Some Nashvillians won nationwide acclaim with their military exploits. For example, Admiral Albert Gleaves convoyed a million troops to Europe without a single loss, and Colonel Luke Lea devised a daring though unsuccessful plan to kidnap Germany's Kaiser Wilhelm II.

When the war ended and the country returned to what President Warren Harding called "nor-

By the time this photograph was taken, early in 1900, workmen had placed the figure of Mercury atop the station tower and were completing the train shed.
Photograph by Robert S. Patterson; courtesy of Joe B. Sills.

Pedestrians watch as workmen add finishing touches to the Union Station train shed during the summer of 1900.
Photograph courtesy of Tennessee State Library and Archives.

malcy," Nashvillians joined in the mood of the times. Voters returned popular pre-war mayor Hilary Howse to office, and flappers and their raccoon-coated dates danced the charleston at roaring nightspots like the Kit-Kat Club in the Hermitage Hotel.

Nashvillians were not preoccupied with politics and jazz in these years, though. They watched Chancellor James H. Kirkland of Vanderbilt and President Bruce R. Payne of Peabody lead those institutions to new heights in education. They saw Rogers Caldwell earn the title "Morgan of the South" by building a financial empire that encompassed banks, insurance companies, factories, newspapers, and the local professional baseball team. And they participated themselves in transportation and communication revolutions. Preston Dorris had introduced Nashvillians to automobiles in 1896 and these "devil wagons" had gained considerable use before the war. They did not

become commonplace, however, until the twenties, when automobile ownership tripled. Similarly, Nashvillians had shown interest in airplanes as early as 1910, when on the evening of June 22 hundreds of people gathered at Cumberland Park to watch the world's first night flight. After the war some Nashville residents served in the Tennessee National Guard's 105th Air Observation Squadron at Blackwood Field, and others used the Nashville-to-Chicago airmail service which originated at that same field in 1924. Many more enjoyed commercial radio after National Life put WSM on the air in 1925 and Life and Casualty established WLAC in 1926.

By 1929 citizens who paused to reflect on Nashville's progress since the turn of the century could be proud. The city had expanded its boundaries, improved public services, embraced popular reforms, defended the flag overseas, and become the leading financial center in the South. The future seemed secure. ❧

Unhappy with what he considered monopolistic practices by the L & N and N, C & St. L lines, Jere Baxter founded the Tennessee Central Railroad in 1901. His battles with his larger competitors made him the most popular railroad man in the city's history, and in 1907, three years after his death, Nashvillians erected a statue in his honor at the intersection of West End and Broadway. The statue has since been removed, and the Tennessee Central no longer exists, but Baxter remains a hero to many residents.
Engraving by E.G. Williams & Brothers (circa 1890); from Wooldridge, History of Nashville.

This circa 1905 southeastward view shows switching and freight operations in the "gulch" area north of Union Station. By World War I the volume of freight passing through here became so great that the L & N moved its switching facilities to the Radnor Yards in South Nashville and left the "gulch" to the N, C & St. L line. The N, C & St. L headquarters buildings, now demolished, are at center, left of the station.
Postcard courtesy of Public Library of Metropolitan Nashville-Davidson County.

Despite fierce competition from the railroads, river steamers continued to play an important role in Nashville commerce. Early twentieth-century photographs of the Nashville Wharf show that grain and building materials were mainstays of the river trade.

In 1903 two large Mississippi River packets, the side-wheeler Lotus W. Sims, *second from left,* and the Belle of Calhoun, *first from right,* are nuzzled up to the Nashville Wharf along with several Cumberland steamers, including the J.B. Richard and R. Dunbar, *second and third from right.*

Photograph by Calvert Brothers; courtesy of Tennessee State Library and Archives.

Docked at the Nashville Wharf in 1906 are the Electra, H.W. Buttorff, R. Dunbar, and Henry Harley. All were built in the 1890s.

Photograph by Robert S. Patterson; courtesy of Tennessee State Library and Archives.

Although gasoline automobiles had appeared occasionally on Nashville streets since the mid 1890s, horse-drawn buggies and wagons remained the chief private conveyances for individuals and businesses when this picture was taken on Union Street in 1906. Electric power lines, such as those shown here, had been cluttering city streetscapes since the 1880s.

Photograph courtesy of Tennessee State Library and Archives.

Percy Warner had just embarked on a successful business career when he posed for this portrait with his daughter Sadie (later Mrs. George Washington Frazer) in the late 1880s. Although today Nashvillians remember Warner largely for the park named in his honor, residents in the early 1900s associated his name with municipal progress. In 1902, while general manager of the Nashville Railway Company, Warner helped get Centennial Park transferred to city ownership. The following year he helped arrange a merger of the United Electric Railway with two newer streetcar lines and the Cumberland Electric Light and Power Company. Afterward he served for many years as president of the new firm, the Nashville Railway and Light Company.

Photograph by Poole Art Company; courtesy of Tennessee State Library and Archives.

Nashville boasted a variety of industries early in the twentieth century. Among them was the William Gerst Brewing Company, shown here about 1901. Gerst, who came to Nashville from Cincinnati, established the brewery in 1890. By the time Tennessee went dry in 1910, the firm was marketing beer in almost every Southern state. During prohibition it produced "near beer." After prohibition it resumed beer production and remained in business until the early 1950s. Today only the bottling building, at the corner of Vine and Ewing streets, remains.

From Nashville in the 20th Century.

Nashville Cotton Mills erected this building in 1881 for the manufacture of sheetings, twines, and other cotton goods. In the early 1900s Southern Motor Works acquired the structure and used it for four years to produce Marathon automobiles. All were touring cars powered by four- and six-cylinder engines that generated between thirty-five and fifty horsepower. Unable to compete with Henry Ford and other mass producers, the company turned to parts manufacturing in 1914 and ceased operating just four years later. Since about 1920 the Werthan Bag Company, a major manufacturer in its field, has used the structure, which is situated on the northwest corner of Twelfth Avenue North and Clinton Street.
Photograph courtesy of The Tennessean.

Nashville's first skyscrapers were erected soon after the turn of the century. Banker Frank Overton Watts built the twelve-story First National Bank Building (now the J.C. Bradford Building) at Church Street and Fourth Avenue in 1904, and in 1906 the Mecklenburg Real Estate Company completed the twelve-story Stahlman Building at Third Avenue and Union Street. Both structures featured the Renaissance revival style characterized by a distinctive two-story base, eight-story midsection, and two-story crown. The Stahlman Building, named in honor of newspaper publisher Edward Bushrod Stahlman, is shown here about 1915. Architect Otto Eggers designed the edifice, and the firm of Carpenter and Blair constructed it.
Photograph by Marvin W. Wiles; courtesy of Nashville Area Chamber of Commerce.

Another early twentieth-century Nashville industry was May Hosiery Mills. Jacob May, who previously had operated Rock City Hosiery Mills at the Tennessee State Penitentiary, founded the company built it into a successful regional enterprise. The May Hosiery structures pictured here in the 1920s are still standing on Houston Street, but they are largely obscured by later additions to the plant. At left in the background is Saint Cloud Hill, site of Fort Negley.
Photograph courtesy of The Tennessean.

During the 1920s Nashville emerged as an important regional banking center. Some of the city's financial institutions marked that achievement by erecting new headquarters. The Commerce Union Bank built this Renaissance revival structure at the corner of Union Street and Fourth Avenue in 1921. It housed the bank for fifty years before being demolished to make room for a new financial complex.

Photograph courtesy of Tennessee State Library and Archives.

Edward Bushrod Stahlman, founder of the Mecklenberg Real Estate Company, immigrated to America from Germany in 1853. He came to Nashville in 1866 as an agent for the Adams Express Company. Later he worked for the Louisville and Nashville Railroad and eventually became its vice-president. In 1893, shortly after this engraving was made, Stahlman bought the Nashville *Banner* and assumed an active role as its publisher. By the time of his death in 1930 he was known throughout the South for his journalistic donnybrooks.

Engraving by E.G. Williams and Brothers; from Wooldridge, History of Nashville.

Eng. by E.C. Williams & Bro. N.Y

In 1901 Cornelius Abernathy Craig, pictured here in his later years, helped establish a business that had an enormous impact on the city's future. With six other men he bought the fledgling National Sick and Accident Association at public auction for $17,250. The next year he and his partners changed the firm's name to National Life and Accident Insurance Company, and in the decades that followed they made it one of the leading industrial insurance companies in the nation. Craig served as president of National Life until 1931 and remained active in its management until the early 1950s. He died in 1957.
Photograph courtesy of National Life and Accident Insurance Company.

This structure, at the corner of Seventh Avenue and Union Street, served as headquarters for the National Life and Accident Insurance Company from 1924 until the late 1960s. It also housed the firm's radio station, WSM, for many years. Today it is a state office building, and National Life occupies a new structure that is situated in the same block and, at thirty-one stories, is Nashville's tallest building.
Photograph courtesy of Nashville Life and Accident Insurance Company.

This postcard depicts the Nashville skyline from the Union Station tower about 1910. Notice the Tennessee State Capitol at the upper left, the Stahlman and Bradford buildings at center on the horizon, the Ryman Auditorium near the top right, the old Methodist Publishing House (rectangular with decorative crosses along the roofline) below the Ryman, and the N C & St. L headquarters in the center foreground. The street at right is Broadway.
Postcard courtesy of Public Library of Metropolitan Nashville-Davidson County.

Bird's Eye View showing (from left to right)
State Capitol, Polk-Watauga Apartments, Hermitage Hotel,
Stahlman Building, First National Bank, Methodist Publishing House,
Custom House and Post Office and Broadway,
Nashville, Tenn.

Moses McKissack III was a particularly active participant in Nashville's twentieth-century growth. After working several years in the building trades, he founded his own architectural firm in 1918. Two years later he took his brother Calvin as a partner, and in 1922 they secured architectural licenses from the state of Tennessee. Since then the firm of McKissack and McKissack has designed more than two thousand buildings in the mid-South.

Photograph by Hooks Brothers; courtesy of The Tennessean.

The Morris Memorial Building, erected in 1923-25 at the northeast corner of Charlotte Avenue and Fourth Avenue North, is an example of the work of McKissack and McKissack. Present occupants of the building include the Citizen's Savings Bank and Trust Company. Established as the One Cent Savings Bank in January 1904, the firm is the second oldest black-owned bank in the United States. Among its founders were attorney James C. Napier and publisher Richard H. Boyd.

Photograph by Edwin C. P'Pool; courtesy of Historical Commission of Metropolitan Nashville-Davidson County.

By the time this photo was taken in the 1920s, Nashville, like the rest of the country, had entered the age of the automobile. In just ten years motor vehicle registrations tripled in the city, and horses and wagons almost disappeared from the streets. This view is from near Church Street southward along Second Avenue. Except for the vintage autos, paving stones, and contemporary advertising signs, this streetscape looks much the same today. Compare this view with the one on page 176.

Photograph courtesy of The Tennessean.

In the golden age of steamboating on the Cumberland, river packets brought supplies to commission merchants and other entrepreneurs whose businesses backed onto Water Street (First Avenue) and the Nashville Wharf, and draymen dispersed the goods in freight wagons drawn by horses and mules. By the 1920s railroad cars brought freight to these businesses on rail spurs that ran within a few feet of the buildings, and truck drivers dispersed the goods in gasoline-powered vehicles.

Photograph by Marvin W. Wiles; courtesy of Nashville Area Chamber of Commerce.

When Angelo, Louis, Charles, and Volley Rottero posed for this early twentieth-century photograph in front of their grocery store at 430 Twelfth Avenue North, they were just beginning to replace their delivery wagons with trucks. Having the latest in delivery equipment was especially important to grocers because many housewives rarely set foot in food stores. They phoned in their orders or had their husbands or children drop off shopping lists, then the grocer filled the orders and delivered them to the customers' doorsteps. Today descendants of the Rottero Brothers operate a supermarket on the Nashville-Clarksville highway.

Photograph courtesy of Public Library of Metropolitan Nashville-Davidson County.

The Nashville Gas and Heating Company, founded in 1851, kept up with the times with this shiny new Model T Ford truck. Notice the wood frame cab and solid rubber tires.

Photograph courtesy of Nashville Gas Company.

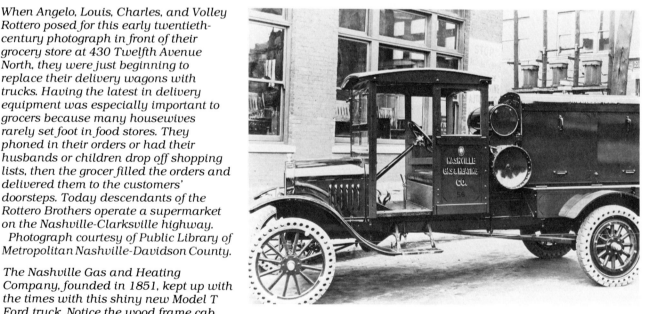

The deliverymen posing here with their Jackson truck worked for Lebeck Brothers, a leading Nashville dry goods and department store from its founding in 1874 until the 1930s.
Photograph courtesy of Harveys Department Stores.

In a scene reminiscent of a western gunfight, the automobile and horse in this 1910 photograph appear ready for a showdown at Ninth Avenue and Union Street. Actually the Buick is being readied for the Nashville Automobile Club's Pathfinder Trip to Chattanooga. The car is parked next to Duncan R. Dorris' Nashville Motor Car Company garage. Dorris, a former bicycle dealer, played a major role in popularizing the automobile in Nashville. In 1903 he opened the city's first auto dealership, and during the next few years he sold several makes, including the "Dorris," an automobile manufactured in Saint Louis by his brother Preston. Duncan R. Dorris was also the first Nashvillian arrested and tried for speeding and reckless driving. He was acquitted.
Photograph courtesy of Catherine T. Avery.

Prior to World War I automobile dealers used speed and endurance runs between distant points to attract public attention and to sell cars. On such excursions well-prepared motorists traveled with a watering can, a tire repair kit, and plenty of spare parts. Here Duncan R. Dorris, Merrit S. Pilcher, and an unidentified friend stop near Clarksville to fill their car's radiator before proceeding on to Saint Louis.
Photograph courtesy of Catherine T. Avery.

Automobiles quickly became popular with families, who used them increasingly for weekend excursions and vacation trips. The Rufus D. Goad, front, and Roy Martin, rear, families are shown here on an outing. Despite winter weather they put the convertible top down so that the cameraman could photograph them in their machine.
Photograph courtesy of Don L. Goad.

In 1931, automobile owners could buy Texaco gasoline at this Firestone tire store, at the corner of West End and Twenty-Fifth Avenue North, for 13½ cents a gallon plus tax. The store is still a West End landmark.

Photograph courtesy of Tennessee State Library and Archives.

The dramatic increase in the number of automobiles in the 1920s created a need for more and better paved streets, and scenes such as this one became commonplace in Nashville. Here workmen are paving Concrete (later Woodmont) Boulevard, the first street in the city constructed of the new material. Note the steam-powered cement mixer and mule-drawn wagons.

Photograph by Charles Henry Butler, Jr.; courtesy of Richard W. Weesner.

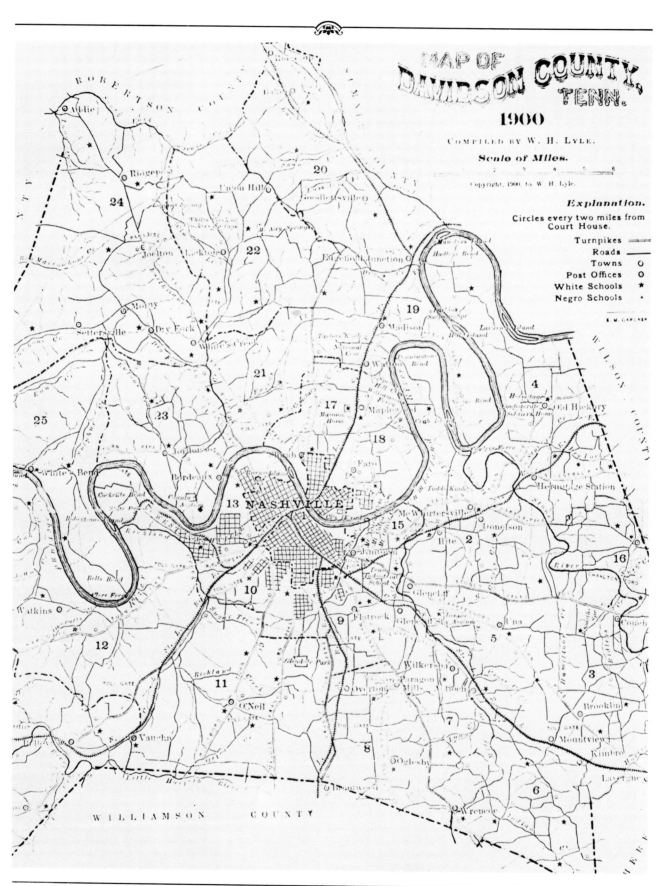

MAP OF
DAVIDSON COUNTY,
TENN.
1900

COMPILED BY W. H. LYLE.

Scale of Miles.

Copyright, 1900, by W. H. Lyle.

Explanation.

Circles every two miles from
Court House.

Turnpikes	═══
Roads	──
Towns	O
Post Offices	O
White Schools	★
Negro Schools	·

When surveyor William H. Lyle prepared this map of Davidson County in 1900, he delineated Nashville and its suburbs with a tiny grid (center). The city had a population of more than 80,000. Another 25,000 people lived just outside the city limits. Four years after the map appeared, the city council substituted numbers for the names of north-south streets west of the river. The chamber of commerce suggested the change so that shoppers from the outlying areas could more easily find their way to downtown businesses.

Map compiled by William H. Lyle; courtesy of Public Library of Metropolitan Nashville-Davidson County.

Park Place, a short street east of the capitol, became an extension of Sixth Avenue in 1904. Before the turn of the century these stately Park Place residences were among the city's most fashionable dwellings. They have since given way to the Tennessee State Office Building (1939) and Cordell Hull Building (1952).

Photograph courtesy of The Tennessean.

In the late nineteenth century Gay Street, shown here westward from the north side of Capitol Hill, passed through Hell's Half Acre, one of the city's largest black neighborhoods. Many of its residents worked as domestic servants in white homes on Park Place and other fashionable downtown residential streets. By the time this picture was snapped, in 1918, the center of this neighborhood had shifted north toward Jefferson Street and west toward Fisk University. These houses were demolished in the 1950s as part of the Capitol Hill Redevelopment Project. Many of the displaced residents moved into public housing units elsewhere in the city.

Photograph courtesy of Tennessee State Library and Archives.

At the turn of the century many elegant Nashville houses were situated on Russell Street in Edgefield. By the 1920s however, when this view was taken westward from Fifth Street, the area had begun to decline. Recently it has undergone revitalization with creation of the Edgefield Historic District and listing on the National Register of Historic Places.

Photograph by Marvin W. Wiles; courtesy of The Tennessean.

Although Nashville boasted four schools of medicine—University of Nashville, Meharry, Vanderbilt, and Nashville Medical School—in the late nineteenth century, the city's reputation as a regional medical center was enhanced considerably by the expansion of hospital facilities after 1900. Nashville City Hospital, pictured here soon after its construction on Hermitage Avenue in 1890, received a new charter and board in 1921, and in 1932 it added a wing that increased its capacity from 65 to 260 patients. Known now as Metropolitan General Hospital, it retains only a portion of the north, or left, wing of the original building.
Photograph courtesy of Tennessee State Library and Archives.

In 1898 Bishop Thomas Byrne bought the Jacob McGavock Dickinson estate, between Hayes and Church streets and present Twentieth and Twenty-first avenues, for the construction of a Catholic hospital. The Daughters of Charity of Saint Vincent DePaul opened the institution, named Saint Thomas, in the former Dickinson residence while awaiting completion of a hospital building. The new structure, pictured here shortly after its erection, began receiving patients in 1902. The sisters expanded the hospital several times over the years, and in the early 1970s they moved to new quarters on Harding Road. Only a portion of the earlier facility remains.
Photograph by Calvert Brothers; courtesy of Tennessee State Library and Archives.

This structure, which stood on the northwest corner of Eighth Avenue and Union Street until replaced by the Federal Reserve Bank, housed several hospitals early in this century. Dr. Matthew McGannon, a professor at the University of Nashville medical department, operated an infirmary here for a number of years, and during the 1910s and 1920s the Woman's Hospital of the State of Tennessee occupied the building. In 1930, shortly after this picture was taken, it became the home of newly established Baptist Hospital. A few years later Baptist merged with the Dozier and Nashville Protestant hospitals and occupied the latter's quarters on Church Street at Twentieth Avenue, across from Saint Thomas Hospital. In 1948 the Tennessee Baptist State Convention bought the Church Street facility and in subsequent years built it into one of the city's largest health care institutions.

Photograph by Calvert Brothers; courtesy of Tennessee State Library and Archives.

As in previous years, Nashville boasted a number of architecturally outstanding churches during the early 1900s. Among them was Christ Church, Episcopal, shown here about 1920. Christ Church was founded in 1829, and from 1831 to 1889 its congregation met in a church building at Sixth Avenue and Church Street where Harveys Department Store is now situated. Francis H. Kimball designed this building at 900 Broadway in the late 1880s, and the congregation occupied it in 1894. Its tower was completed in 1947, and today it is considered the finest Victorian Gothic structure in the city.

Photograph courtesy of Public Library of Metropolitan Nashville-Davidson County.

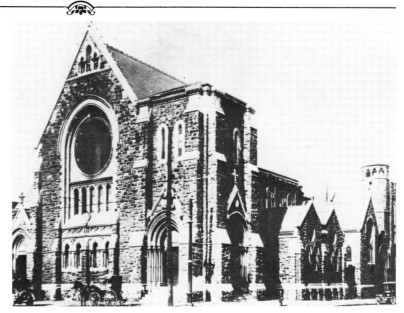

Onion-domed Vine Street Temple, pictured here about 1900, graced Seventh Avenue South for more than eighty years. Former president Andrew Johnson and Rabbi Isaac Wise, the founder of Reform Judaism in the United States, helped lay the cornerstone for the building in 1874. Congregation Ohavai Sholom worshipped in it until 1955, when they moved to The Temple on Harding Road. The old Byzantine-style temple was demolished soon afterward.

Photograph courtesy of Public Library of Metropolitan Nashville-Davidson County.

Before it moved to its present campus near Fisk University in 1931, Meharry Medical College occupied these now-demolished buildings on First Avenue South at Chestnut Street. They are the auditorium, anatomical hall, and administration building. The college, which was nearing its fiftieth anniversary when this photograph was taken, traces its origins to 1874 when the Meharry brothers, Hugh, Samuel, and Alexander, provided funds for the addition of a medical department to Tennessee Central College, a school founded in 1866 to educate freedmen. In 1900 Tenneseee Central College became Walden University, and in 1916 the medical department obtained a separate charter as Meharry Medical College.

Photograph courtesy of The Tennessean.

This sanctuary, at 1524-26 Broadway, housed the West End Methodist Church from 1887 to 1930. The West End congregation began as a small Sunday school on Laurel Street and became a formally organized church in 1870. Members assembled in a tiny frame building for seventeen years before erecting this structure at a cost of $55,000. In 1927, shortly after this picture was taken, they decided to escape the commercialization along this section of Broadway by moving to new quarters on West End. The congregation met in Vanderbilt's Neely Chapel for ten years before moving into their present building in 1940. Today an automobile dealership occupies this site.

Photograph courtesy of Public Library of Metropolitan Nashville-Davidson County.

Lay Brothers, one of three early twentieth-century black photography studios in Nashville, snapped these young people at the Church of the Holy Family. They have completed their first Holy Communion class and are about to be confirmed in the Roman Catholic faith. Holy Family, often called the "Colored Catholic Church," was the first black Catholic congregation in Nashville. The church was formally dedicated at 458 Third Avenue North in 1902. Later it moved to 508 Seventh Avenue South. Neither building survives; the congregation has dispersed to other churches.

Photograph by Lay Brothers; courtesy of Deborah Cooney

Although early twentieth-century Nashville did not enjoy the kind of political influence that the city had wielded in the Jacksonian era, it still drew considerable national attention. For example, President Theodore Roosevelt made a whirlwind visit to Nashville on October 22, 1907, and paused briefly for this photograph at Andrew Jackson's tomb. The president arrived at Union Station at 9:00 a.m., delivered a speech at Ryman Auditorium, visited the Peabody Normal College campus, and went on a guided tour of the Hermitage, all before noon, when he departed by train from Hermitage Station. Roosevelt was no stranger to Nashville. He had sojourned in the city several years earlier while researching his book Winning of the West at the State Library.

Photograph by Robert S. Patterson; courtesy of Tennessee State Library and Archives.

William Howard Taft, left, was a familiar figure to Nashville residents long before he won the presidency in 1908. As a federal judge on the Sixth Circuit Court from 1892 to 1900, he had often held court in Nashville. Here he poses with Nashvillians Horace H. Lurton, center, and Jacob McGavock Dickinson, right, at Belle Meade in 1908. After he entered the White House, Taft appointed Lurton to the United States Supreme Court and made Dickinson secretary of war.

Postcard courtesy of Public Library of Metropolitan Nashville-Davidson County.

Prohibition of alcoholic beverages was a major reform everywhere in the early 1900s. In Nashville the struggle resulted in the assassination of one of the state's leading politicians, Edward Ward Carmack. A former congressman, United States senator, and editor of the Nashville American and Memphis Commercial Appeal, Carmack was an especially sharp-tongued exponent of statewide prohibition during the elections of 1906 and 1908. On November 9, 1908, two of his foremost opponents, Duncan B. Cooper and his son Robin, killed Carmack in a gunfight near the intersection of Seventh Avenue North and Union Street. The circumstances of Carmack's death drew national attention, made him a martyr, and led to the passage of a state prohibition law in 1909.

Photograph courtesy of The Tennessean.

Woman's suffrage was another great reform of the early twentieth century. In August 1920 both its advocates and its opponents throughout the nation riveted their attention on Nashville, and particularly on the state capitol and the Hermitage Hotel, center. Congress had passed a proposed nineteenth constitutional amendment making it illegal to deny the right to vote on account of sex. Approval by one more state legislature was needed for ratification, and the suffragettes, led by Carrie Chapman Catt, had decided to try to win that approval in Tennessee. During most of August, Catt and her colleagues lobbied the Tennessee legislature from headquarters in the Hermitage Hotel, and on the eighteenth the legislators voted for the amendment. At that time the Hermitage, designed by J. Edwin Carpenter and completed in 1910, was considered the city's finest hotel, surpassing even the Maxwell House. In subsequent years the Hermitage served as headquarters for numerous state and local political campaigns and hosted myriad important social functions. Now undergoing renovation for adaptive use, the grand structure stands at 231 Sixth Avenue North.

Photograph courtesy of Nashville Area Chamber of Commerce.

The East Nashville fire of March 22, 1916, was one of the most devastating events in the city's history. Accounts about the cause of the blaze differ: some say that a child started it while trying to retrieve a ball of yarn from a burning pile of leaves at Sixth and Ninth streets; official city records suggest that the conflagration started in a planing mill on First Street. Whatever the cause, the fire was fanned by high winds and raged out of control for four hours. Luckily, the holocaust took only one human life. However, it destroyed 978 buildings and left three thousand persons homeless.

Photograph by Marvin W. Wiles; courtesy of Public Library of Metropolitan Nashville-Davidson County.

To insure an adequate water supply for Nashville's growing population, the city built a fifty-one-million-gallon reservoir on Kirkpatrick Hill, near Eighth Avenue South, in 1887-89. City Engineer James A. Jowett designed the structure, and the firm of Whitsett and Adams built it. This postcard view shows the north side of the reservoir and its pumphouse about 1900. Now a National Water Landmark, the facility is still in use. It is elliptical rather than round and measures 603 feet along its east-west axis and 463.4 feet along its north-south axis. It has two thirty-one-foot-deep compartments.

Postcard courtesy of Public Library of Metropolitan Nashville-Davidson County.

At 12:10 a.m. on November 5, 1912, a portion of the Kirkpatrick Hill reservoir's twenty-two-foot-thick southeast wall gave way, and twenty-five million gallons of water cascaded down the slope, destroying houses and leaving three feet of mud and stone on Eighth Avenue. Amazingly, no one was killed. For several days afterward Nashvillians flocked to the site to examine the damage. Eventually the city repaired and refilled the $364,000 structure, and today it remains a major water storage facility.

Photograph courtesy of Public Library of Metropolitan Nashville-Davidson County.

Broadway, viewed eastward from Union Station, seemed tranquil when Robert S. Patterson snapped this photograph on April 4, 1917. However, in Washington and in the capitals of Europe events were transpiring that would change many lives both in Nashville and elsewhere in the world. Two days earlier President Wilson had asked Congress to declare war on Germany. On April 6 the solons complied. Within days this street was bustling with conveyances bringing young men and women to trains that would take them to military training camps throughout the country.

Photograph courtesy of Tennessee State Library and Archives.

Many Davidson County families had more than one son or daughter in military or other war-related service in 1917-18, and at least one hundred families had three or more. Sue Howell (Mrs. A.G.) Adams had six sons in the armed forces and a seventh who helped build warships.

Photograph by Calvert Brothers; courtesy of Tennessee State Library and Archives.

Lieutenant McMurray was one of many Nashville men in the armed forces during World War I.
Photograph by Calvert Brothers; courtesy of Tennessee State Library and Archives.

Tennessee's War Governor and Troop Commander

Like a host of other Middle Tennesseans who served, most Nashvillians who went overseas were assigned either to the 114th Field Artillery under Colonel Luke Lea, to the 115th Field Artillery under Colonel Harry S. Berry, or to the 117th Infantry under General Lawrence D. Tyson. More than two hundred local men in those and other units did not return.
Photograph by Calvert Brothers; courtesy of Tennessee State Library and Archives.

A number of Nashville women served abroad along with men from the city. When photographed on the S.S. Turrealba in New York in April 1919, these nurses, from Vanderbilt Unit S, had just returned from Europe. The group included head nurse Fannie O. Walton, Elizabeth Beal, Alberta Mills, Effie M. Buchanan, Anna Eastland, Bertha Grunwell, May Shannahan, Lula Shannahan, Bernice Hall, Mayne Merritt, Beulah Taylor, and Katherine Swager.

Photograph courtesy of The Tennessean.

The Centennial Club was headquarters for the auxiliary activities of many Nashville women during World War I. Former members of the Women's Board of the Tennessee Centennial Exposition established the club in 1905. In 1917 and 1918, members sold bonds, operated canteens, and planned patriotic events. Today the Centennial Club occupies a building on Abbott Martin Road, and this structure, on Eighth Avenue South between McGavock and Demonbreum streets, houses a mission for transients.

From Gilmore, Davidson County Women in the World War.

Among the Nashville women who served on the home front was Helen Pickslay (Mrs. Will) Cheek, dressed here in her Motor Corps Department captain's uniform. Under the auspices of the American Red Cross, the Motor Corps was charged with supplying automobiles and drivers for government agencies during emergencies. The corps was organized along military lines, and women who joined had to provide their own uniforms, cars, and gasoline. They were on call at all times.

From Gilmore, Davidson County Women in the World War.

Dozens of Nashville women helped make the Red Cross Emergency Canteen Service a success. They met each of the many troop trains that stopped at Union Station during the war, and from a large hut at track level they provided the soldiers with food, drink, restrooms, bathing facilities, and good cheer. Here Mary Ramage and Sadie Cauvin serve breakfast to a group of doughboys.
From Gilmore, Davidson County Women in the World War.

In May 1917 President Woodrow Wilson's daughter Margaret visited Nashville to encourage support for the war effort. While here she posed for this photograph at the Edmund W. Cole house on Murfreesboro Road. She is flanked on the left by Mrs. Dempsey Weaver and on the right by Mrs. Cole. The children are, left to right: Henriette Weaver, Dempsey Weaver, Jr., Anna Russell Cole Weaver, Elizabeth Glasgow, Mary Weaver Harris, and William Weaver, Jr.
Photograph courtesy of The Tennessean.

In January 1918 U.S. Army engineers selected Hadley's Bend on the Cumberland River northeast of Nashville as the site for a government gunpowder plant. When completed in July of that same year, it boasted more than three thousand structures, including workers' houses, and was the largest smokeless powder plant in the United States. With the signing of the armistice in November 1918 the government ordered the plant shut down, and shortly afterward it was declared surplus property. This aerial photograph shows the plant in 1923 around the time that E.I. duPont deNemours and Company purchased it and changed its name from Jacksonville to Old Hickory. Few of these structures are extant.
Photograph by Albert W. Stevens; courtesy of Public Library of Metropolitan Nashville-Davidson County.

All through the war Nashvillians, like other Americans, anxiously awaited the return of friends and relatives from military service. On April 1, 1919, when the first local men came home from Europe, residents gathered at the N, C & St. L railroad shops, north of Centennial Park, to welcome them. While men and boys who had been unable to fight gawked at those who had, the disembarking doughboys peered into the crowds for familiar faces.

From Gilmore, Davidson County
Women in the World War.

Between March 31 and April 6, 1919, Nashvillians treated several trainloads of returning soldiers to feasts of turkey and ham and then watched them parade through a temporary Victory Arch on Capitol Boulevard.

*Photograph courtesy of
Tennessee State Library and Archives.*

To commemorate the services of Tennesseans who died in World War I, the state legislature appropriated two million dollars in 1919 for a War Memorial Building and Square. Designed by Edward E. Dougherty and constructed of granite and marble, the structure was completed in 1925. The central portion housed Belle Kinney's statue of Victory and plaques bearing names of 3,400 deceased veterans. The north wing, next to the capitol, contained state offices, while the south wing held a public auditorium. Shown here a few years after its dedication, the War Memorial Building has changed little over the decades. The square has been replaced by the Tennessee Memorial Plaza.

*Photograph courtesy of
National Archives.*

After World War I some Nashvillians began to explore peacetime uses for the airplane. Rufus D. Goad, right, purchased this Curtiss aircraft in March 1920 with the intention of using it to complement his Hermitage Taxi Service. He vowed to fly customers to any spot on the globe, but he attracted few passengers and utilized the plane primarily to drop circulars for local merchants. Goad went out of the flying business when his plane, overloaded with Lebeck Brothers Department Store brochures, crashed into a fence.

Photograph courtesy of Don L. Goad.

The war exploits of Sergeant Alvin York, a resident of Pall Mall, Tennessee, captured the imagination of the entire nation and especially enthralled Nashvillians. On October 8, 1918, York almost singlehandedly knocked out 35 German machine guns, killed 25 enemy soldiers, and captured 132 others in the Argonne Forest. Shortly after returning to Tennessee in May 1919, he posed in uniform for this picture while touring the Hermitage with his wife and a group of Rotarians and other prominent citizens. Later the Rotary Club and the Nashville Banner raised enough money to build York a substantial house on a farm given to him by the state.

Photograph by A.J. Thuss; courtesy of Andy Corn.

The 1920s, often called the Jazz Age, witnessed a number of changes in American customs, including new styles of dress, particularly for women. These unidentified Nashvillians were typical of those who adopted shorter hairstyles and thin, short-sleeved "flapper" dresses. Photographs courtesy of Public Library of Metropolitan Nashville-Davidson County.

In 1925 National Life and Accident Insurance Company executives decided to experiment with a new advertising and public service medium—radio. On October 5, they put WSM on the air from this room, Studio A, on the fifth floor of the company headquarters. A few weeks later, on November 28, veteran fiddler Uncle Jimmy Thompson appeared on a Saturday night musical show here and helped launch what eventually became the Grand Ole Opry. Over the years the Opry outgrew this and several other locations, and today it is the nation's longest-running radio program.
Photograph courtesy of Country Music Foundation Library.

Margret Garette, Miss Nashville of 1928, models the latest fashion in Jazz Age women's swimwear.
Photograph courtesy of Don L. Goad.

When WSM hired George D. Hay from Chicago radio station WLS in 1925, he was the most popular announcer in America. Having hosted WLS's National Barn Dance and arrived in Nashville just when an old-time fiddling craze was sweeping the South, Hay started a country music show on WSM. For a time he called it the WSM Barn Dance, and in 1926 he supposedly gave it its present name, the Grand Ole Opry. According to legend Hay coined the title on the air one night after NBC's classical music appreciation hour. "For the past hour," Hay reportedly said, "we have been listening to music taken largely from the Grand Opera, but from now on we will present the Grand Ole Opry."

Photograph courtesy of Country Music Foundation Library.

For years Dr. Humphrey Bate and the Possum Hunters opened every Grand Ole Opry program with "There'll Be a Hot Time in the Old Town Tonight." Contrary to the image they projected in this publicity photograph, the group frequently performed in business suits. Bate, seated second from left, was a Vanderbilt Medical School graduate and practicing physician who often played light classical pieces on his harmonica. He is credited with starting the tradition of informality and comradeship that characterizes the Opry today.

Photograph courtesy of Country Music Foundation Library.

Uncle Dave Macon, center, the "Dixie Dewdrop" from Smart Station, Tennessee, was the best-known performer on the Grand Ole Opry in the late 1920s and early 1930s. He began picking and singing on vaudeville stages and in rural schoolhouses soon after World War I, and when the Opry started in 1925, he was already recording songs like "Keep My Skillet Good and Greasy" and "I'll Tickle Nancy." Over the years he probably did more than any other artist to turn nineteenth-century folk music into twentieth-century country music. With Uncle Dave in this photograph, taken late in his career, are his son Dorris Macon and Rachel Veach.

Photograph courtesy of Country Music Foundation Library

While the Grand Ole Opry was getting started in WSM's home office at Seventh Avenue and Union Street, the Ryman Auditorium, which later became synonymous with the Opry, was hosting a variety of entertainment programs. The John Philip Sousa Band, Ziegfield Follies, and Metropolitan Opera Company were among the many touring attractions that helped make the Ryman the best "one night stand" in America during the 1920s and 1930s.

Programs courtesy of Public Library of Metropolitan Nashville-Davidson County.

Nashville's first symphony orchestra was organized in 1920. Conducted by F. Arthur Henkel, it performed at the Princess Theater on Church Street. The sixty-two members included William E. Von Otto, concert master; Tony Rose, trumpet; Bill Hudson, clarinet; Frank White, trombone; Sid Grooms, trombone; Gil Valdez, clarinet; and "Pop" Gadston, bassoon. The group disbanded after ten seasons, and the city remained without a symphony orchestra until 1946.

Photograph by Marvin W. Wiles; courtesy of Nashville Association of Musicians.

Nashvillians enjoyed a variety of sports in the early twentieth century. High school and college athletic teams, such as the 1911 Vanderbilt baseball club shown here on old Dudley Field, drew enthusiastic followings. In fact, the Vanderbilt football team, which also used this field, attracted such large crowds that in 1922 the university built twenty-thousand-seat Dudley Stadium to accommodate them. It was the largest facility of its kind in the South. This playing area, renamed Curry Field, continued for some years to serve baseball and other teams. Today the university uses a portion of the field for spring commencement ceremonies.

Photograph courtesy of Public Library of Metropolitan Nashville-Davidson County.

In 1922-23 this Hume-Fogg basketball team ran up a remarkable 18-3 won-lost record against such opponents as Knoxville High, Memphis High, Clarksville High, and the Vanderbilt freshman squad. In their final game they defeated Tullahoma 86-10. Their coach, Alfred T. Adams, later became one of Nashville's most successful attorneys.

Photograph by Calvert Brothers; courtesy of Tennessee State Library and Archives.

GOLF AND COUNTRY CLUB
NASHVILLE, TENN.

Golf became popular in Nashville after a group of prominent citizens organized the Nashville Golf and Country Club in 1901. For fifteen years the members' course and clubhouse, left, were situated off present-day Bowling Avenue in West Nashville. Then in 1916 the club changed its name to Belle Meade Country Club and moved to new quarters on 144 acres donated by Luke Lea in the Belle Meade subdivision. Edward E. Dougherty designed the new clubhouse, below, which is still in use at Belle Meade Boulevard and Harding Place.

Postcard courtesy of Public Library of Metropolitan Nashville-Davidson County.

Photograph by Marvin W. Wiles; courtesy of Nashville Area Chamber of Commerce.

Along with their new sporting facilities, commercial buildings, and hospitals, Nashvillians also built new educational structures in the early twentieth century. In 1904 the city used funds from steel magnate Andrew Carnegie to erect the Carnegie Library on the southeast corner of Eighth Avenue and Union Street. Shown here in the 1920s, it was Nashville's first public library building. Previously the library had been housed at the Watkins Institute on Church Street. In the mid-1960s the city demolished the Carnegie Library and erected the new Public Library of Metropolitan Nashville-Davidson County on this site.

Photograph by Marwin W. Wiles; courtesy of Public Library of Metropolitan Nashville-Davidson County.

The public library staff posed for this photograph soon after moving into the new Carnegie Library building in 1904. They are, left to right, top row: Nellie W. Cecil, Elizabeth Carter, Kate B. Jones, and Mary Maury; bottom row: Meriweather L. Lewis, Pearl Kelly, Hannah Johnson, Margaret Kercheval, Florence Kellam, Felicia G. Porter, and Lillian J. Crockett.

Photograph by W.G. and A.J., Thuss, Photographers; courtesy of Public Library of Metropolitan Nashville-Davidson County.

Another proud group that gathered to be photographed in front of a new building was President William J. Hale, center, and the staff and faculty of the Agricultural and Industrial State Normal School for Negroes, now Tennessee State University. Situated on Centennial Boulevard in North Nashville, it opened for classes in June 1912, about the time this picture was taken. As a state land-grant college for blacks, it offered teacher certification courses and training in agriculture and manual arts. In 1922 it expanded that curriculum and began granting bachelor's degrees, and in 1951 it achieved university status.

Photograph courtesy of Tennessee State University.

While Tennessee State Normal School was getting started, Fisk University continued to grow and prosper. Many Fisk graduates earned national prominence, but none became better known than William Edward Brughardt DuBois of the class of 1888. As the country's principal champion of equal rights for blacks, DuBois organized the Niagara Movement for political and economic equality in 1905. Four years later he helped found the National Association for the Advancement of Colored People (NAACP), and afterward he directed its research and publicity departments and edited its magazine, The Crisis, for nearly twenty-five years. Oil on canvas by Laura Wheeler Waring; photograph courtesy of National Portrait Gallery, Smithsonian Institution.

The classical architectural style and quadrangular arrangement of these buildings on the campus of George Peabody College for Teachers is based on Thomas Jefferson's plan for the University of Virginia. Bruce R. Payne brought the concept to Nashville when he left Virginia to accept the presidency of Peabody in 1911. An outgrowth of the University of Nashville and Peabody Normal College, George Peabody College for Teachers was incorporated in 1909. The following year its trustees bought this site on Twenty-First Avenue from Roger Williams University, a black institution that had occupied it since 1874. Until the first new buildings were ready in 1914, Peabody held classes in the old University of Nashville structures on Lindsley Avenue.
Photograph courtesy of George Peabody College for Teachers.

Bruce R. Payne contributed more than any other individual to the early development of George Peabody College. As president of the school from 1911 to 1937, he supervised its move from South Nashville to Twenty-First Avenue, helped raise money to complete construction, and selected a faculty and curriculum that made Peabody the most influential teacher training institution in the South. In fact, he almost literally worked himself to death for the school. On April 21, 1937, after a full day in his office, he went home and died suddenly and quietly. He posed for this portrait only a few years before his death.
Photograph courtesy of Public Library of Metropolitan Nashville-Davidson County.

With its neighbor, George Peabody College for Teachers, top right, growing on the east side of Twenty-First Avenue, Vanderbilt University, center, launched an expansion plan of its own on the west side of the street. The H-shaped building near the upper right of this 1928 aerial view is the School of Medicine and Vanderbilt University Hospital designed by Day and Klauder Architects. It opened in 1925. At the lower left is stately old Kirkland Hall, with tower, and to its left is Curry Field.
Photograph by Walter M. Williams; courtesy of The Tennessean.

Although thousands of people in and around Nashville lost their jobs during the Great Depression of the 1930s, the city did not suffer as much as some other more heavily industrialized communities. Nashville continued to function as a service center and seat of government, and its downtown business district remained busy. Here automobiles and pedestrians line Church Street in front of Lebeck Brothers (now Harveys) department store, right, and the Doctor's Building, right center. The newly erected Sudekum Building, left, stands opposite Lebeck Brothers. Photograph courtesy of Nashville Area Chamber of Commerce.

Two dramatic events, unrelated except that both occurred without warning, shaped the lives of Nashvillians and all other Americans between 1929 and 1945. The first was the crash of the stock market on October 29, 1929; the second was the Japanese attack on Pearl Harbor on December 7, 1941. Each produced a crisis with shocking consequences. The market collapse exposed hidden problems in the American economy and triggered the Great Depression of the 1930s. Thousands in Nashville and millions elsewhere lost their jobs and went on relief. The attack on Pearl Harbor forced the nation into World War II. The catastrophic struggle hastened economic recovery both in Nashville and throughout the United States, but city and nation alike paid a heavy toll in human lives.

Much has been written about the causes of the depression, but all explanations suggest that the prosperity of the 1920s was not as solid as it seemed. Farm income was down, industrial wages were not keeping pace with profits, and many banks and investors were engaging in unsound speculation. When suddenly almost everyone wanted to sell stocks but few wanted to buy them, the market plummeted. This led to the failure of shaky financial institutions everywhere, leaving thousands of investors penniless and hundreds of banks unable to meet demands on deposits.

The most spectacular series of failures in the mid-South began in Nashville with the collapse of Caldwell and Company. As the value of that firm's stock and property continued to decline early in 1930, its controlling partners, Rogers Caldwell and Luke Lea, tried to stop the skid by merging with the Banco Kentucky Company of Louisville. In scrambling for cash to complete this transaction, however, Caldwell and Lea made several questionable financial maneuvers, and on November 7, 1930, their principal subsidiary, the Bank of Tennessee, went into receivership. Failure of another Caldwell bank on November 13 sparked a chain reaction that toppled some 120 other banks in seven states. In the political and financial tumult that followed, Luke Lea and a North Carolina bank president went to prison, a North Carolina mayor committed suicide, and Tennesseans tried to impeach Governor Henry

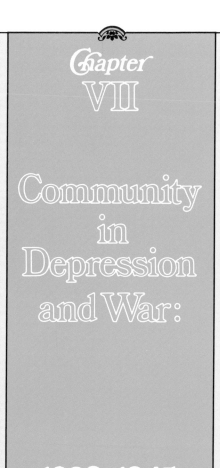

Chapter
VII

Community
in
Depression
and War:

1929-1945

H. Horton, a Caldwell political ally.

During the next two years in Nashville and elsewhere, banks folded, businesses failed, wages dropped, and workers lost their jobs. Nashville suffered less than many more heavily industrialized cities, but that fact did not comfort citizens who suddenly had no money for food and shelter.

In 1932 American voters, dissatisfied with President Herbert Hoover's apparent inability to halt the spiraling effects of depression, sent Democrat Franklin D. Roosevelt to the White House. Immediately upon taking office in 1933 he proposed a number of bold "New Deal" measures designed to provide jobs and to stimulate economic recovery. The resulting programs, which were expedited through Congress by Speaker of the House Joseph W. Byrns of Nashville, proved controversial. The extent to which they succeeded remains a matter of debate among historians. However, several helped Nashville immeasurably. Chief among these were the Tennessee Valley Authority, created in 1933, and the Works Progress Administration, established in 1935. The TVA provided jobs and electricity in the Nashville trade area by constructing dams and powerhouses and implementing flood control, soil conservation, and reforestation projects. The WPA provided jobs and numerous permanent civic improvements by funding a variety of special projects.

Tennessee's allotment of WPA funds ranked among the highest in the country, and a sizeable portion of it was spent in and around Nashville. Colonel Harry S. Berry headed the state WPA office and personally supervised the agency's activities in the Nashville district. In keeping with WPA policy to provide as many jobs as possible, Berry channeled more than half of the money into city and farm-to-market road projects that cost little in material and equipment but employed thousands of men. The improved streets and roads served Nashvillians and other Tennesseans for many years after the depression ended. Other WPA projects in Nashville included the construction of a new airport, erection of schools and other public edifices, restoration of Fort Negley, and construction and improvement of the Percy and Edwin Warner parks.

Despite the economic hard times of the 1930s,

In 1929 Rogers Caldwell was the most powerful financial figure in Nashville. The son of a prominent banker, he had founded Caldwell and Company in 1917 and built it from a distributor of state and municipal bonds into a major holding company that traded real estate bonds and industrial securities and owned such diverse enterprises as banks, newspapers, and Nashville's professional baseball team. The collapse of Caldwell's empire in 1930 cost the state of Tennessee $6.5 million in deposits and made many Nashvillians realize that the prosperity of the 1920s had not been as solid as they thought.
Photograph courtesy of The Tennessean.

Nashvillians tried desperately to hang onto their accustomed life-styles. For many residents this meant listening every Saturday night to a local radio program called the "Grand Ole Opry." Begun in 1925 by WSM station manager George D. Hay, the Opry had initially featured a variety of musical acts. By the thirties, however, the program's largely rural audience had dictated its evolution into a "hillbilly" or country music show starring such performers as Uncle Jimmy Thompson, a fiddler; Uncle Dave Macon, a banjo picker; DeFord Bailey, a harmonica player; and Dr. Humphrey Bate, leader of a popular group known as the "Possum Hunters."

Although probably no one in Nashville realized it at the time, the city was progressing, even while in the depths of depression, toward its future as a center of the American music industry. In 1932 WSM obtained a clear-channel frequency and began broadcasting with fifty thousand watts of power. This made it one of the strongest stations in the country and made the Opry popular throughout the eastern United States. It also hastened the evolution of Opry performers from part-time amateurs into full-time professionals. By 1934 Harry Stone, who had replaced Hay as WSM station manager, had established the Artists' Service Bureau to promote tours and outside bookings for Opry performers and had hired a music librarian, Vito Pellettieri, to advise them about copyrights, performance rights, and publishing royalties. The growing popularity of cowboy music and western swing in Hollywood films boosted the Opry's audience still further, and in 1939 singer Roy Acuff became the show's first national star. His popularity rested partly on his musical style, which resembled earlier, more traditional, southern country music, and partly on his appearance in a 1939 movie, *The Grand Ole Opry*. That film signaled the arrival of country as an acceptable music form and helped insure Nashville's place in its continuing development.

Despite Roosevelt's New Deal programs and the early growth of the country music industry, Nashville, along with the rest of the nation, was still feeling the effects of the depression in December

President Franklin D. Roosevelt was a symbol of hope to millions of Americans during the Great Depression. Many Nashvillians were among those who benefited from the Tennessee Valley Authority, Works Progress Administration, and other programs that he sponsored. When he and Mrs. Roosevelt visited Nashville in 1934, people turned out in droves to meet them. The president is shown here during a brief stop at Fisk University.

Photograph by Wiles Photographers; courtesy of Fisk University Library's Special Collections.

1941 when Japan bombed Pearl Harbor. As a result of that surprise attack, the next four years brought Nashvillians both anguish and prosperity. Some residents went abroad to fight the Axis powers and did not return. Others spent months and years away from Nashville in trying, even terrifying, circumstances. Those who remained at home suffered both temporary and permanent losses of family members and friends to military service. While local men and women who entered the armed forces were generally assigned elsewhere, hundreds of thousands of soldiers from other states saw duty in Middle Tennessee. Their presence and the money that the federal government spent to maintain them helped spur economic recovery in the area.

Because Middle Tennessee had a varied landscape that could be used to train troops for almost any terrain they might encounter overseas, the army sent more than 600,000 men here for maneuvers and war games between 1941 and 1945. Tens of thousands more were stationed at one time or another at Camp Campbell near the Kentucky border, Camp Forrest near Tullahoma, and Smyrna Army Air Field. Other thousands passed through Nashville on troop trains every month. By 1942, 80,000 soldiers crowded into the city each weekend for recreation, and Nashvillians by the hundreds volunteered to entertain them at United Service Organization centers.

Nashville industries contributed significantly to the war effort, too, and profited in return. The new Vultee plant, near the airport, manufactured hundreds of military aircraft, and the Nashville Bridge Company, on the east bank of the Cumberland across from lower Broadway, built two navy mine sweepers, fourteen submarine chasers, and dozens of navy barges. Both firms remained major maufacturers after the war.

For four long years Nashvillians kept up a frenzied pace in support of the war. When peace came, on V-J Day, September 2, 1945, they celebrated in the streets. Both the depression and the war were over, and the city seemed on the threshold of a new, more prosperous era.

The Works Progress Administration spent $84,000 to restore Fort Negley and provide jobs for 800 men. In this photograph, taken in March 1936, some of them are constructing a stone entrance to the fort on the northwest side of Saint Cloud Hill. Visible in the distance is Union Station, top center, and the newly completed post office. The residences and other buildings directly below the hill have now given way to interstate highways, and the Cumberland Science Museum occupies a portion of the slope below the work site.

Photograph courtesy of National Archives.

Between 1938 and 1940 the WPA spent $2.5 million to improve existing Nashville streets and build twenty-two miles of new ones. These WPA workers are resurfacing Second Avenue North near the Public Square on June 3, 1940. They are spreading the road material by hand and packing it with steam-powered rollers.

Photograph courtesy of The Tennessean.

Although the WPA reduced its Nashville spending considerably after 1939, it continued to fund some projects until the spring of 1943. One of the agency's last undertakings was removal of streetcar rails following the cessation of service in 1941. These workmen are taking up rails on Twelfth Avenue South in February 1942.

Photograph courtesy of The Tennessean.

Much of the money that the WPA spent in areas surrounding Nashville went to pave farm-to-market roads. Such projects employed thousands, helped make scenes like this one on old Allen Branch Road in Williamson County a thing of the past, and enabled Nashville to continue its role as a vital trade center.
Photograph courtesy of National Archives.

The WPA constructed parks as well as buildings. In 1936 it employed three hundred men to build and improve the Percy and Edwin Warner parks in southwest Nashville. In addition to providing paychecks for the jobless, the project gave the city two fine recreational areas which its citizens still enjoy. This is the main entrance to Percy Warner Park on Belle Meade Boulevard.
Photograph by Gerald Holly; courtesy of Tennessee State Library and Archives.

The Public Works Administration, another New Deal agency, also provided numerous jobs in Nashville during the early years of the depression. PWA workers erected this City Market near the Public Square just north of the present Davidson County Courthouse. The extensively altered market facility serves today as the Metro Safety Building and Police Headquarters.
Photograph courtesy of National Archives.

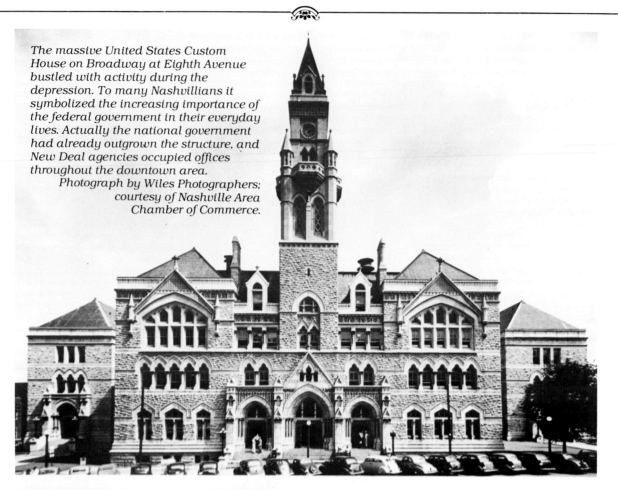

The massive United States Custom House on Broadway at Eighth Avenue bustled with activity during the depression. To many Nashvillians it symbolized the increasing importance of the federal government in their everyday lives. Actually the national government had already outgrown the structure, and New Deal agencies occupied offices throughout the downtown area.
Photograph by Wiles Photographers; courtesy of Nashville Area Chamber of Commerce.

Despite the obvious benefits of many of the New Deal programs, a number of prominent Americans found much in them to criticize. One of the most outspoken critics was Louisiana's Senator Huey Long. Known to millions as the "kingfish," he did everything in a big way, including running for president and promoting the Louisiana State University football team. Here he is pictured with Nashville Mayor Hiliary Howse, left, shortly after arriving at Union Station with five thousand students for the 1934 LSU-Vanderbilt game. Long arranged the trip by pressuring the Illinois Central Railroad into offering special six-dollar round-trip fares to students. The railroad used six fourteen-car trains to transport virtually the entire LSU student body to Nashville. After the youths got off the train, Long led them along Broadway to Centennial Park, where the LSU band played for thousands of Nashvillians. Afterward all marched to Dudley Field and watched the LSU Tigers roll over Vanderbilt by a score of 29-0.
Photograph courtesy of The Tennessean.

Vanderbilt University's "fugitive" poets, shown here at a 1956 reunion, also gained national attention as social critics. They first came to prominence in the 1920s, when literary experts hailed them the most influential group of American writers since Ralph Waldo Emerson, Henry David Thoreau, and other New England transcendentalists. Taking their name from a magazine entitled The Fugitive, which they began publishing in Nashville in 1922, the Vanderbilt authors developed an influential "new criticism" in literature. They decried materialism and industrialism in American society and defended Southern regionalism and agrarianism. Four members of the group—Allen Tate, top row, left; Robert Penn Warren, bottom row, left; John Crowe Ransom, bottom row, fourth from left; and Donald Davidson, bottom row, third from right—became especially well known. In 1930 they and eight others published a collection of essays entitled I'll Take My Stand, and it so eloquently defended the South and rural way of life that literary critics labeled it an agrarian manifesto and its authors "agrarians."

Photograph by Joe Rudis; courtesy of Vanderbilt University Photographic Archive.

Natural disasters compounded the economic difficulties that many Nashvillians faced in the thirties. In 1933 a tornado smashed hundreds of houses in East Nashville, and four years later the Cumberland River crested at 53.8 feet and flooded much of the city.

High water damaged property and stopped traffic in the streets, but it didn't keep these milkmen from making their deliveries.

Photograph by Wiles Photographers; courtesy of The Tennessean.

In 1930 the signs in this idle electric streetcar claimed that it could "save money for every rider." A little more than a decade later, however, such vehicles disappeared from Nashville thoroughfares. The interior view shows the last car during its final run along the Radnor line on Fourth Avenue and Nolensville Road on February 2, 1941. Buses replaced the streetcars and ran generally along the same routes.

Photograph by Wiles Photographers; Courtesy of Tennessee State Library and Archives.

Photograph by Ed Clark; Courtesy of The Tennessean.

While electric streetcars were beginning to disappear in the 1930s, airplanes were serving more and more Nashvillians. American Airways, now American Airlines, brought this Curtiss/Condor aircraft to Nashville's old Sky Harbor airport on a public relations flight in October 1933. Dignitaries who made the trip included United States Postmaster General James Farley, fifth from left, and entrepreneur Howard Hughes, extreme left. Tennessean publisher Silliman Evans, fifth from right, posed with the visitors for this photograph.

Photograph courtesy of
Tennessee State Museum.

Nashville's new Municipal Airport, off Murfreesboro Road, was only partially complete when American Airlines inaugurated passenger service to the city on June 24, 1936. To celebrate the occasion the airline took leading citizens on courtesy flights over Davidson County. Among the first passengers was Nashville Banner publisher James G. Stahlman, one of the many Nashvillians who became regular users of the new service. He is shown here returning to Nashville following his election as president of the American Newspaper Publishers Association in 1937.

Photograph courtesy of
Mildred Stahlman.

On October 10, 1939, the Municipal Airport was officially renamed Berry Field in honor of Colonel Harry S. Berry. As statewide administrator of WPA programs he had wrangled government funds for modernization of the facility in 1935-36. The improvements, which were expected to cost $380,000, ran eventually to $1.2 million and helped lead to a congressional investigation of "boondoggling" in Tennessee. Berry is shown here speaking during the airfield dedication ceremony. Nashville Mayor Thomas L. Cummings, fourth from right, and businessman Will T. Cheek, third from right, were among those in attendance.
Photograph by Ed Clark; courtesy of The Tennessean.

During World War II Berry Field was headquarters for the army's 20th Ferrying Group. This view to the northeast shows military aircraft parked along the taxi strip, center. The small structure to the right of the strip and near the circular drive is the airfield's passenger terminal and administration building. The two structures on the left are a drill hall and office erected in 1936 for the national guard's 105th Observation Squadron.
Photograph by Robert Yarnell Richie; courtesy of Nashville Area Chamber of Commerce.

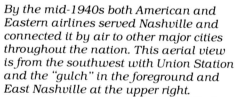

By the mid-1940s both American and Eastern airlines served Nashville and connected it by air to other major cities throughout the nation. This aerial view is from the southwest with Union Station and the "gulch" in the foreground and East Nashville at the upper right.
Photograph courtesy of Nashville Area Chamber of Commerce.

*Ward-Belmont was a well-known
Nashville women's college in the 1930s.
Established in 1913 through the merger
of Ward's Seminary and Belmont
College, it occupied the old Belmont
Mansion, shown here in a 1939 WPA
photograph. Ward-Belmont had an
ambitious academic program and an
outstanding "lecture and artist" series,
but it expanded its physical plant too
rapidly, and in 1951 its bankers
foreclosed its mortgages. That same year
Tennessee Baptists bought the property
and founded a new Belmont College.*
            *Photograph courtesy of
            National Archives.*

Despite the economic uncertainty of the 1930s, Nashville's cultural institutions flourished. Like Vanderbilt's "fugitive" and "agrarian" writers, several Fisk University faculty members won national acclaim for their work. Charles S. Johnson, right, a sociologist, influenced New Deal agricultural policy with his studies of Southern farm tenancy and helped persuade President Roosevelt to establish a "black cabinet" of paid advisors to inform him about Negro opnion. James Weldon Johnson, below left, enjoyed a distinguished career as a songwriter, playwright, novelist, and NAACP field secretary before coming to Fisk in 1932 to teach creative literature. He completed his famous autobiography, Along This Way, in Nashville and remained at Fisk until his death in 1938. Arna Bontemps, below right, head librarian at Fisk for many years, wrote a number of well-received histories and children's books and a widely acclaimed novel, Black Thunder, about Gabriel Prosser and the 1800 Virginia slave insurrection.

Oil on canvas by Betsy Graves Reyneau; photograph courtesy of National Portrait Gallery, Smithsonian Institution.

Oil on canvas by Laura Wheeler Waring; photograph courtesy of National Portrait Gallery, Smithsonian Institution.

Oil on canvas by Betsy Graves Reyneau; photograph courtesy of National Portrait Gallery, Smithsonian Institution.

In 1928 Sara Jeter, left, and Louise Smith, right, were members of the first faculty of the Nashville Conservatory of Music. Both as teachers at that institution and in other capacities, Jeter and Smith instructed many Nashvillians in dance and helped stage dozens of musical revues during the twenties and thirties. Here they are discussing cues with band leader Jimmy Gallagher while planning a show in 1933.
Photograph courtesy of Public Library of Metropolitan Nashville-Davidson County.

Among those Nashvillians with whom dance teachers Sarah Jeter and Louise Smith worked were, left to right, Mary McComas, Joanne Hampton, Mary Manthey, and Dollie Dearman. They are performing "Girls in White" during a revue entitled By Request *in April 1939.*
Photograph courtesy of Public Library of Metropolitan Nashville-Davidson County.

Nashvillians enjoyed two well-known "big bands" in the twenties and thirties. Francis Craig, extreme right, and Beasley Smith went from playing piano duets while students in a Clarksville, Tennessee, elementary school to organizing dance orchestras while attending Vanderbilt University in the 1920s. When WSM radio went on the air in 1925, Craig's band was performing in the dining room of the Hermitage Hotel and Smith's in the Andrew Jackson Hotel. Both began appearing on WSM, and soon afterward they signed successful recording contracts and began touring the country. The female vocalist pictured at left with Craig's orchestra is Alpha Louise Morton.
Photograph courtesy of Country Music Foundation Library.

In 1932 WSM radio obtained a clear-channel frequency and erected this 50,000-watt transmitting tower off Franklin Road. Rising to a height of 878 feet, it was the tallest radio tower in North America. More important, it enabled WSM's signal to reach most of the eastern half of the United States and gave the Grand Ole Opry the beginnings of a national audience. Although WSM joined the new NBC radio network about this time, it preempted all but one of the network's Saturday night shows in order to broadcast the Opry. The exception was "Amos 'n Andy."
Photograph courtesy of Country Music Foundation Library.

By the time WSM opened its new broadcasting facility, Harry Stone, shown here in 1932, replaced George D. Hay as station manager. While Hay continued as announcer for the Opry, Stone busied himself helping Opry performers find enough outside work to support themselves. In 1934 he founded the Artists' Service Bureau to promote tours and other bookings for Opry musicians, and he hired Vito Pellettieri to advise them about copyrights, performance rights, and royalties. As a result the Opry's part-time amateur performers soon became full-time professionals.
Photograph by Todd Studios; courtesy of Country Music Foundation Library.

When the Grand Ole Opry began in 1925 the harmonica was an especially popular instrument in Middle Tennessee. As a result harmonica music became an Opry tradition. Dr. Humphrey Bate and at least two members of the famous Crook Brothers band played harmonicas during the Opry's early years, but DeFord Bailey was the show's first star harmonica soloist. He performed on the Opry from the late 1920s through the early 1940s and is recognized today as one of the most creative harmonica players ever to appear in Nashville. He played in a style that he called "black hillbilly." It combined expressions of early blues and old-time string band music.

Photograph by Dennis Utile; courtesy of Country Music Foundation Library.

Eventually the Grand Ole Opry outgrew WSM's studios, and during the late 1930s the station moved the show to a succession of locations. From 1937 to 1939 the Opry occupied this building, the Dixie Tabernacle, in East Nashville. In 1939 the Opry moved to the War Memorial Auditorium, and in 1941 it shifted to the Ryman Auditorium, where it remained until completion of the new Opry House in 1974. The Dixie Tabernacle has been demolished.

Photograph courtesy of Public Library of Metropolitan Nashville-Davidson County.

Roy Acuff, center, joined the Grand Ole Opry in 1938 and became an instant hit. Born in Maynardville, Tennessee, in 1903, Acuff grew up in the Knoxville suburb of Fountain City and attempted a career in professional baseball. When a sunstroke ended his playing days in 1929 he took up the fiddle, and soon he was touring East Tennessee in a medicine show. He developed a distinct singing style, began performing on a Knoxville radio station, and in 1936 received an invitation to record for the American Record Corporation. In only two sessions Acuff and his band recorded thirty tunes. Sears, Roebuck and Company selected some of them for mail-order distribution, and one, "The Great Speckle Bird," sold tremendously. Its popularity helped Acuff wrangle an invitation to appear on the Opry, and in 1939 his success on the show helped persuade NBC to carry a thirty-minute segment of it every Saturday. He is shown here performing on the Opry about 1940. Left to right are Jess Easterly, Lonnie Wilson, Acuff, and Oswald Kirby.

Photograph courtesy of Country Music Foundation Library.

In 1941 steadily increasing demand for tickets to Opry performances forced WSM to move the show to the largest available auditorium in the city, the Ryman at 116 Fifth Avenue North. It was an appropriate choice. Erected between 1889 and 1892 as the Union Gospel Tabernacle, the building had important cultural ties with Southern music and was already a Nashville landmark. Dwight L. Moody, Billy Sunday, and other famous evangelists had preached in it; William Jennings Bryan, Champ Clark, and other national political leaders had spoken from its podium; and John Philip Sousa, Enrico Caruso, and other internationally known artists had performed its stage. WSM leased the building until 1963, and then the station's parent company, National Life and Accident Insurance, bought it. When the Opry moved to a new building on Briley Parkway in 1974, the Ryman remained open for tours by country music fans.
Photograph by Jack E. Boucher; courtesy of Historic American Buildings Survey.

In 1939, the same year that NBC began broadcasting a segment of the Grand Ole Opry nationally, Roy Acuff starred in a movie entitled The Grand Ole Opry. Although the picture was only the first of several that Acuff made, it was by far the most important. Despite a medium budget, contrived plot, and corny jokes, the movie effectively depicted Southern country music as honest, open, and reflective of conservative values shared by people in all regions of America. In short, the picture signaled the arrival of country as an acceptable music form and helped insure Nashville's place in its continuing development. Uncle Dave Macon and George D. Hay, right, with hat, appeared with Acuff, left, with fiddle, in the movie.
Republic movie poster courtesy of Country Music Foundation Library.

During all the years that it occupied the Ryman Auditorium, the Grand Ole Opry retained the building's old church pews. To meet the demand for tickets, the Opry eventually began offering two shows on Saturday night and at least one on Fridays. For more than thirty years, each time the auditorium doors swung open 3,500 persons crowded into these seats to see Roy Acuff, Red Foley, Bill Monroe, Kitty Wells, Minnie Pearl, and other country performers.
Photograph by Jack E. Boucher; courtesy of Historic American Buildings Survey.

In addition to the Grand Ole Opry, WSM boasted a number of other well-known shows in the thirties and forties. They included musical variety programs such as "Sunday Down South" and the "Lion Oil Show"; Alfred Leland Crabb's "Teachers College of the South"; a history program called "Adventures that Made America"; and Mary Lyle Wilson's "Radio Kitchen," shown here. All of these, plus others, were broadcast live from WSM studios.
Photograph courtesy of Country Music Foundation Library.

Nashville's police force also had radio equipment to be proud of in the thirties. Dispatcher H.B. Beazley, right, sits behind the console of a brand new two-way system reputed to be among the largest in the country. It went into operation on January 1, 1936.
Photograph by Wiles-Photographers; courtesy of Public Library of Metropolitan Nashville-Davidson County.

Complementing the police force's new two-way radio system were new radio cars that could be dispatched to any part of the city. Here Officer Carney Patterson, at extreme right in light overcoat and hat, poses with the "Black Maria," a bullet-proof 1937 Dodge riot car. Note the shields around the front tires and over the radiator.
Photograph by Wiles-Photographers; courtesy of Public Library of Metropolitan Nashville-Davidson County.

Although they were still concerned with the lingering effects of the Great Depression. Nashvillians watched intently as war spread over much of Europe and Asia in the late 1930s. Long before the Japanese attacked Pearl Harbor and plunged the United States into armed conflict in December 1941, some residents were preparing for that eventuality. In December 1940, A.G. Masters, right, became one of the first three Nashville donors in a military blood drive. He was assisted by Dr. Fred Cooper, left, at the Vanderbilt University Hospital.
Photograph courtesy of Vanderbilt University Photographic Archives.

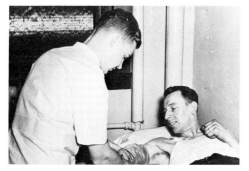

When war came the draft brought millions of Americans into military service. Despite the success of the draft, the armed forces conducted aggressive recruiting campaigns to get top-notch volunteers for highly specialized assignments. In March 1942 Army Air Corps recruiters parked this mobile recruiting station at the corner of Church Street and Capitol Boulevard in downtown Nashville and began signing up young men for pilot's training. Inside the trailer Sergeants John W. Greer, David B. Everett, and LaRue Washburn, left to right,explained the aviation cadet program to prospective recruits and helped them fill out applications.
Photographs by Ed Clark; courtesy of The Tennessean.

Because of Middle Tennessee's varied terrain and central location the army used it as a training ground for more than 600,000 men during World War II. This scene was repeated in rural areas all around Nashville as troops from Camp Campbell, Camp Forrest, Smyrna Army Air Field, and other installations conducted war games and other training exercises almost nonstop. These men are trainees of the Army Air Corps' 20th Ferrying Group stationed at Berry Field. They have just completed a twelve-mile march in full field equipment in February 1944 and are preparing to bed down for the night.
Photograph courtesy of The Tennessean.

Scenes like this one at Union Station on January 16, 1944, were also common in wartime Nashville, as military personnel from all over the nation waited for trains to take them home on furlough or back to camp. Private First Class James Aylsworth, left, of Council Bluffs, Iowa, and Sergeant Claude Boarman, center, of Shawano, Wisconsin, have just come off maneuvers near Nashville and are headed home. Sailor Oscar Brown, right, of McMinnville, Tennessee, has used up his leave and is returning to his ship.
Photograph courtesy of The Tennessean.

Nashville civic and charitable organizations helped entertain thousands of servicemen and women who flocked into the city from area military bases every weekend. On this night in July 1942, four hundred couples were swinging and swaying to the latest dance music in the YMCA gym at Seventh Avenue and Union Street, where the Hyatt Regency Hotel now stands. The men were new arrivals at the Army Air Force Classification Center on Thompson Lane. The women were from Nashville and surrounding communities.
Photograph by Campbell Bligh; courtesy of The Tennessean.

In addition to being a service center for military bases, Nashville was a major producer of war material. The Aviation Manufacturing Corportion built this plant next to Berry Field shortly before the United States entered the war. Vultee Aircraft, Inc., bought it in 1940, and on May 4, 1941, former Republican presidential nominee Wendall Willkie, dedicated it to "Defense of the Democracies." Hundreds of Nashvillians found jobs here, as war production all over the country provided work for millions who couldn't find it during the Great Depression. The large orchards in this photograph are gone now, having given way to other factories and dozens of residences, but the plant remains as part of AVCO Aerostructures Division.

Photograph courtesy of The Tennessean.

Photograph courtesy of AVCO Aerostructures Division, Vultee Boulevard, Nashville.

Workers on this Vultee assembly line produced hundreds of these Vengeance aircraft during the war. They had a top speed of 279 miles per hour and each plane carried four to six .50 caliber machine guns and two 500-pound bombs. British Royal Air Force and Indian Royal Air Force units used most of these planes in the India-Burma theater.

Photograph courtesy of Tennessee State Museum.

This Vultee employee is towing a completed Lockheed P-38 Lightning fighter-bomber off the assembly line. Powered by two 1,425-horsepower engines, these planes flew at speeds of more than 400 miles per hour and carried one 20-millimeter cannon, four .50-caliber machine guns, and either two 1,000-pound bombs or ten 5-inch rockets. Lightnings claimed more Japanese planes than any other American aircraft.

Photograph courtesy of AVCO Aerostructures Divison, Vultee Boulevard, Nashville.

Nashville's role in the war brought a steady stream of dignitaries to the city. Here World War I air ace Eddie Rickenbacker, left, inspects an assembly line at the Vultee plant. As special consultant to Secretary of War Henry L. Stimson, Rickenbacker toured United States military installations all over the world.

Photograph courtesy of AVCO Aerostructures Division, Vultee Boulevard, Nashville.

In addition to serving in the armed forces, manufacturing war material, and playing host to military personnel from area bases, Nashvillians contributed to the war effort by buying and selling government bonds. Here Hollywood actress Loraine Day addresses Vultee employees during a bond sale at the plant.

Photograph courtesy of AVCO Aerostructures Division, Vultee Boulevard, Nashville.

World War II brought military vessels back to the Cumberland River for the first time since the Civil War. Instead of coming down the river to Nashville like the Union gunboats in 1862, these minesweepers were built in the city. The Nashville Bridge Company manufactured them for the navy early in 1942.

Photograph courtesy of The Tennessean.

At this war bond rally in downtown Nashville, citizens were invited to buy bonds and to sign bombs to be dropped on Berlin and Tokyo. Country music stars Roy Acuff, right, and Bill Monroe, second from right, were first in line to buy a bond and sign a bomb.

Photograph courtesy of Country Music Foundation Library.

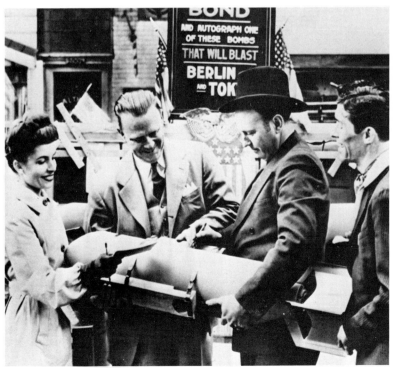

Even entertainment often had a military flavor during the war. These Nashvillians are standing in line in January 1944 to see Gary Cooper and Ingrid Bergman in the movie version of Ernest Hemingway's For Whom the Bell Tolls, a novel set in the Spanish Civil War of the 1930s. With gasoline, tires, and most other consumer goods rationed, in short supply, or not available at all, motion pictures provided a welcome diversion. This theater, the Paramount, stood on Church Street and served residents until it was demolished in 1979.

Photograph by John Malone; courtesy of The Tennessean.

The 693rd Army Air Force Band interrupted a practice session to pose for this photograph in the Berry Field gymnasium. The group was getting ready for a 1944 Labor Day concert at the Centennial Park bandstand. Entitled "Democracy in Words, Music, and Prayer," the event was co-sponsored by the 20th Ferrying Group and Nashville's Gold Star Mothers. Most of these men were professional musicians before the war.

Photograph courtesy of The Tennessean.

On August 15, 1945, news of Japan's surrender set off a resounding celebration in Nashville. To the accompaniment of loud cheering and trumpet tooting, soldiers and civilians alike hopped aboard automobiles and conducted impromptu parades along Church and other downtown streets. The victory party lasted long into the night, and when the revelers began to tire, they rested on the curbs rather than quit the celebration.
Photographs courtesy of The Tennessean.

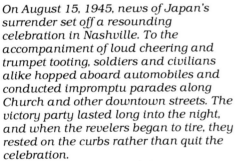

No Nashvillians welcomed the end of the war more than those who had family members and friends overseas. Mrs. Thomas E. Harvey, who had four sons in Europe, listens to news of Germany's surrender on May 8, 1945. In her hand is a picture of Lieutenant Colonel Robert H. Harvey, an army medical officer in France. On the radio, left to right, are photographs of Staff Sergeant Benson Harvey, Chief Petty Officer Frank D. Harvey, and Chief Warrant Officer James L. Harvey.
Photograph by John Malone; courtesy of The Tennessean.

When Andrew Jackson came to Middle Tennessee in October 1788, Nashville was only a frontier crossroads. In May 1960, when these workmen moved Jackson's equestrian statue from the capitol grounds to the courtyard of the state archives, Nashville was one of the largest metropolitan areas in the South. The population of Davidson County had grown more than fifty percent, to 400,000, since the end of World War II, and voters were on the verge of approving an innovative countywide metropolitan government. Workmen returned the statue to its original location following completion of remodeling at the capitol. Photograph by Jimmy Ellis; courtesy of The Tennessean.

Chapter VIII

Metropolitan Nashville:

1945-1964

The end of World War II marked a turning point for Nashville. For nearly two decades its citizens had concentrated their public attention on problems of depression and war. Now, with the dawning of peace, they were able to focus more of their talent and energy on purely local concerns. As a result, during the next seventeen years the city enjoyed tremendous growth and expansion. It also pioneered a new kind of urban government and earned national recognition for innovative approaches to urban problems.

In 1946 Nashvillians joined most other Americans in a spending spree, and after a minor recession in 1948-49, boomtime conditions existed in all sectors of the economy. At first wartime savings fueled this growth. Later it was fed by the postwar baby boom, cold-war defense spending, and people's continued desire for more and better automobiles, homes, and other consumer goods.

In Nashville, as elsewhere, the most sought-after commodity was housing. There had been little new residential construction since 1929, and the severe shortage of homes remained critical well into the 1950s, despite the construction of 22,000 new housing units by 1949. Nashville contractors built 30,000 more units in the fifties, however, and by 1960 only 11,000 of Davidson County's 115,000 families lived in the same houses they had occupied twenty years earlier.

Between 1946 and 1960 the combined population of Nashville and Davidson County increased from about 260,000 to almost 400,000. This rapid growth produced new problems for the community and magnified a number of old ones. For example, most new housing lay outside the city limits in suburbs subject to a county government that was designed to meet rural needs and which therefore lacked authority to provide urban services. Within Nashville proper, many older houses were becoming uninhabitable. Streets and water lines were showing effects of neglect dictated by wartime shortages of asphalt and lead pipe, and improper sewerage disposal was threatening public health. Heavy pollution fouled the Cumberland River below the city, and Richland Creek in West Nashville served as an open conduit of waste. Increased traffic caused problems, too, as automobile ownership tripled in Davidson County between 1946 and 1957. Most residents drove the family car back and forth to work and clogged city streets and suburban roads twice each day.

In their search for solutions to these problems, both county and city dwellers sought new political leadership. Suburbanites rallied in 1950 behind attorney Beverly Briley in his successful bid to unseat Judge Litton Hickman, who had headed the Davidson County Quarterly Court since 1917. One year later Nashville voters narrowly elected Ben West mayor over incumbent Thomas L. Cummings, who had held that office since Hilary Howse's death in 1938. Briley and West quickly emerged as powerful political figures and effective champions of their respective constituencies. Briley became a nationally known defender of suburbia and advocate of modernized county government, while West earned a national reputation as a champion of the central city.

With West at the helm Nashville underwent a virtual renaissance. In the early 1950s the Capitol Hill Redevelopment Project, one of the first urban renewal projects in the nation, cleared ninety-six acres north of the capitol and central business district. The area was then utilized for the four-lane James Robertson Parkway, several public and private office buildings, apartments, a motel-restaurant complex, and eventually the Municipal Auditorium. In 1954 West obtained a major Federal Housing Act urban renewal grant for East Nashville. This project, which covered 2,052 acres and included 8,617 dwellings and 5,750 other buildings was the nation's largest in number of structures, and second in acreage. West's accomplishments in the public sector spurred new private investment, too. Between 1955 and 1959 developers spent $50 million to erect new buildings or to refurbish old ones in the downtown business district.

Despite West's efforts, however, the central city continued to lose population to the suburbs. In 1950 Nashville, with 174,000 people, still outnumbered the rest of the county, which had 147,000, but by 1960 the reverse was true. The suburban population outnumbered Nashville 229,000 to 171,000. With the city's tax base

When World War II ended, some Nashville soldiers, like thousands elsewhere, brought home foreign brides. To help orient them to American customs, the local Red Cross chapter gave cooking classes. Here, left to right, Joan Davis from England, Nora Schubert from New Zealand, and Jeannie Bowen from France are learning how to prepare Southern fried chicken, grits, fried okra, chess pie, and other regional dishes. Their instructor is Jeannie G. (Mrs. R.K.) Webb, right.
Photograph courtesy of The Tennessean.

During the postwar housing crunch Nashville builders erected small, one-story, frame houses such as these in tract developments all around the city. Although built rapidly, inexpensively, and to uniform designs, they helped fill a desperate need for housing, because the depression and war had almost halted residential construction.
Photograph by Photography, Inc.; courtesy of Nashville Gas Company.

shrinking rapidly, some citizens thought Nashville should annex the suburbs. West and other city leaders were hesitant to propose such a controversial solution, however.

Meanwhile, Judge Briley suggested a different remedy, not only for the city's problems but for those of the suburbs as well. Speaking to the Nashville Rotary Club on June 21, 1955, he urged a single, consolidated, metropolitan government for Nashville and Davidson County. Planning for such a government began a few weeks later, and in October 1956 a special city-county committee announced a design for consolidation. It called for a common executive and council but divided the county into general and urban service districts. Briley, West,

most other community leaders, and both newspapers approved the plan, but suburban voters, fearing higher taxes and urban problems, defeated it in a special referendum on June 17, 1958.

This vote proved only a temporary setback, thanks largely to Mayor West and the city council. Shortly after the referendum the council began annexing outlying industrial areas, and in 1959 it enacted a law requiring all motorists who used the city streets more than thirty days a year to purchase a ten-dollar automobile sticker. The following year the council annexed forty-two square miles with 82,000 residents. This caused a revolt in the suburbs and a drastic shift in opinion toward a consolidated city-county government. On June 28,

The postwar building boom continued through the 1950s, and by 1960 Davidson County had more than 50,000 new housing units. Many were situated in suburban communities outside the city limits. Only a few months before this photograph was taken in January 1961 the Parkwood Estates subdivision, near Dickerson Road several miles north of downtown Nashville, was peaceful farm land. This view northward along Richmond Hill Drive shows more than half-a-dozen finished houses and thirty others under construction.
Photograph by Jack Corn; courtesy of The Tennessean.

Automobile ownership increased sharply in Nashville after World War II, but city streets remained relatively unchanged. Traffic snarls such as this one on Broadway between Fifth and Sixth avenues were commonplace. On this day, January 20, 1947, motorists needed twenty minutes to go from Fifth to First Avenue.
Photograph by Charles Cowden; courtesy of The Tennessean.

1962, despite an active campaign by Mayor West who now opposed the plan, voters approved consolidation by a count of 36,961 to 28,133. In November Judge Briley defeated Clifford Allen for the office of metropolitan mayor, and on April 1, 1963, the new government went into effect. It was one of the first of its kind in the nation.

Nashville progressed on other fronts in the postwar years, too, most notably in race relations. Unlike many of its sister cities in the South, where public officials and white citizens often joined to block the demands of Negro citizens for their rights, Nashville seemed by comparison to be too busy to hate. The city desegregated its schools with relatively little difficulty in 1957, and following sit-ins at downtown lunch counters in 1960, it desegregated eating places in dime, drug, and department stores. By the summer of 1963 almost all public facilities had been opened to black citizens. Probably the best indication of forward-looking racial attitudes in Nashville came in 1964 when Richard Fulton joined a handful of other Southern congressmen in voting for the far-reaching Civil Rights Act.

By the mid-1960s Nashville, with its innovative metropolitan government and its increasingly positive approach to race relations, seemed to have made significant progress toward solving some difficult problems shared by nearly all major American cities.

Increased traffic put a strain on the city's bridges and viaducts as well as on its streets. None had been adequately maintained during the war. By 1947 the Broadway viaduct had deteriorated so much that motorists nicknamed it "Old Shakey." Finally the city closed it to traffic, and after winter weather caused long delays, workmen commenced removing the surface in February 1948. They completed the rebuilding by the end of the year.

Photograph by Robert C. Holt, Jr.; courtesy of The Tennessean.

To insure an adequate supply of water for its rapidly growing population, Nashville spent four million dollars to improve and expand the city water system in 1951-52. These men are removing worn-out equipment at the waterworks on Pumping Station Road near Lebanon Pike and Mill Creek. Superintendent Robert Pattison, standing at upper right, supervises the work.
Photograph by James Dorris; courtesy of The Tennessean.

Once known as Hell's Half Acre, this predominantly black neighborhood was destined for the wrecking ball when this photograph was taken in 1950. The Capitol Hill Redevelopment Project, one of the first federal urban renewal projects in the nation, cleared ninety-six acres here to make room for the James Robertson Parkway and a variety of new public and private buildings. Compare this view with the one on page 169.

Photograph courtesy of The Tennessean.

In June 1958 fire almost destroyed the Maxwell House Hotel, a Nashville landmark since the 1860s. The conflagration started in a fifth floor restroom and spread quickly, but firemen, shown here using ladders to reach the roof, contained the blaze. Three years later another fire gutted the stately old edifice and forced its demolition. The Third National Bank Building now stands on this site at Fourth Avenue and Church Street.
Photograph by Jimmy Lunsford; courtesy of The Tennessean.

The success of Harveys Department Store, here decorated for the 1952 Christmas season, revitalized competition among downtown retailers in the late forties and early fifties. Fred Harvey, a merchandising genius with a flair for showmanship, bought the financially troubled Lebeck Brothers store at the corner of Sixth and Union in 1941, renamed it Harveys, and within a year had it operating at a profit. Eventually he expanded the store into adjoining buildings, installed the first escalators in Middle Tennessee, and attracted the attention of retailers and shoppers all over the nation. His circus-like promotions led the Saint Louis Post-Dispatch to proclaim that shopping at Harveys was "more fun than a cageful of monkeys."
Photograph courtesy of Harveys Department Stores.

Railroads, which had played an important role in Nashville's development after the Civil War, were also crucial to the city's economic vitality following World War II. The Radnor Yards, situated between Sidco and Trousdale drives in South Nashville, became a significant center of suburban industry and wholesale activity. The Louisville and Nashville Railroad established the yards in 1918 to escape crowded conditions at the Union Station "gulch," and during the early 1950s the company enlarged them and installed automatic switching equipment. In 1955 the Nashville, Chattanooga, and Saint Louis Railroad moved its switching operations here, too. This view shows the yards in 1959.
Photograph by Howard Cooper; courtesy of The Tennessean.

Like the railroads, the Cumberland River remained an important artery of commerce in the postwar years. Once plied by steamboats, the river was traversed after World War II by huge barges such as this one being launched by the Nashville Bridge Company in September 1963. This craft measured 12 feet deep, 50 feet wide, and 290 feet long and could carry 28,000 barrels of petroleum products.

Photograph by Frank Empson; courtesy of The Tennessean.

Nashvillians have always shown a keen interest in politics, and scenes such as this one in 1947 were common before election laws required that campaign workers and posters be kept at a distance from the polls. The women at left are campaigning in front of the polling place for the sixth ward, fifth precinct, at 151 North First Street. The man in the checkered jacket and tie is election officer Joe Halliburton.

Photograph courtesy of The Tennessean.

The interstate highway system, begun in the 1950s, changed traffic patterns and landscapes in Nashville and most other major American cities. This early 1960s view shows the junction of interstates 40 and 65 at Lebanon Road southeast of downtown. The western portion of the interstate loop is incomplete, and the finished section ends near the old Howard School and University of Nashville buildings on Second Avenue in old South Nashville, left.

Photograph courtesy of Nashville Area Chamber of Commerce.

In 1948 country music star Roy Acuff entered the political arena and won the Republican gubernatorial nomination. His campaign rallies featured as much music as politics, and the huge crowds that attended them caused considerable alarm among Democrats. On November 1, the night before the election, Acuff concluded his campaign with a rally at War Memorial Square, and several thousand people turned out to hear him and forty other Grand Old Opry performers. Shortly before Acuff appeared, B. Carroll Reece, the Republican candidate for United States senator, tried to speak, but the crowd booed him off stage amid cries of "bring on Roy." Acuff fared better on election day than any Republican gubernatorial candidate had in years, but most Tennessee voters apparently preferred his music to his politics. He lost the election to Democratic reform candidate Gordon Browning.

Photograph by Charles Cowden; courtesy of The Tennessean.

The 1951 mayoral race between the incumbent Thomas L. Cummings and challenger Ben West was so close that the outcome remained unknown until a canvass of the vote a few days after the election. Here John Pritchett, center, secretary of the Davidson County Election Commission, explains the canvass procedure to Cummings and West supporters. Left to right, in front, are: Albert Williams, West's law partner; Elkin Garfinkle, first district magistrate and West supporter; Kenneth Harwell, a member of West's law firm; Pritchett; John C. Askew, Jr., and Dr. Leonard Edwards, members of the election commission; and E.C. Yokley, Nashville city attorney and a Cummings supporter. Standing behind Harwell near the window are police Lieutenant Ted Nannie, left, and Sheriff Garner Robinson. Ben West emerged the winner by fifty-five votes.

Photograph by Eldred Reaney; courtesy of The Tennessean.

During most of the 1950s, area residents debated consolidating the Nashville and Davidson County governments. In 1958 a special charter commission drew up a plan to place the city and county under metropolitan administration. When photographed in March the commissioners had just completed that document. The members included, left to right: attorney K. Harlan Dodson, commission chairman Carmack Cochran, commission secretary Rebecca Thomas, Ed Hicks, businessman Victor S. Johnson, labor lawyer Cecil Branstetter, city councilman Z. Alexander Looby, commission counsel Edwin Hunt, E.C. Yokely, retired druggist G.S. Meadors; and school principal R.N. Chenault. Voters defeated the metro plan in a referendum on June 17, but proponents resurrected the idea in 1962. Another commission, identical to the first except for the absence of Hicks and Yokely, drafted a similar charter, and 56.8 percent of the voters approved it.

Photograph by Eldred Reaney;
courtesy of The Tennessean.

Ben West, right, the last mayor of the old city of Nashville, congratulates the first metropolitan mayor, Beverly Briley, left, after his inaugural address on April 1, 1963. Between them West and Briley held the office of mayor for nearly a quarter of a century.
Photograph by J.T. Phillips;
courtesy of The Tennessean.

Soon after the new metropolitan government went into effect in April 1963, the old Nashville city limit signs came down. Mayor Beverly Briley personally removed this one in front of Schwab School on Dickerson Road.
Photograph by Harold Lowe, Jr.;
courtesy of The Tennessean.

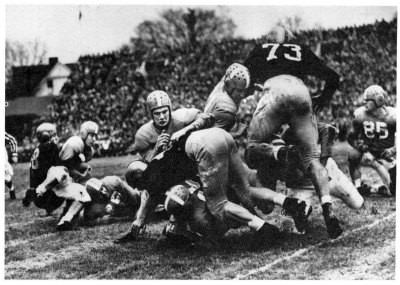

In the postwar years, as before, sporting events attracted large crowds in Nashville. The biennial Vanderbilt-Tennessee football game at Dudley Field was always a sell-out. Vandy fans festooned in black and gold and Tennessee fans wearing Volunteer orange rooted fervently for their favorites, and tensions ran high both on and off the playing field. In the 1948 game Vanderbilt defeated Tennessee 28-6. Here Vandy linebacker Bill Powell (number 48, left) drives through the Tennessee line to throw Big Orange quarterback Jack Beeler for a three-yard loss. Also in the play is Commodore tackle Carl Copp (number 73).
Photograph by Eldred Reaney;
courtesy of The Tennessean.

Except for the last year of World War II, Nashvillians by the thousands have been turning out one Saturday each May since 1941 for the annual running of the Iroquois Steeplechase in Percy Warner Park. The Works Progress Administration built the three-mile-long, eighteen-jump course in 1938 at a cost of $45,000. Many steeplechase enthusiasts consider it more beautiful than the site of England's famed Grand National race. This scene is from the 1951 Iroquois.
Photograph by Robert C. Holt, Jr.;
courtesy of The Tennessean.

An era of sports history ended on December 9, 1963, when the Nashville Vols played their last game in Sulfur Dell stadium north of downtown. The team won, but they played to virtually empty stands. Union soldiers had brought baseball to Nashville in 1862, and residents had watched the city's first professional game on this site in 1885. During the middle years of the twentieth century the Vols had been a stellar minor league team, but by 1963 television and other forms of entertainment had cut significantly into attendance. Thus the franchise folded, and Sulfur Dell was leveled to make room for a used car lot. In 1978, however, Nashville got a new ball park and a new professional team, the Sounds. In their second year of play in the Southern League, the Sounds set an all-time minor league season attendance record of 504,401.
Photograph by Jimmy Ellis;
courtesy of The Tennessean.

Music continued to grow in importance in Nashville during the postwar years. Programs like "Sunday Down South" with Snooky Lanson and Margaret Whiting played to large regional audiences and helped WSM Radio earn the nickname "Air Castle of the South." Lanson, who later became a star on both the radio and television versions of "Your Hit Parade," still performs often in Nashville.

Photograph courtesy of Country Music Foundation Library.

Nashville's first symphony orchestra disbanded before World War II, and in 1946 Walter Sharp returned home from the army determined to form another one. Within a few months he organized the Nashville Civic Music Association and raised enough money for a concert season. He also proved instrumental in persuading New Yorker William Strickland to serve as conductor. The new Nashville Symphony Orchestra made its debut in War Memorial Auditorium on December 10, 1946, with Helen Jepson as soloist. Here she is congratulated by Sharp, right, and Strickland, left, following the performance.

Photograph courtesy of Nashville Symphony Association.

These two Nashvillians, Tennessee State University women's track and field coach Ed Temple and sprinter Wilma Rudolph, made international sports news in the late 1950s and early 1960s. They also helped make TSU's Tigerbelles one of the best-known track and field teams in history. Since 1956 thirty-two Tigerbelles have participated in the Olympic Games and won eleven gold, five silver, and four bronze medals for the United States. Temple coached the 1960 and 1964 American women's teams, and Rudolph won three gold medals in the 1960 games in Rome.

Photograph courtesy of Tennessee State University.

Tickets to the Nashville Symphony Orchestra's first season are now prized mementos for the city's many classical music lovers. The Nashville Civic Music Association, predecessor of today's Nashville Symphony Association, had an annual budget of only $60,000 in 1946-47 but made maximum use of it. In fact, the orchestra became so successful that in 1949 when *Look* magazine did a feature on the postwar symphony boom in America, it began the story with Nashville.

Ticket courtesy of Nashville Symphony Association.

The Nashville Symphony Orchestra won its first national recognition on January 15, 1949, when the NBC radio network broadcast one of its concerts coast-to-coast on the "Orchestras of the Nation" program. A few minutes before the show went on the air from the Ryman Auditorium, Mayor Thomas L. Cummings, left, presented a citation to Walter Sharp, right, for his role in founding and boosting the orchestra.

Photograph courtesy of Nashville Symphony Association.

THE NASHVILLE CIVIC MUSIC ASSOCIATION

Presents the

NASHVILLE SYMPHONY ORCHESTRA

Season 1946-47

ONE SEASON TICKET

Concerts December 10, January 14, February 11, March 11, April 8, and April 29

Balcony

ECTION UB ROW G SEAT 15

War Memorial Auditorium   8:30 P. M.

Some female country music artists, such as Maybelle and Sara Carter, earned recognition as early as the 1920s while performing in duos and groups. Few women, however, became well-known as individual performers until mid-century. Comedienne Minne Pearl, whose real name is Sarah Ophelia Colley Cannon, was among those who rose to stardom in that era. She joined the Grand Ole Opry in 1940, toured widely with the Camel Caravan during World War II, and eventually became an Opry Superstar. Here she signs autographs for American servicemen curing the Korean War.

Photograph courtesy of
Country Music Foundation Library.

The national appeal of the Grand Ole Opry continued to grow in the 1950s. Some of the thousands of country music fans who traveled to Nashville to attend the performances in the Ryman Auditorium, top center, came by bus. At that time the Greyhound station stood just around the corner at Sixth Avenue and Commerce Street. Since then the depot and most of the other buildings shown here in the foreground have given way to parking lots.

Photograph by Floyd Evans;
courtesy of The Tennessean.

Nashville native Kitty Wells was the first female country singer to achieve widespread success as a soloist. She began her career as a gospel performer, joined the Grand Ole Opry in 1952, and won the nickname "Queen of Country Music" with hit records such as "It Wasn't God Who Made Honky Tonk Angels." Between 1952 and 1963 nineteen of her recordings made Billboard *magazine's "Top Ten" list. Photograph by Fabry Studios; courtesy of Country Music Foundation Library.*

Nashvillians who preferred pop music to classical and country could hear it in one of the clubs along Printers' Alley in the heart of downtown. The alley became a celebrated nightspot during prohibition when the bars on Fourth Avenue North closed and speakeasies opened in the narrow thoroughfare behind them. When this photograph was taken in 1962, the featured entertainer at the Voo Doo Room was Teddy Bart, now a popular local radio and television personality.
Photograph by Jack Corn;
courtesy of The Tennessean.

President John F. Kennedy visited Nashville on May 20, 1963. After speaking at Vanderbilt University and lunching with Governor Frank Clement, the president met with officials of George Peabody College for Teachers to discuss Kennedy Foundation visiting professorships. Here he greets Peabody president Felix Robb at the Governor's Mansion on Curtiswood Lane. To Kennedy's right are Governor and Mrs. Clement.

Photograph by Vic Cooley; courtesy of The Tennessean.

The postwar years were a time of growth for Nashville's institutions of higher learning. At Vanderbilt, Chancellor Harvie Branscomb, left, oversaw a campus expansion program that doubled the number of buildings during his eighteen-year tenure. He posed for this photograph with Vice Chancellor Madison Sarratt, right, in 1947, one year after taking office.

Photograph by Durwood B. White; courtesy of Vanderbilt University Photographic Archive.

Compared with most other Southern cities, Nashville made considerable progress in race relations in the late 1950s and early 1960s. In the summer of 1955, a year after the United States Supreme Court outlawed racial discrimination in public schools, A.Z. Kelley, a Negro barber who lived in East Nashville, decided that his son Robert should not be bused across town to Pearl High School when East High was only a few blocks from the family's home. In September Kelley filed a class action suit, Robert W. Kelley v. Board of Education of Nashville, asking for desegregation of the Nashville schools. Eventually Kelley's suit led to a plan to integrate the public schools one grade at a time, beginning with the first in 1957. Here Kelley, left, in suit and hat, escorts black children to Caldwell School on the first day of desegregation.
   Photograph courtesy of The Tennessean.

Nashville's public parks and other recreational facilities were desegregated in 1956. Jerry Folston and several companions broke the color barrier at the Shelby Park golf course on February 11. Five Days later Robert Smith and other blacks played the McCabe Park course. Here Smith prepares to hit a tee shot while Wesley Dennis, left, and Arthur Clay, center, watch.
   Photograph by Eldred Reaney; courtesy of The Tennessean.

Early in 1960 hundreds of Negroes and a few white supporters began a series of sit-ins to try to desegregate downtown eating places. On February 13 nearly one hundred persons, many of them students at Fisk and Tennessee State, trudged through heavy snow and entered three stores that had lunch counters. Although refused service, the protesters remained seated for five hours. Two days later two hundred individuals conducted sit-ins in four stores, and by the end of the week three hundred people were protesting in five stores. This photograph, taken on March 26, shows student leader Rodney Powell and two companions at the Walgreen's counter. Eventually the protesters prevailed, and on May 10 most of the downtown eating places began serving blacks.

Photograph by Jimmy Ellis; courtesy of The Tennessean.

A number of students from Nashville's black colleges and universities were active in the civil rights movement throughout the South. In May 1961 some joined the "freedom riders" who boarded interstate buses to test desegregation of public transportation. Later that summer Tennessee State officials, acting under heavy political pressure, expelled fourteen students for "freedom riding," and in September many of their Tennessee State classmates marched to the capitol to protest the dismissals. At right, the demonstrators are crossing James Robertson Parkway.

Photograph by Harold Lowe, Jr.; courtesy of The Tennessean.

By 1964 Nashville had made considerable progress toward solving some difficult problems shared by nearly all major American cities. The innovative consolidated government was attracting nationwide attention, and its seat, the old "Davidson County Public Building and Court House," was becoming symbolic of a new era in the city's development. Designed by F.C. Hirons and Emmons H. Woolwine and erected in 1937, the building is known now as the Metropolitan Nashville-Davidson County Courthouse.

Photograph by Polly Wiley.

The Third National Bank Building was the first of several modern banking edifices erected in downtown Nashville in the sixties and seventies. Designed by Brush, Hutchinson, and Gwinn, it stands on the site of the old Maxwell House Hotel and features an aluminum and glass tower that rises sixteen stories above a four-story base with landscaped roof. Photograph by Russell Ray Studio; courtesy of Public Library of Metropolitan Nashville-Davidson County.

The story of Nashville in the last sixteen years is largely one of continued growth and influence in regional and national affairs. Today three-quarters of a million people live in the metropolitan area. They work at a variety of jobs in financial and educational institutions, government agencies, industrial firms, construction companies, and myriad other places. They shop in the revitalized downtown business district and several modern malls. They send their children to diverse public and private schools and a dozen colleges and universities. They attend more than seven hundred churches, many of whose denominational headquarters are located in the city. And they enjoy an outstanding assortment of recreational activities in a community that has become known throughout much of the world as "Music City, U.S.A."

In recent years, just as in Andrew Jackson's time, political leaders have helped keep Nashville in the national limelight. Among those have been four United States Senators who, while not natives of Nashville, maintained offices in the city and drew attention to it. Estes Kefauver and Albert Gore enjoyed considerable support for the presidency in the 1950s, as did Howard Baker in the 1970s. The fourth, William Brock, became national chairman of the Republican party in 1976. The Watergate scandal brought Nashville attention, too, as local attorneys Fred Thompson and James Neal played critical investigatory roles.

Commercial and industrial enterprises have done even more to give Nashville influence beyond Tennessee. The printing industry has been especially important in this respect. In addition to accounting for one-fifth of Nashville's annual manufacturing payroll, it makes the local post office the sixth largest second-class postage center in the United States. Nashville has been a magnet for printing firms, both denominational and secular, since the Methodist Publishing House opened here in 1854. Today the Southern Baptist Sunday School Board is the largest of some half-dozen church-owned publishing concerns in Nashville. The Southern Baptists print 100 new book titles, 140 monthly and quarterly periodicals, and 90 million church bulletins each year. These go to all fifty

Chapter IX

Music City, U.S.A.:

1964-1980

states and ninety-two foreign countries. The commercial publishers reach a wide audience, too. Thomas Nelson, Inc., turns out more Bibles than any other firm in the nation, and Baird-Ward Printing Company prints such popular national and regional magazines as *Southern Living, Field and Stream, Progressive Farmer,* and *Changing Times.*

A variety of other Nashville industries also send products throughout the country. For example, Genesco, which once owned the famous Tiffany and Bonwit-Teller stores in New York and still is one of the world's largest producers of footwear and clothing, is headquartered in Nashville. DuPont has one of its biggest chemical plants in northern Davidson County, Ford operates a gigantic automobile glass plant in West Nashville, and AVCO produces Galaxy C5A aircraft wing assemblies in its huge Vultee plant near the airport.

Nashville's financial institutions are well known outside the metropolitan area, too. In fact, Union Street, around which many of them are situated, is often called the "Wall Street of the South." Three of Tennessee's largest bank holding companies have their headquarters in Nashville. They are Tennessee Valley Bancorp, First Amtenn Corporation, and Third National Corporation. The city also boasts a branch of the Federal Reserve Bank of Atlanta and remains the home of the National Life and Accident Insurance Company and the Life and Casualty Insurance Company.

Another major Nashville enterprise, the one that most Americans associate with the city, is music. Depending upon the method of calculation, it is the second or third biggest business in the community. It is also multifaceted, encompassing activities that range from performing and recording to publishing and accounting. Its growth after World War II is attributable largely to the continued popularity of the Grand Ole Opry, the pool of talent that the Opry drew to Nashville, the increasing professionalization of performers, and the determined imagination and entrepreneurial instincts of a number of individuals.

Although RCA Victor had attempted to record in Nashville as early as 1928 and several major record labels plus a number of independents had

As Nashville entered the 1970s several major new buildings adorned the skyline, and more were being planned. In this view from the northwest the thirty-one-story National Life Center rises one block west of the capitol, the sixteen-story Andrew Jackson State Office Building nears completion one block east of the capitol, and the twenty-story Third National Bank Building stands next to the thirty-story Life and Casualty Tower erected in the 1950s.

The twenty-one story Parkway Towers Office Building is partially visible at left near the Municipal Auditorium. Before the end of the seventies these were joined by the twenty-eight-story Hyatt Regency Hotel, twenty-four-story James K. Polk State Office Building (Tennessee Performing Arts Center and Museum), and twenty-story Commerce Union Bank Building.

Photograph courtesy of Nashville Area Chamber of Commerce.

172

With the erection of new office buildings, renovation of Church Street, and construction of the Legislative Plaza south of the capitol, Nashvillians became accustomed to downtown scenes such as these in the late 1960s and early 1970s. In the view above, Oman Construction Company workers are excavating the site of the National Life Center between Seventh and Eighth Avenues.

Photograph courtesy of Public Library of Metropolitan Nashville-Davidson County.

At right, Melvin Norris, foreground, and other Nashville Gas Company employees are installing a new gas line under Capitol Boulevard.

Photograph courtesy of Nashville Gas Company.

173

CAIN-SLOAN

successfully renewed those efforts in the late forties, it was not until the mid-1950s that Owen Bradley and Chet Atkins, working independently, created what became known as the "Nashville Sound" and established the city as a recording center. About 1952 Bradley, who had once played with the famous Ted Weems dance band and had been musical director of WSM, set up a recording studio in the basement of an old house on Sixteenth Avenue South, just east of Vanderbilt. This was the first of many studios on what is now known as "Music Row." In his basement Bradley recorded such emerging stars as Sonny James, Johnny Cash, and Marty Robbins, but he was not satisfied merely with that success. He built another studio next door in a quonset hut, put an echo chamber in it, invented a new way to record drums, and began giving his recordings a kind of polish or flair that appealed to wider audiences. In 1962 he sold the then-famous hut to Columbia Records for $300,000.

Meanwhile Chet Atkins, a skilled guitar player and Opry performer, began organizing recording sessions for RCA Victor. Eventually he persuaded the company to build a studio in Nashville, and by 1957 he was managing it and producing records. Because he could perform any kind of music—country, pop, jazz, or classical—Atkins followed a trend already being set by artists like Eddy Arnold and Tennessee Ernie Ford and put a popular or "easy listening" touch on many of the records he produced. Atkins also started or perfected such innovations as overdubbing in records, using vocal groups to back up a singer, and adding horns and strings. He also acknowledged the popularity of rock. In all these ways he, like Bradley, helped develop a different, more modern, more relaxed style of country music that was both widely popular and distinctly Nashville. This in turn opened the way for pop, rock, and gospel recording in the city, attracted more artists and record labels, and helped make Nashville, along with New York and Los Angeles, one of the top three recording centers in the nation.

When recording boomed in Nashville, so did music publishing. Although Roy Acuff and Fred

Rose organized the first Nashville music publishing house, Acuff-Rose, in 1942, it did not have a national hit until "Tennessee Waltz" in 1950. From there the firm went on to build its own recording studio and win awards for both pop and country music. In the mid-1950s Cedarwood Publishing Company and Tree International Publishing Company were established in Nashville, and by the mid-1970s the city had nearly 250 such firms.

Following the record companies and music publishers, there came branches of the nation's three major music licensing corporations, trade and fan magazines, talent agencies, musicians' unions, syndicated television productions, and manufacturers of sophisticated recording equipment. Tourists came, too, by the hundreds of thousands. And in the early 1970s National Life, which still owned the Grand Ole Opry, capitalized on their enthusiasm for Nashville by opening a gigantic musical theme park with a new multi-million-dollar home for the Opry.

In 1975 Hollywood took notice of Nashville again, and acclaimed director Robert Altman made a major motion picture about the city and its most visible industry. He called the movie *Nashville*. He could have called it *Music City, U.S.A.* The industry's power to draw talent has merely highlighted an abiding interest that Nashvillians have always shown in music of many kinds. Today the city continues to enjoy the Fisk Jubilee Singers, enthusiastically supports the highly regarded Nashville Symphony, listens daily to WSM's "Waking Crew" band (which is the last "live" radio studio orchestra in the country), dances often to the nostalgic sounds of Louis Brown's "big band," attends countless vocal and instrumental concerts put on by several outstanding college music departments, and frequents an abundance of night spots that feature some of the best musical acts available anywhere.

Nashville *is* "Music City, U.S.A."

Efforts by Nashvillians to save Union Station attracted nationwide attention among historic preservationists in the late 1970s. Now a National Historic Landmark, the grand structure is undergoing restoration and conversion into a federal office complex.
Photograph by Jack E. Boucher; courtesy of Historic American Buildings Survey.

Despite much new construction, Nashvillians have worked in recent years to preserve many of the city's historic buildings. The Historical Commission of Metropolitan Nashville-Davidson County and Historic Nashville, Inc., have been especially influential in saving significant structures. Both organizations are headquartered in the old Silver Dollar Saloon at the Broadway end of the Second Avenue Historic District, which is shown here from Church Street. Except for some modernization of first-floor facades, these buildings have changed little since the turn of the century.
Photograph by Jack E. Boucher; courtesy of Historic American Buildings Survey.

The Downtown Presbyterian Church, formerly First Presbyterian, has been a focal point of architectural interest in downtown Nashville since 1851. It is one of the few Egyptian revival-style churches in the United States. Designed by capitol architect William Strickland, it sits on the corner of Church Street and Fifth Avenue and is listed on the National Register of Historic Places.
Photograph by Jack E. Boucher; courtesy of Historic American Buildings Survey.

This 1964 view of the east side of the Second Avenue Historic District, taken from the east bank of the Cumberland, shows the Avalon, an excursion steamer, docked at what remains of the Nashville Wharf.
Photograph courtesy of The Tennessean.

Near the turn of the century a number of
American cities had shopping arcades
such as this one between Fourth and
Fifth avenues downtown. Few have
survived, however. The Nashville Arcade
was designed by Thompson, Gibel, and
Asmus and erected by the Nashville
Manufacturing Company in 1903. It
measures 75 feet wide and 360 feet long,
houses a variety of shops, and is a
National Historic Place.
 *Photograph by Jack E. Boucher; courtesy
 of Historic American Buildings Survey.*

Although Nashville still has a number of
meat packing firms, the Union
Stockyards, shown here in 1966, are
among the historic structures that have
not survived. Only the brick
headquarters building, now vacant,
remains at the corner of Whiteside and
Second avenues north of downtown. At
this writing, plans had been announced
to renovate it for adaptive use as a
restaurant.
 *Photograph by Gerald Holly;
 courtesy of The Tennessean.*

Since the mid-1950s four United States Senators have helped keep Nashville in the national political limelight. None have been natives of Nashville, but all have maintained offices in and drawn attention to the city. All have either sought or been prominently mentioned for the presidency or vice-presidency of the United States. Democrat Estes Kefauver, far left, served in the Senate from 1949 to 1963; Democrat Albert Gore, left, from 1953 to 1971; Republican William Brock, bottom left, from 1971 to 1977; and Republican Howard Baker, bottom right, from 1967 to present.

On March 16, 1974, the nation watched on television as President Richard M. Nixon helped dedicate the new Grand Ole Opry House. Welcoming an opportunity to try to boost his public image in the midst of the Watergate crisis, Nixon, left, played the piano and took a yo-yo lesson from Roy Acuff, right. Less than five months later, on August 9, 1974, Nixon became the first person in history to resign from the office of president of the United States.
  Photograph courtesy of The Tennessean.

Among other Nashvillians influential in national governmental affairs in the 1970s was Wade H. McCree, Jr. A graduate of Fisk University, McCree became Solicitor General of the United States under President Jimmy Carter.
  Photograph courtesy of Fisk University Library's Special Collections.

Nashville's colleges and universities continued to grow and change in the 1970s. After years of informal discussion, Vanderbilt University and George Peabody College for Teachers merged in 1979, as did Tennessee State University and the University of Tennessee in Nashville. In 1977 Fisk University inaugurated a new president, Walter J. Leonard, left. Formerly a special assistant to the president of Harvard, he poses here with 1935 Fisk alumnus John Hope Franklin, an internationally known scholar and former president of both the Organization of American Historians and the American Historical Association.
Photograph by Murphy Photography, Inc.; courtesy of Fisk University.

These three Nashville Democrats dominated local political headlines in the 1970s. Businessman John Jay Hooker, left, sought statewide office on several occasions and in 1979 became the publisher of the Nashville Banner. *The late Clifford Allen, center, served for many years as Davidson County tax assessor and represented the fifth congressional district in Washington from 1975 to 1978. Richard Fulton, right, served fourteen years in Congress before succeeding Beverly Briley as mayor of Nashville in 1975, the year this photograph was taken. After an unsuccessful try for the governorship in 1978, Fulton won a second four-year term as the city's chief executive in 1979.*
Photograph by Jack Gunter; courtesy of Nashville Banner.

Nashvillians maintained a lively interest in sports in the 1960s and 1970s. Thousands of children and adults took up jogging, participated in competitive team sports such as baseball and softball, and enjoyed watching a variety of high school and college athletic squads. Vanderbilt and Tennessee State football games continued to draw large crowds, and the Nashville Sounds professional baseball team, which began playing in 1978, attracted national interest. For many Nashvillians, however, the number one game in the city remained Vanderbilt basketball. During those two decades the Commodore roundballers ranked consistently among the best in the South. At left in this action photograph is Vandy's Perry Wallace, who in 1967 became the first black basketball player in the Southeastern Conference.

Photograph courtesy of Vanderbilt University Photographic Archive.

Although the origins of Nashville's recording industry lie in the 1920s, the city's emergence as a national recording center began in the 1950s. One of the men most responsible for developing both the industry and the now-famous "Nashville Sound" was Owen Bradley, seated. He pioneered the use of echo chambers and drums in Nashville recordings and encouraged informality and improvisation in studio sessions. With Bradley in this 1950s photograph is Vito Pellettieri, left, who for many years was stage manager of the Grand Ole Opry, and Bill McElhiney, center, WSM musical director.

Photograph courtesy of Country Music Foundation Library.

The "Nashville Sound" has been described as easygoing, relaxed, and tensionless. Chet Atkins, center, helped develop that distinctive style both as a performer and a producer of records for RCA. Here he greets pop singer Perry Como at the Nashville airport in the mid-1960s. Como recorded numerous hits in Nashville.

Photograph courtesy of Country Music Foundation Library.

Although Nashville recording sessions are informal, a modern studio is a maze of wire and electronic equipment where one twenty-four-track recording console can cost up to $100,000.

Photograph by Polly Wiley; courtesy of RCA Records.

In the late 1960s and early 1970s Grand Ole Opry stars Dolly Parton and Porter Wagoner were country music's most popular duo. Today Wagoner has one of the nation's most successful syndicated country music television programs, and Parton is an entertaiment superstar with songs listed on pop as well as country rating charts. Their success is indicative of both country music's continued rise in popularity and the music industry's expansion in Nashville.

Photograph courtesy of Country Music Foundation Library.

Elvis Presley, Eddy Arnold, Charley Pride, and a host of other well-known entertainers recorded many of their hit songs in RCA's Studio B. Erected in the late 1950s largely at the urging of Chet Atkins, the famous Music Row facility is now a popular attraction of the Country Music Hall of Fame and Museum. Here a guide explains the recording process. During sessions the stars performed from the podium in the foreground.

Photograph courtesy of Nashville Area Chamber of Commerce.

During the 1960s a number of country music stars began taping television shows in Nashville and distributing them through syndication. Instead of selling the programs to networks, the performers sold them directly to individual broadcasting stations. This technique enabled Jimmy Dean, Johnny Cash, Bill Anderson, and others to appear regularly in hundreds of television markets all over the United States. The best-known current syndicated series produced in Nashville is "Hee Haw," a comedy and music program that began in 1969. "Hee Haw" features Buck Owens, with guitar, and Roy Clark, with banjo, and a supporting cast that includes Archie Campbell, second from left, back row, Grandpa Jones, fifth from left, back row, and George "Goober" Lindsay, sixth from left, back row.

Photograph courtesy of Henderson, Kelly, and Ward, Inc.

Roy Acuff and Fred Rose established Nashville's first music publishing house, Acuff-Rose, in 1942. Today there are nearly 250 such firms in the city, as well as branches of the nation's three music licensing corporations. Broadcast Music Incorporated (BMI) opened an office in Nashville in 1958, and the American Society of Composers, Authors, and Publishers (ASCAP) and Selected Editions of Standard American Catalogs (SESAC) followed in the 1960s. These organizations license the right to perform copyrighted musical works in public for profit. ASCAP completed this headquarters building on Music Square West (Seventeenth Avenue South) in 1969.

Photograph by Polly Wiley.

SOUVENIR PROGRAM

THE GRAND OLE OPRY

THE MOTHER CHURCH OF COUNTRY MUSIC

On March 15, 1974, the Grand Ole Opry held its final performance in the Ryman Auditorium on Fifth Avenue North. The program included Roy Drusky, Dottie West, Roy Acuff, Wilma and Stoney Cooper, the Wilburn Brothers, Grandpa Jones, Bill Anderson, the Willis Brothers, Jim Ed Brown, and many others. Although vacant, the Ryman remains a popular attraction for the hundreds of thousands of country music fans who travel to Nashville each year to see their favorite stars and "Music City, U.S.A."

Souvenir program from the collection of Ralph Jerry Christian.

In 1975 acclaimed Hollywood movie director Robert Altman made a major motion picture about "Music City U.S.A." Entitled simply Nashville, the film received mixed reviews from the music industry, but it proved popular with moviegoers and reflected Nashville's national identification with music. In this scene from the picture, country music entertainers are performing at a political rally in Centennial Park.

Photograph courtesy of The Tennessean.

WSM began planning a new Grand Ole Opry House in 1968. Construction commenced in November 1971, and the completed structure was dedicated in March 1974. Designed by Welton Becket and Associates to reflect the intimacy and informality of the Ryman, the new Opry House is situated in Opryland, U.S.A., a music theme park off Briley Parkway in East Nashville. The main auditorium seats 4,400 people and contains the best available electronic light and sound equipment. Also in the building is a 300-seat television production studio.

Photograph by Les Leverett; courtesy of Historical Commission of Metropolitan Nashville-Davidson County.

The stage of the new Grand Ole Opry House is 110 feet wide and 68 feet deep. It is covered with maple flooring laid over subflooring on concrete. In the center there is a six-foot disc of original oak flooring from the stage of the Ryman Auditorium. Back of the stage there hangs a curtain painted to resemble the set at the Ryman, and in the seating area there are upholstered benches designed to resemble the Ryman's bare church pews. All of this represents an effort to recall the mood of Opry performances at the Ryman, but none of it succeeds as well as the Opry stars themselves. Here two Opry veterans of almost forty years, Minnie Pearl and Roy Acuff, trade jokes on the stage of the new house.

Photograph courtesy of Nashville Area Chamber of Commerce.

Nashville's radio stations contribute significantly to the city's reputation as a music center. There are twenty-five in the metropolitan area, more in relation to population than in New York City. WSM, which started the Grand Ole Opry in 1925 and today boasts the last "live" studio orchestra in the nation, is the best known. But the list also includes WLAC, which is almost as old, and WAMB, which is one of only eight "big band" stations remaining in the United States. Here Nashville's own "big band," the Louis Brown Orchestra, plays at one of WAMB's frequent tea dances.

Photograph courtesy of WAMB Radio.

The Fisk Jazz Ensemble is one of the many fine student musical groups in Nashville. Here they perform under the direction of Roby George.

Photograph courtesy of Fisk University.

The musicians of the Nashville Symphony Orchestra come from a variety of musical backgrounds. Some are college and university teachers; some are television and recording studio performers. Together they add still another important dimension to the Nashville music scene. In this 1967 photograph Willis Page leads the orchestra in War Memorial Auditorium. In 1980 the symphony moved into the new Tennessee Performing Arts Center.

Photograph by Joe Rudis; courtesy of The Tennessean.

Michael Charry, a New Yorker of Russian ancestry, became musical director and conductor of the Nashville Symphony Orchestra in 1976. Under his leadership the symphony has continued its tradition of featuring such guest artists as Robert Shaw, Leontyne Price, and Van Cliburn and offering Nashvillians a variety of special programs ranging from ballet to park concerts.
Photograph courtesy of Nashville Symphony Association.

Tenneseee Governor Lamar Alexander, at the piano, joins the Nashville Symphony Orchestra in a Sunday-afternoon concert at the Centennial Park band shell.
Photograph by Dana P. Thomas.

Photograph by Polly Wiley.

The skyline of "Music City, U.S.A." from the north, left, and the south, right, in 1979.

Photograph by George Rollie Adams.

This bird's eye view of Nashville symbolizes the city's vision for the future and illustrates the density of downtown development during the 1980s. The historic Tennessee State Capitol stands to the left of the thirty-one-story American General Building (formerly the National Life Center) in the foreground, and the remaining downtown structures stretch eastward toward the Cumberland River, which cuts across the top of the photograph from right to left. Photograph by Gary Layda; courtesy of the Government of Metropolitan Nashville-Davidson County.

The closing years of the 1970s marked not only the end of Nashville's second century, but the convergence of forces that catapulted the city into its next 100 years with growth and advancement on almost every front. Economically, politically and culturally, Nashville marched during the 1980s to a song of progress. More than any previous song, this one contained a harmonious blend of verses that called for both daring new ventures and renewed efforts to preserve the best of the past.

To a large degree, Nashville's song of the eighties followed the tone of the city's two-hundredth-anniversary celebration. The bicentennial Century III Commission, established in 1978, played a leading role in writing the song. The commission supported and helped arrange pageants and all the other hoopla usually associated with historical celebrations, but it also emphasized long-term projects designed to move Nashville ahead.

Under the motto "Celebrating the Past while Looking into the Future," the commission proposed to transform the city's landscape. It called for building a convention center in Sulphur Dell, constructing a riverfront park and renovating Union Station. Although none of these projects took exactly the form envisioned, or was finished in time for the anniversary, they helped shape Nashville's vision of its future. By focusing attention on downtown redevelopment and historic preservation, the commission advanced the notion, shared by many, that the city could grow and expand while retaining its individual identity and accepting stewardship for its unique architectural heritage.

As the bicentennial celebration ended, Nashville was poised to pursue this vision. The city stood on the threshold of development that would change its appearance more in a single decade than any other series of events had since the arrival of the pioneers, or since the building boom after World War II.

In part the city's experience in the 1980s reflected the national trend of economic decline in many northern industrial areas and simultaneous growth in the Sunbelt. But as in previous years, Nashville also enjoyed the advantage of economic diversity. Davidson County retained a healthy mix of commerce, industry, education and government, plus a surrounding trade area of smaller cities, towns and agricultural com-

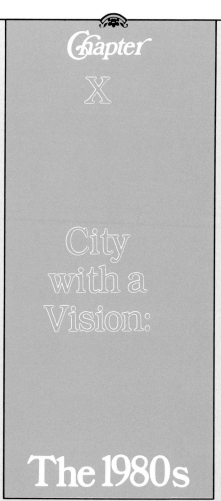

Chapter

X

City
with a
Vision:

The 1980s

munities. This economy was largely service-oriented and integrated, and it resisted recession while encouraging growth. Consequently, when the national economy turned sharply downward in 1981-82, Nashville was able to weather the decline more easily than most other cities and then move quickly forward again.

Between 1980 and 1988 Nashville-Davidson County's population grew from almost 478,000 to an estimated 513,000. Although this increase was somewhat modest compared to some Sunbelt cities, it was well ahead of 1980 census projections. Meanwhile, the surrounding areas grew much more rapidly, and total metropolitan population approached one million. More significantly, during this same period Nashville's retail space increased from 9.4 to 14.5 million square feet, and retail sales jumped almost ninety-five percent, from $2.4 to $4.7 billion. As a consequence, one national business publication ranked Nashville's economy eighth among the country's most healthy, and another listed the city among the three best locations for new business success.

Nashville's strong economy also made it and surrounding communities attractive to already established, outside businesses. In the eight years following 1980, more than 250 firms relocated or opened branches in the area, bringing with them 86,000 additional jobs. In 1986-87 alone, four new banks—Boatmen's Bancshares of St. Louis, SunTrust of Atlanta, Dominion Bankshares of Roanoke, and Sovran Financial Corporation of Norfolk—either opened branches or acquired existing financial institutions in Nashville.

The most publicized newcomer was Saturn Corporation, a new General Motors division organized to manufacture automobiles that would compete with imports. After a lengthy study and efforts by several states and communities to entice Saturn to their localities, General Motors announced in 1985 that it would build the new facility in Spring Hill, a small community south of Nashville. Construction was well underway by the late 1980s, with production scheduled to begin in 1990. Saturn officials planned initially to employ 3,000 workers and produce 250,000 automobiles a year, and in time they expected to double these figures.

When Richard Fulton completed his third term as mayor following the 1987 elections, business leaders and preservationists alike saluted him for his contributions to the revitalization of downtown. Early in his twelve-year tenure, however, some of his proposals were known as "Fulton's Follies." Riverfront Park, the Convention Center and the beautification of Church Street, shown here, were among the ideas that some observers deemed unsound. All succeeded, though.

Photograph by Gary Layda; courtesy of the Government of Metropolitan Nashville-Davidson County.

Flanking the Life and Casualty Tower, erected in the 1950s, are two of Nashville's newest skyscrapers. They are, to the right, twenty-five-story One Nashville Place completed in 1985 and now known as Dominion Tower at One Nashville Place, and to the left, the thirty-story Third National Financial Center, completed in 1986. In the background to the extreme left is the thirty-two-story James K. Polk State Office Building and Tennessee Performing Arts Center, completed in 1980.

Photograph by Gary Layda.

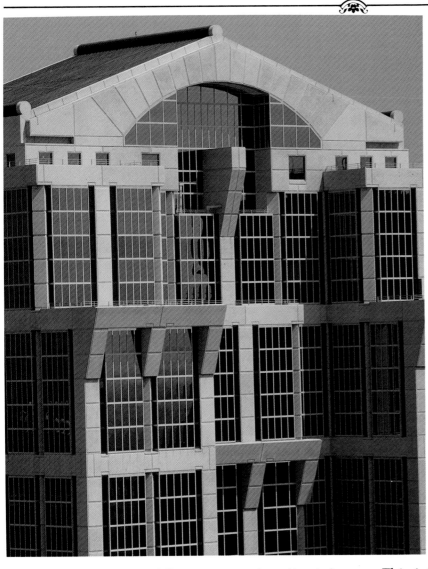

Nashville and Middle Tennessee also attracted major foreign investment. Between 1975 and 1988, a number of foreign firms built new plants in the region, and others bought existing facilities. The principal investors were Japanese. Nissan built a huge truck factory in Smyrna, and Bridgestone Tire acquired the Firestone plant at nearby La Vergne. The Japanese came partly because state agencies worked hard to attract them, partly because Middle Tennessee had available labor, partly because locating in America might help circumvent trade barriers, and partly because the dollar declined in value against the yen. In some instances, the Japanese believed they might even produce their own domestic-market goods more cheaply in the United States than in Japan. In just the first four months of 1987 seven more Japanese companies announced plans to build facilities near Nashville. Financial observers anticipated that by the time these were completed, Tennessee would have approximately ten percent of the total Japanese investment in the United States.

This influx of new business, coupled with the expansion of many existing firms, sparked a construction boom that began early in the decade and was proceeding virtually unabated near its close. As in past decades, growth continued strong in the suburbs. South, into Brentwood, aggressive developers and the impact of the Saturn plant spurred both residential and office construction. And east, along Briley Parkway, further expansion of Opryland and completion of a new forty-six-gate, $200 million air terminal stimulated the building of more hotels and office complexes.

More dramatic, however, was the construction and rehabilitation of older buildings and historic districts, such as St. Cloud Corner, Second Avenue, the Custom House, Rutledge Hill and lower Broadway. The educational efforts of preservation groups such as Historic Nashville helped promote interest in and concern for significant older properties, and federal income tax incentives made the rehabilitation of historic buildings as appealing as new construction

Nashville's vision of the 1980s has
been a blend of the old and the new. Here
Dominion Tower at One Nashville Place
looms above historic Ryman Auditorium.
Home of the Grand Ole Opry from 1941 to
1974, the Ryman remains a must-see site
for the millions of country music fans who
visit Nashville each year.
Photograph by Gary Layda.

Restoration of Nashville's Union Station
was finally completed in 1986, after years
of effort by many individuals and groups.
One of those groups, Historic Nashville,
Inc., sprang from early endeavors to save
the station and became a major force for
preservation throughout the city. The
stationhouse is now Union Station Hotel,
but unfortunately efforts to find an
adaptive use for the nationally significant
historic train shed have not succeeded.
Photograph by Gary Layda.

Passengers have not scurried through the barrel-vaulted lobby of Union Station for many years. But since Union Station Hotel opened in December 1986, overnight travelers booked into one of the 128 guest rooms and suites and Nashvillians headed to one of the hotel's several restaurants have enjoyed its beautifully restored features.
Photograph by Gary Layda; courtesy of the Government of Metropolitan Nashville-Davidson County.

The completion of Nashville's new forty-six-gate airport terminal in 1987 was the result of careful planning to meet the needs of a growing city. Already the new facility has spurred office and hotel development along Briley Parkway, attracted American Airlines to locate a regional hub in Nashville, and given the city's convention recruiters another major selling point. In addition, officials predict that airport-related jobs will combine for an annual payroll of $170 million, another boost to the local economy.
Photograph by Gary Layda; courtesy of the Government of Metropolitan Nashville-Davidson County.

for many investors.

By 1988 all this activity in the Central Business District had begun to reverse historical demographic trends and encourage other development on several fronts. For the first time in recent memory, there was discernible movement toward living downtown, as townhouses in Rutledge Hill and upper floors and lofts along Second Avenue and lower Broadway were renovated for residences. Also, companies seemed more likely to remain in downtown rather than move to the suburbs, and some, such as the regional offices of IBM and Aetna, actually returned from outlying areas. Elsewhere, the Metro Center, Music Row and West End Avenue areas also experienced significant new development. West End had been changing for several years, but its phenomenal acceleration appeared linked in part to the completion of controversial Interstate Highway 440.

As the 1990s approached, it seemed likely that the combination of new construction and historic

rehabilitation would continue to play a major role in the resurgence of Nashville's commercial core. The renovation of Union Station was completed in 1986, and it reopened as a hotel in December of that year. In 1987 construction was completed on a new $45 million Convention Center near lower Broadway. These projects have already helped inspire additional ones, such as the Church Street Center Mall and Ryman Park. Both combine rehabilitation with new construction.

Politically in the 1980s, Nashville maintained a balance between continuity and change. For the most part, the city pursued progressive policies. Metropolitan government, once viewed as experimental and controversial, passed the quarter-century mark as an example for other urban areas to study and emulate. The city also continued its pattern of mayoral stability. Richard Fulton twice won reelection, in 1979 and 1983, and served three full terms, like his predecessor Beverly Briley. Barred by the Metro Charter from

Architect Robert Lamb Hart of New York designed the new Metropolitan Nashville Airport terminal, and the design firm of Gresham, Smith & Partners coordinated the production of drawings and other architectural work for the structure. It has all the amenities of the nation's larger airports, and its staff is determined to make it one of the friendliest and most convenient. The focal point of the terminal design is the large, central atrium, shown here, with its sloping green-tinted, energy-efficient skylights.

Photograph by Gary Layda; courtesy of the Government of Metropolitan Nashville-Davidson County.

seeking a fourth term in 1987, Fulton retired and was succeeded by Congressman William Boner. As Fulton had done earlier, Boner surrendered a relatively safe congressional seat to return to local politics.

The most significant political change in Nashville during the 1980s was the emergence of neighborhood organizations into a major force. This grass roots movement was begun in the late 1960s and early 1970s by political activists who sought change at both national and local levels. The Belmont-Hillsboro Neighbors set the tone for the movement in Nashville. Organized in the early 1970s to promote racial harmony and better urban living, the Belmont-Hillsboro group became a principal opponent of building Interstate Highway 440. They feared the freeway would lead to stagnation and decline by isolating the neighborhoods bordering it from the rest of the city. In preparing to fight the highway, the neighborhood discovered a sense of history, distinctiveness and purpose that helped in time to stabilize property values.

Although eventually the Belmont-Hillsboro Neighbors lost the battle to stop I-440, many of their concerns were addressed in its final design. Perhaps more important, as a cohesive and vital neighborhood organization, they became the model for more than sixty similar groups. Some of these neighborhood organizations focused more than others on historic preservation, but all supported community improvement and opposed unrestrained progress. Over time

The Nashville Convention Center is another 1980s product of the Downtown Nashville Plan and Development Project championed by Mayor Richard Fulton in the late 1970s. Situated on Broadway at the corner of Fifth Avenue North, it offers convention-goers twenty-five meeting rooms and almost 120,000 square feet of exhibition space. In the rear is the adjoining thirty-five-story Stouffer Hotel, which opened in 1987. It offers Nashville's visitors 673 rooms.

Photograph by Gary Layda; courtesy of the Government of Metropolitan Nashville-Davidson County.

As had Nashvillians in the late 1960s and early 1970s, those of the 1980s grew accustomed to the sights, sounds and inconvenience of construction. Here the first of two Nashville City Center structures rises at the corner of Union Street and Sixth Avenue North. Scheduled for completion in 1988, it will house one-half million square feet of leasable office space and parking spaces for 330 automobiles.

Photograph by Gary Layda; courtesy of the Government of Metropolitan Nashville-Davidson County.

Ryman Park, depicted in this architectural rendering, is part of Nashville's current City Center vision of the future. The goal of the City Center Plan is to tie together and renovate the area between Union Station, Riverfront Park, the historic lower Broadway business district, the central business district and the Rutledge Hill office and residential section. As part of that plan, Ryman Park would be a mixed-use development that included a park under glass. The project is a joint venture of the Ryman Group, consisting of Opryland USA, the R. C. Mathews Company and Central Parking Systems.

Photograph by Gary Layda; courtesy of the Government of Metropolitan Nashville-Davidson County.

Envisioned in the late 1970s as a key
ingredient for downtown revitalization,
Riverfront Park is now a reality. Situated
at the foot of Broadway, it helps Nashvillians recall an earlier period in the city's
history, when steamboats plying the
Cumberland were a vital commercial link
with the rest of the nation. The park serves
also as a setting for special events and a
stimulus for further residential development in the lofts and upper floors of historic Broadway and Second Avenue
commercial buildings.
        Photograph by Gary Layda; courtesy
            of the Government of Metropolitan
                Nashville-Davidson County.

Another aspect of Nashville's vision for the
1980s and beyond is improved transportation. Trolleys, such as this one photographed in Riverfront Park, now traverse
downtown on rubber tires and bring back
memories of years when railcars drawn
by horses and mules were the city's only
means of public transportation. Now the
Metropolitan Transit Authority is studying
ways that railroad corridors along West
End Avenue and Gallatin Road can be
developed into special busways or rapid
light rail systems.
        Photograph by Gary Layda; courtesy
            of the Government of Metropolitan
                Nashville-Davidson County.

These colorful restored store fronts along lower Second Avenue North illustrate dramatically the architectural richness and beauty of Nashville's historic waterfront commercial district. In the 1800s the warehouses along this street were home to commission merchants and traders of all kinds, and they served as a focal point for a majority of the city's economic activity. During the 1970s and 1980s they were a focal point for the city's growing interest in historic preservation.
    Photograph by Gary Layda; courtesy of the Government of Metropolitan Nashville-Davidson County.

These new townhouses in the 600 block of Second Avenue South are part of a blend of rehabilitation and new construction that is transforming the Rutledge Hill office and residential area of downtown Nashville.
    Photograph by Gary Layda; courtesy of the Government of Metropolitan Nashville-Davidson County.

*Historic Edgefield, Inc., was one of Nashville's earliest neighborhood associations. Formed in 1976, it worked with the Metropolitan Historical Commission to get the Edgefield Historic District listed in the National Register of Historic Places and to persuade the city to make it Nashville's first locally zoned historic area. Once one of Nashville's most fashionable neighborhoods, Edgefield retains a concentration of Victorian structures and four-square and bungalow style buildings. This view is southeastward along Russell Street and shows some of the earliest restorations.
Photograph by Gary Layda.*

they demonstrated significant ability to work together on common issues and against common foes. The 1987 election for Metro Council proved their combined strength. A coalition of neighborhood groups managed to unseat one-third of the incumbents, replace them with persons sympathetic to neighborhood concerns, and gain the balance of power in the council.

The neighborhood movement helped stimulate historic preservation throughout Nashville. As people organized and looked more closely at their communities, they realized that many houses from the Victorian era and early 1900s were better constructed and contained more amenities than newer homes. This discovery enabled the neighborhood groups to use historic preservation to instill community pride and promote economic revitalization, and it encouraged the Tennessee and metropolitan historical commissions to conduct neighborhood architectural

and historical surveys and nominate individual structures and entire districts to the National Register of Historic Places. These activities contributed, in turn, to the impetus for preservation and rehabilitation downtown.

Culture and tourism also played a vital role in Nashville's growth in the 1980s. For example, in 1982 the Grand Ole Opry, Opryland and the area's museums and historic sites helped attract 7.4 million tourists who spent $525 million in the city. This combination of music and tourism, together with Opryland Hotel, also made Nashville a major location for conventions.

Other cultural activities flourished in the 1980s as well. The Tennessee Performing Arts Center, a joint endeavor of government, business and private citizens, became one of the busiest operations of its kind in the United States. The Italian Street Fair and the Market Street Festival continued to do well, too, and

Interstate Highway 440, here crossing Interstate Highway 65, has been the source of bitter controversy since at least the mid 1970s, when the Tennessee Department of Transportation decided to begin construction. Citizens for Better Neighborhoods stalled the project with a lawsuit until 1981, but ultimately it was completed. It connects Interstate Highways 40 and 24 west and south of the city. Some residents in the vicinity of the highway still complain of noise and reduced property values, but proponents point to reduced traffic on the inner loop, fewer accidents and easier access to various areas of the city.

Photograph by Gary Layda; courtesy of the Government of Metropolitan Nashville-Davidson County.

Metro Center, across Interstate Highway 265 north of downtown, was one of the first areas of midtown Nashville to be developed as alternative office space. Construction began there in the late 1970s and has continued apace since that time. In 1987 Fountain Square, a $20 million marketplace for shopping, eating and entertainment, opened there, and its managers expect to host 10 million visitors a year. This view shows some of the shops and pedestrian areas fronting along the Square's forty-five-acre Lake Amulet.

Photograph by Gary Layda; courtesy of the Government of Metropolitan Nashville-Davidson County.

Opryland USA with its music theme park and Opryland Hotel, played a large role in Nashville's economic success during the 1980s. When its Nashville Network and other enterprises are included, Opryland USA ranks as the city's seventh largest employer. Among its newest ventures is the all-new, nineteenth-century replica showboat General Jackson, *shown here headed down the Cumberland from Opryland to Nashville's Riverfront Park.*

Photograph by Gary Layda; courtesy of the Government of Metropolitan Nashville-Davidson County.

Despite Nashville's new convention center, airport, and downtown revitalization, most of the rest of the world still sees it as "Music City U.S.A." When Broadcast Music, Incorporated (BMI), a licensing agent that tracts radio broadcasts and collects royalties for songwriters and performers, moved into this new headquarters on Music Row in 1964, the development of that area was still in its infancy. Since then it has boomed. Although country music record sales slumped in the early 1980s, they are rising again now. And Nashville ranks only behind New York and Los Angeles in television and video production.

Photograph by Gary Layda.

by 1985 the three-day Summer Lights Festival was filling downtown Nashville every year with tens of thousands of people to see and hear local artists, musicians, singers, dancers, actors, mimes and storytellers. Unfortunately, one important cultural organization did not fare as well. Financial difficulties forced the Nashville Symphony Orchestra to cancel its concert season in 1988.

Not all Nashvillians shared in the economic progress of the 1980s either, and some of the changes themselves had disturbing aspects. To a substantial degree the economic gains passed over Nashville's blacks. They made some limited additional political progress, but their business community continued to suffer from the negative impact of Interstate Highway 40, which years earlier had largely isolated the predominantly black area north of Nashville.

In addition, as the decade drew to a close, some Nashvillians were becoming concerned about the

city's growing dependence on outside capital. The acquisition of the Cain-Sloan Department Stores by Dillard Department Stores of Little Rock and the mergers of many of Nashville's largest banks with out-of-state financial institutions made the city increasingly subject to outside economic forces and business decisions made elsewhere. Equally disturbing were federal income tax provisions that made tax credits for historic rehabilitation less attractive to investors and threatened to change corporate attitudes toward cultural philanthropy.

Despite these concerns, however, when compared to many of the nation's major cities, Nashville could rightfully feel a certain amount of pride and satisfaction about how much of its vision it had achieved. Much remained to be accomplished on all fronts—economically, politically and culturally—but the city could look forward realistically with hope for further progress. ❧

In addition to the Grand Ole Opry and Opryland, the Country Music Hall of Fame and Museum remains a must for every country music fan who visits Nashville. Located at 4 Music Square East, the Hall of Fame and Museum uses its unique collections of memorabilia, instruments, recordings and archival material to preserve and interpret the history of all forms of country music, from western swing and bluegrass to cajun, honky-tonk and rockabilly. In addition to being popular with visitors, it is highly respected by museum professionals throughout the nation.
Photograph by Gary Layda.

The success of the Country Music Hall of Fame and Museum, together with its proximity to the rest of Music Row, has inspired the establishment of numerous commercial museums, both nearby and in outlying areas, over the years. This view, from the north end of the Music Row area northeastward toward downtown, shows some of the newer enterprises.
Photograph by Gary Layda.

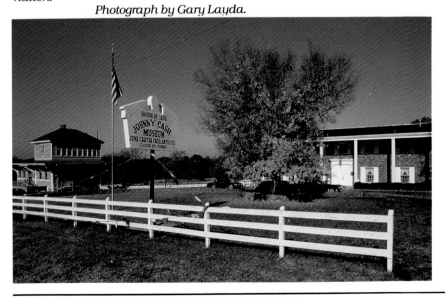

First among the outlying commercial museums of country music was the House of Cash, shown here, on Gallatin Road northeast of Hendersonville, Tennessee, home of many country stars. It was joined in the 1980s by Conway Twitty's Twitty City and by Music Village U.S.A., a complex of museums about the lives and careers of Ferlin Husky, Marty Robbins and Bill Monroe.
Photograph by Gary Layda.

Nashville's rapidly growing Summer Lights Festival is closely related to the city's music industry, but it draws its inspiration, talent and visitors from a wide spectrum of cultural interests. Begun in 1982 and sponsored by the Metro Nashville Arts Commission, it attracts tens of thousands of people downtown every year for three days and nights of fun and entertainment of all kinds. In this view festival goers stretch from the War Memorial Building eastward along Deaderick Street to the Metropolitan Courthouse.

Photograph by Gary Layda; courtesy of the Government of Metropolitan Nashville-Davidson County.

These Summer Lights Festival fans are watching and listening to country music star Skeeter Davis, while the Nashville skyline, with its appealing blend of old and new buildings, provides an attractive background.

Photograph by Gary Layda; courtesy of the Government of Metropolitan Nashville-Davidson County.

Sports loomed large in Nashville's vision of the 1980s and beyond. The Nashville Sounds, shown here in action at Greer Stadium, annually attracted 500,000 fans in the 1980s and moved from class AA professional baseball up to the class AAA American Association, just one rung below the major leagues. Team owners, civic leaders and fans all hope that the Sounds make the final leap upward in the 1990s.
Photograph by Gary Layda; courtesy of the Government of Metropolitan Nashville-Davidson County.

During the 1980s Nashville continued to be a national center for health care and hospital management. Hospital Corporation of America, renamed HCA, The Healthcare Company in 1987, has ranked consistently among the country's largest hospital management firms. Its headquarters building is situated on 25th Avenue North, near Centennial Park.
Photograph by Gary Layda.

HOSPITAL CORPORATION OF AMERICA
ONE PARK PLAZA

Nashville's brilliant new skyline at night, from west to east, with the American General Building in the foreground at left, and Dominion Tower at One Nashville Place on the right.
Photograph by Gary Layda; courtesy of the Government of Metropolitan Nashville-Davidson County.

PROFILES
IN
LEADERSHIP

Cities are in large part a reflection of the quality and success of their economic and cultural institutions and the people who manage them.

From the earliest times Nashville has been blessed with people and institutions of foresight and tenacity. Their collective story is reflected in the preceding pages. The detailed stories of some of the best are told in the following pages.

The Publisher

Brandau Craig Dickerson Company

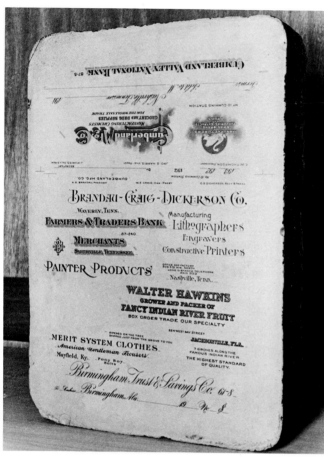

This fine-grained engraving stone, from the 1920s, contains the names of Brandau Craig Dickerson Company customers in Tennessee, Kentucky, Alabama and Florida.

Brandau Craig Dickerson Company is a pioneering color lithography and printing firm. It was founded in 1912, when A. G. Brandau, W. E. Craig, and C. S. Dickerson resigned from Brandon Printing Company and took over Standard Printing Company, a commercial printing and office supply firm.

Soon after moving into offices at 309 Fifth Avenue North, the new company dropped its office supply business and concentrated on lithography and printing. At first Brandau Craig Dickerson artists engraved designs on fine-grained sandstone, and from those the designs were transferred to metal plates and then to paper. Later the company became one of the first to adopt the new process of photo-lithography.

In 1926 Brandau Craig Dickerson purchased property at 304 Tenth Avenue South and constructed a new plant and offices. The company has operated in those facilities since that time.

In 1933, during the Great Depression, President Franklin Roosevelt ordered all U.S. banks closed, and Nashville's financial institutions issued and guaranteed script that local citizens and businesses accepted in place of currency. Because of its printing expertise, Brandau Craig Dickerson was selected to design and print millions of dollars of the new script in four denominations, with each bill serially numbered. The firm did such an outstanding and accurate job that later the state of Tennessee chose it to print millions of dollars of revenue stamps for cigarettes, cigars and pipe tobacco.

Both A. G. Brandau and C. S. Dickerson died during the early 1930s, leaving W. E. Craig as the lone remaining founder. In 1950 he sold his interest to Seawell Brandau, Chester A. Roberts and Thomas B. Walker, who became president, vice president, and secretary-treasurer respectively. Seawell Brandau's son, Seawell John Brandau, joined the company in 1960, following graduation from Vanderbilt University and military duty overseas. Chester A. Robert's son, Allen Roberts, came on board in 1969 following graduation from David Lipscomb College. Today Seawell Brandau is chairman of the board, Seawell John Brandau is president and treasurer, and Allen Roberts is executive vice president and secretary.

Over the years the company has continually updated its manufacturing facilities with new and improved equipment for volume color production. Currently Brandau Craig Dickerson offers such specialized services as aqueous coating, varnishing, dust bronzing, off-press die cutting and small insert folding. Its accounts extend throughout the region and nation, and its production includes labels, point-of-sale materials, package inserts and wraps, posters, maps, and direct-mail pieces.

The firm participates actively in various trade associations, and for years it has contributed regularly to the Graphic Arts Technical Foundation for research and development in the industry.

This business biography provided by Brandau Craig Dickerson Company.

Castner Knott Company

Castner Knott moved into this building at the corner of Church Street and Seventh Avenue, North in 1907.

As the Nashville area's oldest department store, the Castner Knott Company has a long and proud tradition of quality service. Charles Castner and William Knott founded the company and opened its first store at 203-211 North Sumner Street (now Fifth Avenue) in 1898. Their business philosophy was outstanding service, quality merchandise, and realistic prices.

Not long after the new store opened, Knott, who was serving as president, traveled to New York City and opened one of the first buying offices operated by a southern store in the nation's retail capital. This demonstrated from the outset that Castner-Knott was determined to follow progressive business practices.

Within a few years Castner Knott outgrew its first store and began seeking a new site. It considered moving to a suburban location but eventually selected the former site of the Demonville home at the corner of Church Street and Vine (now Seventh Avenue). The firm moved into a new building on this lot in 1907, and its downtown flagship store remains there today.

During its early years the store offered an array of products unusual by today's standards. In addition to fine clothing and household furnishings, Castner

Knott customers could buy wood-burning cookstoves and special cookbooks written by a store employee. And in the basement they could buy groceries and receive special trading stamps.

In 1914 Mercantile Stores, Inc., bought the department store and continued to operate it, making changes over the years as popular styles and tastes changed. Soon after World War II Castner Knott began a period of expansion by opening a branch store in Shelbyvillle, Tennessee. Since then branches have been opened in Green Hills (1955), Donelson (1961), Harding Mall (1966), Bowling Green, Kentucky (1968), Rivergate (1971), Tullahoma (1977), Florence, Alabama (1978), Hickory Hollow (1979), Decatur, Alabama (1979), and Huntsville, Alabama (1984). Many of these stores anchor shopping malls, and in 1990 and 1992 two other Castner Knott stores will perform this function, in Bellevue and Brentwood, Tennessee.

Under the leadership of Ralph Glassford, company president, Castner Knott intends to continue exploring new markets for expansion. The firm also plans to continue developing private label merchandise in order to provide brand-name style and quality at affordable prices while offering customers the latest fashions from America's top designers.

This business biography provided by Castner-Knott Company.

Coca-Cola Bottling Co. of Nashville, Inc.

In 1945 *Fortune Magazine* wrote that the best known and most commercially promising mass-produced item in the world was not an automobile, refrigerator, or gadget. It was Coca-Cola. By 1974 Coca-Cola was being consumed internationally at the rate of 165 million drinks every twenty-four hours, and *New Yorker* writer E. J. Kahn, Jr., called it a symbol of American life.

Next to the unique taste and quality of Coca-Cola, the system of locally owned and operated Coca-Cola bottling plants is considered by most business observers as the most important factor in this phenomenal success story. The Coca-Cola Bottling Company of Nashville is one of the nation's oldest such operations. In fact, the bottling contract that it secured from the parent Coca-Cola Bottling Com-

pany of Chattanooga in 1900 was the first ever issued to another firm.

The origins of Coca-Cola go back to 1886, when pharmacist John S. Pemberton concocted the drink in Atlanta, Georgia. Soda fountains were becoming popular then, and Pemberton was trying to take advantage of the trend. His bookkeeper, Frank Robinson, gave the new drink its name, which he wrote on the first package label in the same flowing script that still characterizes the Coca-Cola trademark.

Fountain operator Willis E. Venable enhanced the appeal of Coca-Cola in 1887, when one day he added carbonated, instead of plain, water to the Coca-Cola syrup. Still, the drink was slow to catch on with the public, and in 1888 Walker, Candler and Company acquired all claims to it. Four years later Asa G.

The advent of bottled Coca-Cola coincided with the development of new means of transportation, and early bottlers used trucks such as these to distribute their popular new product during the early 1900s.

Candler incorporated The Coca-Cola Company and launched an extensive promotion campaign that made the drink a nationwide product by 1895.

The practice of bottling Coca-Cola was begun by Joseph A. Biedenharn in Vicksburg, Mississippi, in 1894. As the manager of Biedenharn Candy Company, a confectionery and wholesale grocery firm, Biedenharn distributed several brands of soda water. He began bottling Coca-Cola almost by accident one day when he lacked enough of his regular products to fill an order. During the next few years, Biedenharn experimented with various bottle and crates for Coca-Cola and sent samples to Candler in Atlanta. Candler even visited Biedenharn several times but chose not to pursue bottling aggressively himself. He thought that soda fountain sales would always be the foundation of his business.

In the meantime, other entrepreneurs were thinking about the commercial possibilities of bottling Coca-Cola. One of those was Chattanooga lawyer-businessman Benjamin F. Thomas, who had observed brisk sales of a carbonated fruit drink while serving with the United States Army Commissary Department during the Spanish-American War. When he returned home to Tennessee, Thomas broached the idea of bottling Coca-Cola to his friend and fellow attorney Joseph B. Whitehead, and they went to Atlanta to secure permission to bottle Candler's product.

Candler remained uninterested in bottling, and after Thomas and Whitehead promised him that they would assume full responsibility for all operations, he signed a simple 600-word contract with them. It gave them exclusive rights to bottle Coca-Cola everywhere in the United States except Mississippi, where Biedenharn was operating; Texas, where syrup distribution negotiations were still pending; and six New England states, where Seth W. Foote & Sons already had a distribution contract.

This arrangement became the basis for the modern soft drink industry. Wasting little time, Thomas and Whitehead formed the Coca-Cola Bottling Company and sold half interest in the enterprise to John T. Lupton to raise the capital needed for their first plant in Chattanooga. Aware that they could not blanket the country with additional plants by themselves, they decided to sell bottling rights for various geographic regions.

The first regional bottling contract issued by the parent company in Chattanooga went to William Heck, Jr., of Nashville in September 1900. He operated a small plant at 1225 College Street, now Third Avenue, North, where he also bottled cider, vinegar and soda water. Heck's contract described Coca-Cola as "a carbonated drink, consisting of a mixture of water and the syrup or preparation known as Coca-Cola, charged with carbonic acid gas, and confined under a pressure of more than one atmosphere."

The contract gave Heck exclusive rights to a territory including Nashville and all of Middle Tennessee within a radius of seventy-five miles. In return he had to furnish all the necessary capital, facilities, machinery, bottles, wagons, horses, mules and workers necessary to bottle and distribute the product. The contract also required that he promote the drink.

Presumably the parent bottling company thought that he would do that, for the R. G. Dun Company, forerunner of the present Dun & Bradstreet, reported that Heck was "economical, hard working and industrious." Apparently, however, Heck did not promote bottled Coca-Cola effectively. He did not even advertise it in the Nashville city directory.

Within three years John M. Kenny acquired the right to bottle and distribute Coca-Cola in Nashville. The 1903 city directory listed his Coca-Cola Bottling Works at 916 Church Street, and under his name the directory carried this neat advertisement: "Drink a Bottle of Coca-Cola 5 Cents."

When Kenny began bottling Coca-Cola, plant equipment and apparatus were still somewhat crude and experimental. They improved steadily, though, and by 1909 a well-organized plant could produce up to 600 cases a day. And more than 375 plants were then doing so throughout the United States. They faced competition, though. By 1916 there were said to be more than 150 imitations of Coca-Cola around the country. One problem created by this multitude of bottled drinks was how to distinguish them in their glass packaging, especially because printed paper labels came off rather easily when wet. This problem was solved for the Coca-Cola bottlers in 1916, when Alex Samuelson of the Root Glass Company in Indiana designed the distinctive bulging bottle that became a Coca-Cola trademark.

In 1919, a year after the end of World War I, a syndicate headed by Ernest Woodruff bought The Coca-Cola Company, and in that same year Julius B. Weil acquired Kenny's bottling works in Nashville. Four years later Robert W. Woodruff became president of The Coca-Cola Company, and in the years that followed, he expanded its operations throughout the world. At the same time Weil expanded the Nashville bottling enterprise by taking advantage of new technology and transporting his product in a fleet of motorized trucks. During the 1930s he moved the company into a new plant at 1600 Church Street.

The Coca-Cola Bottling Co. of Nashville, Inc. moved into this spacious facility at 407 Craighead Street in 1977.

For more than forty years the Weil family operated the Coca-Cola Bottling Co. of Nashville, with Mrs. Weil managing the company herself after her husband's death. According to tradition, she always invited her guests to have cold bottles of Coca-Cola, but she did not serve the drinks herself. Instead, she handed her visitors nickels, from a roll that she kept in her desk, and allowed them to get their own bottles from a dispensing machine. This ritual emphasized the hard work that had gone into developing the product and the Nashville bottling company.

In 1962 Wometco Enterprises, Inc., bought the Coca-Cola Bottling Co. of Nashville, and in 1977 it moved into new facilities at 407 Craighead Street, where it remains headquartered today. Kohlberg, Kravis and Roberts & Co. bought Wometco's bottling operations in 1984 and sold them just a year later to Coca-Cola Bottling Co. Consolidated of Charlotte, North Carolina. At the time of the sale Wometco was operating bottling plants in several southeastern states, the Caribbean and Canada. All were transferred to Coca-Cola Consolidated, which now ranks as the third largest American bottling company. During the year of the sale, it and Wometco together produced nearly fifty million cases of Coke.

Today James Moore is chief executive officer of Coca-Cola Consolidated, and vice president Claude Clements is division manager for the Coca-Cola Bottling Co. of Nashville. In addition to its Craighead Street facility, it operates branch bottling plants in Dickson, Columbia, Springfield, Lebanon, Murfreesboro and Paris, Tennessee.

This business biography provided by Coca-Cola Bottling Co. of Nashville.

David Lipscomb University

Students often gather in Bison Square, located in front of the Willard Collins Alumni Auditorium, to spend leisure time or study between classes.

David Lipscomb University was founded as the Nashville Bible School by Church of Christ evangelists David Lipscomb and James A. Harding on October 5, 1891.

Lipscomb described the school's purpose in the *Gospel Advocate,* of which he was editor. It shall "teach the Bible as the revealed will of God to man," he wrote, and "such other branches of learning may be added as will aid in the understanding and teaching of the Scriptures and . . . promote usefulness and good citizenship among men."

When the school opened in rented quarters on old Fillmore Street, nine boys enrolled for the first session. Before the term ended, twenty-three other students, including two girls, joined them. They studied the Bible, English, Latin, Greek and mathematics, marking the start of a strong liberal arts tradition at the school.

Before the second session began, the school moved to South Cherry Street, now Fourth Avenue, and in 1893 it moved again, to a purchased site near the city reservoir on South Spruce Street. By 1903, the school had outgrown this location, too, and Lipscomb donated his farm for a permanent campus between present Lealand Lane and Belmont Boulevard.

Lipscomb served as chairman of the school's board of trustees and taught classes in the Old and New Testaments until age 82. Following his death in 1917, the school was renamed David Lipscomb College in his honor.

During the 1920s and 1930s the college moved forward, although it struggled, as did most Americans, with the financial complications of the Great Depression. It also survived two campus fires, which destroyed Lindsay Hall and Avalon Home.

In 1944 the college launched the Lipscomb Expansion Program under the direction of A. C. Pullias, assisted by Willard Collins. This effort resulted in completion of the Crisman Memorial Library and the McQuiddy Gymnasiun, then the largest in Nashville.

In 1946 Pullias and Collins became president and vice president, respectively, and two years later David Lipscomb graduated its first senior college class. Over the next few years more facilities were added, and in 1954 the college was accredited by the Southern Association of Colleges and Schools. Pullias continued as president until 1977,

He was succeeded by Collins, whose nine-year administration was marked by more vigorous expansion, a team concept of management, increased scholarships and record enrollments. Chief among new facilities was the Axel Swang Center for Business Administration, the first major new classroom building since the mid-1960s. The department of business administration became the largest of Lipscomb's seventeen academic departments, but the college maintained an emphasis on Bible study as the core of the curriculum, and appropriately, the school's first graduate work was offered in Bible studies, in 1983.

Harold Hazelip succeeded Collins as president in 1986, and under his leadership the college has expanded its graduate program and been accredited by the Southern Association at the master's degree level. In February 1988 the college's board of directors, acting on the new accreditation and a strategic plan developed by the administration, voted to advance Lipscomb to university status.

Today the school boasts 2,300 students and offers more than 100 major fields of study. By the school's centennial anniversary in 1991, it will offer master's degrees in business administration and education.

This business biography provided by David Lipscomb University.

Dozier Equipment International

Hugh Marshall Dozier, Founder

Dozier Equipment occupied this headquarters building at 1530 Demonbreun Street from 1955 to 1963. It was here that the company launched its catalog business.

For nearly forty years, Dozier Equipment International has built its reputation on providing its customers with the highest quality of material handling equipment. Many of these products are produced at our manufacturing facility in Nashville, Tennessee. Other products are acquired from independent manufacturers. Through the medium of a direct mail order catalog, these products are made available both nationally and internationally. Our sales efforts are supported by a team of salesmen who provide professional assistance on a direct sales basis covering the territories in Tennessee, Southern Kentucky and Northern Alabama and also through our telecommunications system—FAX, Telex, WATS lines. In addition, our customer service and satisfaction has always been a top priority of our organization.

Dozier Equipment International is known around the world as a leading manufacturer and distributor of material handling equipment and industrial supplies. The first began, however, as Dozier Equipment Company, a small family business founded by Hugh Marshall Dozier at 319 Sixth Avenue South in 1953.

At first the company distributed Buda fork lift trucks and operated parts and service departments. These efforts proved so successful that in 1955 the company was able to move to larger quarters at 1530 Demonbreun Street and open a branch office in Chattanooga.

In 1960, with the assistance of Material Flow, Inc., a Chicago-based mail-order company, Dozier Equipment went into the catalog business. Operating with only six employees, including Hugh Marshall Dozier and his wife, Anne S. Dozier, the fledgling firm produced its first catalog under the name "Cherokee Products Company." This new sales tool had only twenty pages, including the covers, but it succeeded well enough for the company to add a Dozier Equipment catalog the next year.

By the mid 1960s the company needed more space, and it built a new office and shop at 2933 Armory Drive. About this same time its efforts to manufacture material handling equipment gained momentum, and in 1968 the firm created the Hercules Industries division to produce a variety of material handling equipment.

In 1974 Randolph S. Dozier became president of the company and took over day-to-day operations from his father. Under the son's direction, the pattern of growth continued, and soon a dealer program was established for Hercules products. Catalog sales grew, too, and in 1981 the firm had to lease additional space at Space Park South in Nashville. In 1985 Dozier Equipment bought property at 2940 Foster Creighton Avenue, directly behind the Armory Drive building, and in 1987 the company enlarged both its Armory Drive and Space Park South facilities.

Today Dozier Equipment International owns Material Flow, Inc., the firm that introduced Hugh Marshall Dozier to the mail-order business. Randolph S. Dozier is chairman of the board and chief executive officer. The company he directs has more than 2,200 Hercules dealers and produces four different catalogs that range from 156 to 208 pages each. These are the Cherokee Products Corporation catalog, the Dozier Equipment International catalog, the Material Flow, Inc., catalog, and the Hercules Dealer "Products for Industry" catalog. They serve a customer list of more than 80,000 and illustrate well the Dozier success story.

This business biography provided by Dozier Equipment International.

217

HCA Park View Medical Center

HCA Park View Medical Center is the flagship institution of Hospital Corporation of America, founded in 1968 by Dr. Thomas F. Frist, Sr., Dr. Thomas F. Frist, Jr., and entrepreneur Jack Massey. Headquartered across Centennial Park from the medical center, the corporation was renamed HCA, The Healthcare Company in 1987, and today it is the nation's largest single healthcare firm. It owns and manages hospitals throughout the United States and in seven foreign countries and is a diversified participant in many other healthcare markets.

The origins of both HCA Park View and HCA, The Healthcare Company lie in the 1960s. Known originally as Park Vista Convalescent Hospital and Nursing Home, the medical center was founded in 1961 by a group of twenty-five physicians and businessmen. It had 100 general medical beds, 50 extended care beds, no operating room and only a small emergency room. These helped but did not satisfy the shortage of hospital beds in Nashville, and within four years the hospital added 50 more beds, four operating rooms, a more sophisticated x-ray department, laboratory facilities and a larger pharmacy.

One of the original owners of Park Vista was Dr. Thomas F. Frist, Sr., and when he, his son and Massey formed Hospital Corporation of America in 1968, they bought the hospital. They believed that a hospital could be run as a business by utilizing business management techniques and skills. Within the first year they acquired ten more hospitals, and in 1969 the new corporation became publicly owned.

In 1972, then known as Park View, the hospital added 125 more beds and new support facilities in a $45 million expansion. It also added EKG and EEG laboratories and started a department of nuclear medicine. The following year, on adjacent property, it added Parthenon Pavilion, a $1.5 million, 100-bed facility that was the first private psychiatric hospital in Nashville. Eventually, in 1984, Parthenon Pavilion was expanded by an additional 58 beds.

Meanwhile, Park View continued to expand as well. In 1976 it added a linear accelerator for use in cobalt therapy. In 1977 it made computerized tomography available to its patients and opened the Cardiac Rehabilitation Lab. And in 1978 it renovated the older wings, added two new cardiac surgery rooms and opened the Cardiovascular Catheterization Lab.

The 1980s brought further growth. With a $7.5 million project in 1981 the hospital added a new 109-bed oncology unit for cancer patients and expanded radiation therapy to include three linear accelerators. In 1984 the hospital's board of directors changed its name to Park View Medical Center to reflect the institution's increased status and broad referral base.

Today, The Cancer Center at Park View is one of the most advanced in the southeast, offering patients and their families total care throughout each personal cancer battle.

The Eye Care Center is the only one of its kind in middle Tennessee in that it houses the surgical suites, recovery and post-operative suites all in one area.

The Heart Network Center is the base for cardiac referral within a 100-mile radius of Nashville. This program coordinates the superior cardiology services offered by Park View to enhance the cardiac services of rural hospitals in middle Tennessee, southern Kentucky and northern Alabama.

The Rehab Center, a 20-bed long term rehabilitation Center, provides multi-specialty care for stroke and/or neurological patients.

These diverse "Centers of Excellence" help make HCA Park View Medical Center one of Nashville's leading healthcare providers.

Jane Jones Enterprises, Inc.

*Jane D. Jones, founder and president of
Jane Jones Enterprises, Inc.*
Photograph by Gil Williams.

*Jane Jones Enterprises corporate
headquarters building on Plus Park
Boulevard in Nashville. The company has
branch offices in Fountain Square,
Brentwood and Smyrna.*
Photograph by Gil Williams.

In 1977 Jane Jones was frustrated by the lack of adequate job opportunities for personnel directors in Middle Tennessee. Consequently she established her own temporary employment agency, and within ten years Jane Jones Enterprises grew from a two-person office to a fifty-person operation with three divisions: Jane Jones Temporary Services, Jane Jones Personnel Services and Jane Jones Management/ Technical Services.

According to the *Nashville Business Journal,* by 1987 Jane Jone's Temporary Services division had become the largest temporary personnel agency in Nashville. Today Jane Jones Enterprises ranks as one of the biggest and most diversified personnel service companies in Tennessee.

The firm is also considered a leading innovator in its field. From the start, Jane Jones demonstrated an affinity for predicting trends and staffing needs in the local market. She piloted a special program to train temporary tellers for area banks, and her "Try Before You Hire" program enabled clients of Jane Jones Personnel Services to work with potential employees on a temporary basis to determine if they were suitable for permanent employment.

In 1985 Jane Jones Enterprises converted to an

in-house computerized personnel resources management system, the first in Nashville. This enabled the firm to conduct immediate comprehensive searches for personnel to match clients' specific criteria— such as skill level, education, current work availability and employment history—for each available job.

As a result of her accomplishments, Jane Jones has earned both professional recognition and acclaim as one of Nashville's leading female business executives. She has been selected as the first recipient of *Nashville Business Journal's* Small Business Executive of the Year, Woman Entrepreneur of the Year, NAPS Circle of Excellence Community Service Award in addition to serving as President of Tempnet, a national temporary services association, a Member of the Board of Governors of the Nashville Area Chamber of Commerce and Belmont College.

More than 40,000 Middle Tennesseans have found temporary or permanent employment by following the advice of Jane Jones' slogan, and it seems likely that in the future many others will "Just pick up the phone and call Jane Jones."

This business biography provided by
Jane Jones Enterprises, Inc.

The Kroger Company

Bernard Kroger used colorful display practices in his first store in the 1880s and introduced meat departments into chain food stores in 1904. Both of these features, which were adopted by other food chains, have been important components of Kroger stores throughout this century.

The first great chain stores in America were food stores, and the Kroger Company was one of the earliest and most innovative among them. It was founded in Cincinnati in 1883 by Bernard H. Kroger, who, at age twenty-three, already had ten years of experience as a door-to-door grocery salesman and delivery boy.

Young Kroger launched that first store, which he called "The Great Western Tea Company," with a partner, whom he bought out after the first year. Hard work and an emphasis on quality and strict economies of operation quickly brought Kroger success, and by 1885 he had four stores in Cincinnati.

Over the next twenty years Kroger's chain grew steadily, and by 1902 he had forty stores and a factory in the city. That same year he changed the name of the company to the Kroger Grocery & Baking Company. By then he had become a pioneer in food advertising, taking out newspaper ads almost as large and colorful as the grocery advertisements of today. He also drew attention and customers by insisting that his prices be as low or lower than all his competition's.

More expansion and innovation followed. Kroger's company became the first food chain in the nation to operate bakeries and the first to incorporate meat departments in grocery stores. This helped the Kroger chain expand to fifteen stores in Dayton, Ohio, and eight in Columbus by 1910.

During the years just before World War I, Kroger took advantage of new, motorized transport and spread his organization rapidly throughout the Midwest. His fleet of trucks serviced Kroger stores in Detroit, Indianapolis, Springfield and Toledo. The war in Europe slowed Kroger's expansion, but growth resumed in the 1920s, as the firm bought out smaller, often distressed chains in geographic areas adjacent to existing Kroger operations.

Bernard Kroger sold his interest in the company in 1928, but it survived the Great Depression and continued to expand. The Kroger Company moved into the Nashville area in 1934. It bought the franchise name of Piggly Wiggly, operated it until the franchise name ran out, and then changed the stores to Kroger. From a headquarters building at Nineteenth Avenue North and Joe Johnston Avenue, Kroger officials soon managed stores throughout Tennessee and contiguous states. Eventually this became the Southland Marketing Area, the company's largest, including Tennessee, Kentucky and Alabama, plus a satellite operation in Atlanta.

In 1987 Southland Marketing Area officials moved Kroger's regional operations into a new headquarters at 2620 Elm Hill Pike and introduced the company's new "store of the 1990s." Today, Southland Vice-President Richard Bere operates 162 Kroger Food Stores, 29 of which are in the Nashville metropolitan statistical area.

This business biography provided by The Kroger Company.

McKissack & McKissack & Thompson
Architects & Engineers, Inc.

McKissack & McKissack & Thompson have the distinction of being the first black architectural firm in the state of Tennessee and one of the first in the United States.

When Moses McKissack, III, the founder of the firm, began practicing architecture in Nashville in 1905, he already had more than fifteen years' experience in constructing and designing buildings. His grandfather and father had been trained as master builders while in slavery, and shortly after the Civil War, his father had moved to Pulaski and became a leading building contractor. In the nineteenth and early twentieth centuries, the distinction between architects and builders was often blurred, and master builders like Moses McKissack, II, often planned and designed buildings as well as constructed them.

Mrs. Leatrice B. McKissack has been chief executive officer of McKissack & McKissack & Thompson since May 1983.

Before it became McKissack & McKissack & Thompson, the firm of McKissack & McKissack designed the George W. Hubbard Hospital on the campus of Meharry Medical College. The distinctive building was completed in 1976.

Moses McKissack, III, developed his skills under his father's tutelage and while supervising construction for a number of firms and individuals in the Pulaski area. In 1903 he ventured out on his own and for the next two years built houses in Athens and Decatur, Alabama, as well as in Mt. Pleasant and Pulaski, Tennessee.

In 1905 Moses McKissack, III, moved to Nashville and opened his first office over the One-Cent Savings Bank in the Napier Court Building. Soon he established a friendship with Dr. Richard Henry Boyd, who persuaded him to move his office to the National Baptist Publishing House and helped him get church design commissions. In the meantime, McKissack completed a correspondence course in architecture and engineering to prepare himself for larger projects.

Moses McKissack, III, received his first major commission in 1908, when he was selected to design the Carnegie Library, now the Academic Building, on the campus of Fisk University. Numerous other commissions followed, including several outside the black community, most notably the home of Governor Albert H. Roberts and several houses in Belle Meade. During much of this period, he was assisted by his younger brother, Calvin Lunsford McKissack, who completed a correspondence course in architecture while working as draftsman for the firm.

In 1922 Calvin McKissack, after spending several years practicing architecture in Texas and teaching architectural subjects at several Nashville educational institutions, went into partnership with his brother to establish the firm of McKissack & McKissack. Two years later, they designed the National Baptist Convention's Morris Memorial Building, in which they also placed their own offices.

Over the succeeding years the McKissack partnership proved very successful, as the firm designed more than 3,000 structures, including offices, hospitals, factories, hotels, educational buildings, churches and residences. In 1942 the firm received a $5.7 million contract for an air base in Tuskegee, Alabama, which at that time was the largest government contract ever given to a black firm.

Moses McKissack, III, died in 1952, and the firm was directed by his brother until his death in 1968. In that year William DeBerry McKissack, son of Moses McKissack, III, took over the firm and operated it until illness forced him to relinquish control to Leatrice B. McKissack. On January 1, 1984, McKissack & McKissack merged with Thompson-Miller in order to provide more comprehensive services, combine expertise, and serve a broader geographical area.

This business biography provided by McKissack & McKissack & Thompson, Architects and Engineers, Inc.

McQuiddy Office Designers

Interior of McQuiddy Printing Company sales offices near mid-century, prior to creation of McQuiddy Office Designers.

McQuiddy Office Designers is a modern, comprehensive office design and supply company that traces its history back to the mid-nineteenth century, to one of Nashville's many early religious printing enterprises.

In 1854 John T. S. Fall, Tolbert Fanning and others established a periodical called the *Gospel Advocate* as the organ of the Church of Christ. They published it for only four years, but in 1866 Tolbert, along with David Lipscomb, revived it as a sixteen-page weekly. It was expanded several more times over the next fourteen years, and in 1880 it came under the direction of J. C. McQuiddy.

Although the *Gospel Advocate* continued as an organ of the Church of Christ, eventually the Advocate Publishing Company became the forerunner of the McQuiddy Printing Company. By the turn of the century it was situated at 232 Second Avenue, North, where, in addition to conducting a printing business, it sold stationery and supplies.

After many decades of successfully managing printing and office supply operations together, the company split off its latter operations as a separate division in 1962. Thus McQuiddy Office Designers was launched with a staff of three and high expectations for the future.

Within four years McQuiddy Office Designers became a separate corporation and took complete occupancy of the existing McQuiddy office-warehouse complex in Nashville's downtown business district. Over the next two decades the new company attained prominence in the Central South as a major supplier of office furniture, office supplies, educational equipment, medical facility equipment and contract design services.

From 1978 to 1987 McQuiddy Office Designers was owned by Walter Kidde, Inc., a diversified corporation that also had several other furniture and supply companies. In 1987 it merged with Hanson Industries, the United States division of Hanson Ltd. of London.

Today McQuiddy Office Designers employs 250 people and is headquartered on Seventh Avenue, North in downtown Nashville. The company has retail branches in Nashville, Knoxville and Memphis and is the sole owner of Office Furniture Warehouse, a budget furniture outlet with four locations in Tennessee.

McQuiddy takes pride in providing working environments that improve communication and use interior space to its maximum potential while retaining sensitivity to aesthetics. The company's services range from providing total office furnishing, technical assistance and installation services. These are utilized by clients throughout the entire United States.

This business biography provided by
McQuiddy Office Designers.

These McQuiddy showrooms and completed installations illustrate the modern design capabilities of McQuiddy Office Designers.

Metropolitan Nashville Airport Authority

The New Nashville International Airport terminal.

Pursuant to enabling legislation passed by the 86th Tennessee General Assembly in 1969, the Government of Metropolitan Nashville-Davidson County created the Metropolitan Nashville Airport Authority (MNAA) in 1970 as a separate, self-supporting public corporation to manage, own and operate a regional system of airports.

Within this system, the Authority owns and operates Nashville International Airport, Smyrna Airport and John C. Tune Airport, and operates Springfield Airport under a management contract.

Smyrna Airport is a 1,700-acre general aviation facility approximately fifteen miles southeast of Nashville in Rutherford County. John C. Tune Airport is a 399-acre general aviation reliever facility that began operations in west Nashville in 1986. And Springfield Airport is a 70-acre general aviation facility approximately forty-one miles northwest of Nashville in Robertson County.

Nashville International Airport is a 3,800-acre hub for commercial airline service, a major center for general aviation, and home of the Tennessee Air National Guard. Over the years since 1936 it has been the site of three passenger terminals, including the newest, which opened in 1987.

The first terminal was situated on the east side of the airport, which came to be called Berry Field, in honor of Colonel Harry S. Berry. As state adminis-

trator for WPA funds, he had secured federal support for the facility. Previously, from 1921 to 1928 the city had relied on Blackwood Field, a small, 100-acre airfield west of Shute Lane in Hermitage, and from 1929 to 1936 it had used Sky Harbor, a 188-acre facility that is now the site of farming and light manufacturing near Murfreesboro.

Served initially by American and Eastern airlines, Berry Field boasted a 4,000-foot concrete runway, 80 obstruction lights, runway lights totaling 3 million candlepower, a 1.8 million-candlepower revolving beacon light, two hangars and a three-story terminal. In 1937 the terminal handled 189,000 passengers.

During World War II Berry Field became home to the 4th Ferrying Command and was one of the country's largest clearing stations for military aircraft bound for Africa, India, Italy and Egypt. This necessitated expansion, and when the war ended, Nashville had a 1,500-acre airport.

The city's growth and the coming of the jet age soon required even further changes, and in 1961 a new terminal was completed on the west side of the airport. By that time six airlines were serving the city, and in its first year the new terminal handled 531,000 passengers. Also added were a new 8,000-foot runway and a modern electronically equipped control tower.

By the late 1960s civic and government leaders knew that additional expansion would soon be necessary, and the eventual creation of the Metropolitan Nashville Airport Authority marked a milestone in airport history. As a separate public corporation, governed by a non-paid board of commissioners, managing a regional airport system, and operating without local tax support and in partnership with Nashville's serving airlines, the MNAA is unique.

Since it was established the airport authority has increased airport revenue, expanded aviation services, developed special working relationships with airlines serving the city, and firmly established Nashville and Middle Tennessee as an aviation hub.

The most striking manifestation of these achievements is the city's new terminal. Designed by New York architect Robert Lamb Hart, with Nashville-based Gresham, Smith and Partners, the $104 million, three-level edifice has 750,000 square feet of space and features forty-six gates and a huge central atrium covered by energy-efficient, green-tinted skylights. In 1987 it served 14 airlines and 6.38 million passengers.

Bob Mathews, Jr., is chairman of the Metropolitan Nashville Airport Authority, and General William G. Moore, Jr., is president.

This business biography provided by
Metropolitan Nashville Airport Authority.

Mrs. Grissom's Salads

*Grace and Herbert Grissom, founders of
Mrs. Grissom's Salads.*

Grace and Herbert Grissom founded Mrs. Grissom's Salads in 1955, after she talked him into mortgaging everything they owned to buy a failing company whose sales were less than $1,000 a week.

The Grissoms began their operation in an old restaurant building at 303 South Second Street in East Nashville. At first they had only five employees, whom they paid wages starting at seventy-five cents per hour. Thirty years later Mrs. Grissom's Salads had fifty-five employees and was distributing millions of red-and-green cartons of salad in a three-state area every year.

When they started, the Grissoms had no business experience except what they had learned as employees. She had worked for twelve years as secretary to the division storekeeper of Southern Railway in Knoxville, Tennessee. He had been a salesman for a feed company in Knoxville and later in Nashville. Between them they knew good business practices and understood sales, and that proved sufficient.

From the beginning, Mrs. Grissom was an involved manager. Even now she's often in her kitchens, where employees clad in white uniforms work on immaculate counters to prepare cole slaw and chicken, ham, potato, tuna, congealed and pimento cheese salads.

Since 1960 Mrs. Grissom's Salads has been housed in a modern new plant at Rosedale and Bransford avenues in Nashville. Over the years the facility has undergone several expansions to accommodate the company's growth. Today, Mrs. Grissom's Salads markets its products not only to grocery chains, but directly to hospitals, schools and regional food distributors. The company also acts as distributor for other manufacturers, such as Plumrose Ham and Jimmy Dean Sausage products.

When Mrs. Grissom is not in her kitchens, she is active in a variety of community affairs, especially higher education. She has served on the boards of trustees of Martin College in Pulaski, Tennessee, and of Tennessee Wesleyan, Hiwassee College and Emory and Henry College in East Tennessee. She has also served on the Development Council of Peabody College in Nashville and has been the recipient of several awards as an outstanding female executive.

This business biography provided by
Mrs. Grissom's Salads.

Nashville Cellular Telephone Company

Cellular One®

At Nashville Cellular Telephone Company's downtown Nashville location, 160 Fourth Avenue North, customers can slip behind the wheel of the front half of a Toyota, use an activated cellular telephone, and get the feel of doing business from an automobile.

In June 1985 several local investors, including a group headed by Joe Rogers and JMR Investments and Massey-Burch Investments through Charisma Communications, formed the Nashville Cellular Telephone Company. The firm became an affiliate of the nationwide Cellular One network a month later, when its six employees moved into Grassmere Office Park in July 1985.

Its first installer/technician installed mobile phones under a shade tree for two months, but another installer/technician was soon hired to keep up with demand. The staff tripled to 18 within a year, and by October 1986 sales had doubled projections.

To fill the ever-increasing demand for high-quality, efficient mobile communications, the company uses the most advanced mobile phone service AT&T technology can provide. In July 1987 Cellular One introduced a digital AT&T Autoplex cellular system, the largest cellular telephone system in Tennessee, which combines the latest technology with AT&T standards for quality.

In addition, because of efficient use and re-use of the radio spectrum, modern cellular technology can handle thousands of calls simultaneously in a geo-

graphic area, whereas older systems were limited to a few hundred. Better yet, the transmission quality is comparable to the phone in your home or office.

In August 1987 Cellular One became a subsidiary of McCaw Communications, the largest provider of cellular service in the country. The firm opened its first retail store at 160 Fourth Avenue North in September, and in February 1988 the Rivergate Mall store opened.

The Southeastern Region, which encompasses Kentucky, Alabama, and Tennessee, is headquartered on the 11th floor of American Center One, 3100 West End Avenue. On the roof of this building are a series of antennae that connect the cellular customer, via the cell and the central switch, to another cellular customer or to an ordinary telephone.

Cellular One continues its rapid expansion, both in the number of customers and geographic markets served, as more and more people incorporate the convenience and quality of cellular phones into their hectic lifestyles.

This business biography provided by
Cellular One.

226

Nashville Electric Service

Nashville was one of the first cities in the South to have electric streetcars. The first service began in 1888, and a year later the City Electric Railway Company was incorporated to provide service along Broadway.

The Nashville Railway and Light Company, incorporated in 1903, was one of the forerunners of Nashville Electric Service. It brought Nashville's light, power, and electric railway system under a single management and served the city until it was dissolved in 1930 by merger with the Tennessee Electric Power Company. These workman are repairing electric railway lines in the early 1900s.

Although Nashville Electric Service (NES) dates back only to 1939, its origins can be traced through several firms that preceded it in furnishing electrical current as an energy source. The Brush Electric Company introduced electric power to Nashville in 1882, when it energized one of Thomas Edison's incandescent light bulbs at the State Capitol. The Citizens' Electric Company succeeded it in 1886, and six years later, that company gave way to the Cumberland Electric Light and Power Company.

In 1903 the Nashville Railway Company merged with Cumberland to create the Nashville Railway and Light Company, an enterprise that placed light, power, and transportation systems under central direction. In 1930 Tennessee Electric Power Company, a subsidiary of the Commonwealth and Southern Corporation, acquired Nashville Railway and Light through merger, thus making Nashville an important part of the South's major interconnected power system.

The events that lead to the creation of Nashville Electric Service are closely tied to the development of the Tennessee Valley Authority (TVA) in 1933. After TVA began to generate electricity, many small towns and larger communities in the region began to purchase existing distribution facilities and build new ones to provide their citizens with cheaper TVA power.

In 1936 a TVA Power League was established in Nashville, and a petition campaign was begun to persuade the city to buy power from TVA. A heated private versus public power debate followed, and eventually the public power advocates prevailed. In 1939 the Tennessee Legislature enacted the Electric Power Board bill, which set up an autonomous public body appointed by the mayor and confirmed by the council to have full management and control of electric power distribution for the city. After floating a $15 million bond issue, the city purchased the local Tennessee Electric Power Company system, and on August 16, 1939, TVA power officially came to Nashville.

The impact of low cost energy was lessened somewhat by the onset of World War II, but in the postwar era and after, it played a vital role in Nashville's dramatic suburban and industrial growth. From slightly more than 50,000 customers in 1939, the number jumped to almost 138,000 in 1964. Today it totals over 250,000, and NES is the eighth largest public electric utility in the nation. It services an area of approximately 700 square miles, which includes all of Davidson County and parts of six surrounding counties.

This business biography provided by Nashville Electric Service.

National Baptist Publishing Board

Annual session of the National Congress

The National Baptist Publishing Board is the oldest and largest black-owned-and-operated religious publishing and printing corporation in the United States. Dr. Richard Henry Boyd established it in 1896 to enable black writers to interpret, write and distribute their own religious literature. The corporation has continued this tradition for nearly a century, and today it prints and distributes millions of books and periodicals to enrich the lives and moral awareness of people everywhere.

Born a slave in 1843, Richard Henry Boyd worked as a cowboy in Texas after the Civil War, taught himself to read and write, and became an ordained minister. For a time he supplied religious books and other printed materials to black Texas congregations from an office in San Antonio, and eventually he moved to Nashville because it was a center for publishing.

In 1906, ten years after launching the National Baptist Publishing Board, Boyd founded the National Baptist Sunday School Congress to train clergy and laity through the use of Board materials. Eventually the National Congress became the official training arm of the Publishing Board, and today it convenes annually in a selected major city, where more than 100 instructors and a support staff in excess of 250 teach and work with between 20,000 and 25,000 attendees.

Boyd also had many other entrepreneurial interests. He was a co-founder in 1904 of the One Cent Savings Bank and Trust Company, which today is known as the Citizens Savings Bank and Trust Company and is the nation's second oldest black-owned-and-operated bank. He was also involved in the founding of Bishop College in Texas, and he established a furniture factory to make pews and other items for churches.

Boyd's descendants continued his legacy of leadership. His son, Dr. Henry Allen Boyd, took over the Publishing Board following his father's death in 1922 and continued at the helm until 1959. He implemented new operational procedures and saw the corporation flourish. Like his father, Dr. Henry Allen Boyd was active in many civic and other business organizations. He served as president of Citizens Savings Bank and Trust Company, was an

Dr. Theophilus B. Boyd, III, President,
C.E.O. is the fourth generation to lead this
national organization in the field of
religious publication.

organizer of the National Association for the Advancement of Colored People, and sat on the board of trustees of Fisk University and Meharry Medical College.

In 1959 Dr. Theophilus B. Boyd, Jr., became the chief executive of the National Baptist Publishing Board and led it into its most prosperous and productive period. Under his direction the corporation built a new million-dollar headquarters in 1974, installed new and more efficient printing equipment, and adopted increased employee benefits.

Since 1979 Dr. Theophilus B. Boyd, III, has served as President, C.E.O. of the board, continuing the company's tradition of family service. The Publishing Board still strives for excellence, uses the latest methods in publishing and printing, and insists on

quality customer assistance through its field sales program, data center and customer service program. It publishes Bibles, Sunday church school literature, Baptist Training Union materials, Vacation Bible School study aids, missionary books, sermons and pastoral aids, religious reference works, hymn books, church bulletins, church administration guides, and many kinds of church management forms.

The corporation is also involved in a number of charities and educational organizations. Each year it donates grants and scholarships to churches, colleges, universities and charitable groups throughout the country.

This business biography provided by
the National Baptist Publishing Board.

Neely Coble Company

The Cobles Maintain The Family Tradition At Neely Coble Company

The company was founded in 1951 by Neely B. Coble and Neely Coble Jr. as a Heavy Duty Truck Distributor, and now sells Mack, Freightliner, Isuzu and Nissan Trucks.

Bill Coble, another son, was President of Leaseco Truck Rental which has been sold. Two grandsons are in the business, Will Coble, and Neely Coble III, President.

Starting with only five employees, the company now has 179 in five locations.

In general the company's success is based on having Ambitious and Capable Associates in the business. Also a strong company policy of Fairness... Dependability... Enthusiasm... Hard Work... and Willfully taking care of our customers' Best Interest.

At age 88 Coble Sr. remains active, and loves the business challenge.

This business biography provided by Neely Coble Company.

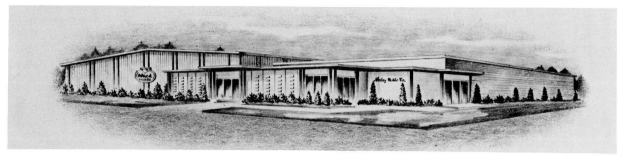

Nashville Headquarters

Opryland USA Inc.

The barn backdrop of WSM's Grand Ole Opry is a familiar sight to country music lovers. Nearly a million people attend performances of the Opry every year, and millions more listen to the broadcasts on the radio and TNN.

Opryland USA Inc., is the parent company of a number of entertainment, broadcasting, and hospitality businesses that have played a major role in making Nashville the world capital of country music and helping earn it the title "Music City USA." The origins of the present enterprise can be traced back to November 28, 1925, when the National Life and Accident Insurance Company's newly established WSM Radio introduced a program known as the "WSM Barn Dance." Two years later it became the "Grand Ole Opry" and went on to be the longest running program in radio history.

In its early years, the Opry emphasized instrumental performance, and its first stars included individuals who were virtuosos of the fiddle, banjo, and other instruments. Uncle Jimmy Thompson, the 80 year old who had been the solo performer on the first broadcast, reportedly knew a thousand fiddle rounds and claimed he could fiddle the "taters off the vine." DeFord Bailey, the first black member of the Opry and a performer from the late 1920s to the early 1940s, became the show's first star harmonica soloist and played in a style that became known as "black hillbilly" because it combined early blues and traditional string-band music. The first really big

name Opry star, however, was Uncle Dave Macon from Smart Station, Tennessee. Nicknamed the "Dixie Dewdrop," Macon was an outstanding banjo picker and crowd pleaser, who over the course of the years did more than any other performer to transform nineteenth-century folk music into twentieth-century country music.

In the late 1930s and early 1940s, singing began to take on increasing importance in the Opry with the arrival of new stars like Roy Acuff and his Smoky Mountain Boys and Eddy Arnold, "The Tennessee Plowboy." The popularity of these and other vocal performers led to increased interest not only in country music but in attending Opry broadcasts as well. Originally, the show had been broadcast in a regular radio studio, but because of public interest, WSM constructed Studio C, an acoustically designed auditorium that could hold 500 fans. As the popularity of the show increased, large numbers of people had to be turned away, and the show was moved to the Hillsboro Theatre, which soon proved inadequate as well. In 1936 the Opry moved into the Dixie Tabernacle in East Nashville, but within three years it outgrew this location. In 1939 the show moved to the new War Memorial Auditorium, and for the first time began charging admission (twenty-five cents) in the hope of curbing the crowds. This had little impact, however, and weekly crowds averaged better than 3,000. Finally, in 1943 the Opry moved to the Ryman Auditorium, the famed red brick building destined to become synonymous with the program.

The period from the late 1930s until the mid 1950s were years of substantial growth for country music in general. In 1939 NBC Radio began to carry the Opry nationally, and in 1940 Roy Acuff, Uncle Dave Macon, and George D. Hay starred in a movie entitled "Grand Ole Opry." New performers joined the Opry troupe, including Red Foley, Ernest Tubb, Cowboy Copas, Whitey Ford, Minnie Pearl, Rod Brasfield, Texas Ruby, Bill Monroe and Hank Williams to name only a few. Again and again fans packed the 3,000-seat Ryman for a glimpse at their favorites.

Although country music's growth was slowed somewhat by the rock-and-roll craze of the mid and late 1950s, it and the Opry received a tremendous boost in the early 1960s with revived public interest in folk music. Opry performers like Lester Flatt, Earl Scruggs, Bill Monroe and others too numerous to name found themselves in general demand. The marked interest in the Opry and its performers made obtaining tickets to the performances increasingly difficult. Admission lines began to form early on Saturday morning, and by late afternoon, they extended around the Ryman and down Broadway.

In the summer of 1968, WSM President Irving Waugh and National Life executives Edwin Craig and Bill Weaver began discussing plans to build a new home for the Opry. As their plans matured, however, they developed a diverse entertainment complex that would become known as Opryland USA.

Ground was broken on June 30, 1970, and the first component, the Opryland theme park, began operating less than two years later on May 27, 1972. Its theme was live entertainment featuring many kinds of American music. The Opry moved to Opryland USA on March 16, 1974, when the 4,400-seat Grand Ole Opry House was completed.

The advent of Opryland USA marked the beginning of a period of rapid growth. An interest in television, begun in 1950 when WSM-TV first aired, expanded in 1974 when Opryland Productions began operation. With facilities in the Grand Ole Opry House, Opryland Productions produced shows and commercials for many clients, and it won three Emmy awards for videotape editing for ABC-TV's coverage of the 1976 Montreal Olympics.

In 1975, plans were announced to add a major hotel to Opryland USA. In 1977, the Opryland Hotel opened with 600 guest rooms and a special devotion to meetings and conventions. It added 467 rooms in 1983 and another 824 rooms in 1988, making it the 12th largest hotel in the nation (1,891 rooms and more meeting, exhibit and public space than any

Opryland USA's General Jackson show-boat recalls the showboat days of the 19th Century as it cruises the Cumberland River.

A raft of white-water adventurers tries to avoid the inevitable—getting sprayed by a waterfall on the Grizzly River Rampage at Opryland.

other hotel).

In 1981, a decision was made to enter the field of cable television. Therefore, the company sold WSM-TV and created The Nashville Network, which went on the air on March 7, 1983. TNN set a cable television record for initial subscribers, with a base of nearly seven million homes. In less than five years, that grew to more than 40 million homes, the vast majority of cable television homes in the U.S.

While Opryland USA was evolving, National Life was acquired by the American General Corporation. American General sold the Opryland USA companies on September 1, 1983 to Gaylord Broadcasting Company of Dallas, and a new company was born— Opryland USA Inc. Opryland USA Inc. and Gaylord Broadcasting Company are parts of the Oklahoma

Publishing Company, which is owned by Edward L. Gaylord of Oklahoma City.

Acquisition by Mr. Gaylord heightened the pace of growth. In December 1983, plans were announced for a $12 million paddlewheeler showboat that could carry 1,200 passengers on the Cumberland River. The boat, the *General Jackson*, was christened by Mr. Gaylord's wife, Thelma, in ceremonies at Nashville's Riverfront Park on July 3, 1985. It immediately became one of Nashville's most popular attractions.

Another significant addition to Opryland USA came in 1985 with the purchase of Acuff-Rose, Nashville's first music publishing company. From Acuff-Rose has evolved the Opryland Music Group, which soon created 16th Avenue Records, an independent record label. Acuff-Rose was founded by Opry star Roy Acuff

*The Opryland Hotel Conservatory, with its
distinctive glass roof, features a two-acre
indoor tropical garden surrounded by 468
guest rooms.*

and songwriter/entertainer Fred Rose in 1942, and
its catalog of copyrighted songs includes country and
pop standards by songwriters such as Hank Williams,
Pee Wee King, Dallas Frazier, Ray Orbison and the
Everly Brothers.

Other components of Opryland USA Inc. have
evolved through the years. In the broadcast field,
WSM-FM joined its sister station, WSM-AM, in 1968
and is one of Nashville's most popular stations. WSM-
AM continues to broadcast the Grand Ole Opry every
Friday and Saturday night, and a third station in the
group, WKY in Oklahoma City, carries the Saturday
night Opry.

Gaylord Syndicom, a component created in 1984,
develops television shows for syndication, and it is

responsible for "Hee Haw," the long-running country
music and entertainment show that is one of the
most successful shows in syndication history.

Other elements of Opryland USA Inc. include Opryland Productions Duplicating Service, which dupli-
cates videotapes; Opryland Travel, a travel company
that arranges a variety of package vacations both in
Nashville and other travel destinations; Grand Ole
Opry Sightseeing Tours, which offers a variety of tour
itineraries throughout Nashville; and Opryland Talent, which produces shows and arranges entertainment for clients in Nashville and practically any place
else in the world.

This business biography provided by
Opryland USA Inc.

Roy Acuff

Roy Acuff on stage at the Grand Ole Opry with Minnie Pearl.

Probably no single performer has influenced the Grand Ole Opry and country music in general as much as Roy Acuff, the "King of country Music." Born in 1903 in Maynardsville, Tennessee, Acuff grew up in the Knoxville suburb of Fountain City, where his principal interests were sports and not music. A three-letter man in high school, his primary passion was baseball, his heroes were Ruth and Gehrig, and his career ambition was to follow in their path and become a major leaguer. Unfortunately Acuff suffered sunstroke on three different occasions when trying out for a professional club, and he never realized his baseball ambitions.

With his playing days behind him, Acuff took up the fiddle, largely at the inspiration of hisminister-attorney father who played the instrument and collected records of mountain fiddle songs. Roy used these records to teach himself, and around 1932 he joined a traveling medicine show in the mountains of Virginia and East Tennessee, performing both as a fiddler and a singer. By 1936 he had made his first recording and had begun singing on WNOX and WROL in Knoxville. In 1936 he and his band recorded thirty tunes in just two sessions for the American Record Corporation. Several of these songs were selected by Sears, Roebuck and Company for mail-order distribution, and one of them, "The Great Speckled Bird," had tremendous sales.

The popularity of the "Great Speckled Bird" brought Acuff an invitation to appear on the Grand Ole Opry, where he soon became a regular. He is generally credited with transforming the Opry from a show that was predominantly instrumental into one in which vocals became increasingly important. Acuff's popularity was so great that in 1939 NBC Radio began broadcasting a thirty-minute segment of the Opry every Saturday night.

That same year Acuff starred in the movie *Grand Ole Opry,* the first of several he would make. This film proved especially important because it effectively depicted country music as honest, open, and reflective of conservative values shared by Americans in all regions of the country. In essence, the film signaled the arrival of country as an acceptable music form and helped to insure Nashville's place in its continuing development.

In 1942 Acuff branched out further when he and Fred Rose founded Acuff-Rose Publications, the first music publishing company in Nashville, and eventually one of the largest in the music industry. Acuff veered furthest from performing in 1948 when he ran for governor of Tennessee as the Republican nominee. Although he lost, he did better than any other Republican had in recent memory, and his performance is generally credited with helping revive the Republican Party in the state.

Today, Roy Acuff continues to appear on the Opry regularly, providing renditions of the "Great Speckled Bird" and the "Wabash Cannonball." He has received many honors, including election to the Country Music Hall of Fame. In 1987 the National Academy of the Recording Arts and Sciences awarded him a lifetime achievement award, and in 1988 the National Association of Broadcasters elected him to their Hall of Fame.

This biography provided by Opryland USA, Inc.

R.P. Industries, Inc.

Established in 1978, R. P. Industries, Inc. has emerged as one of Middle Tennessee's leading construction companies. It was founded by Joseph L. Parkes, Sr., and Walter Rowlette, both of whom had been associated previously with Hardaway Construc-

The Southern Turf Building, erected at 212 Fourth Avenue North in 1895 and a recent renovation project of R. P. Industries.

Interior of Hickory Hollow Mall expansion, an R. P. Industries project.

Joseph L. Parkes, Sr., president of R. P. Industries, and his three sons; Joe, Jr., David, and Gary.

tion Company. Rowlette sold his interest in the new firm in 1982, but Parkes remains as president.

The company concentrates on a few major repeat-oriented clients. These include some well-known names, such as Handy City Stores, Service Merchandise and The Trion Group, developers of shopping centers and office buildings. Another client is Richmond-based Circuit City Stores, for which R. P. Industries has completed or has under construction twenty superstores ranging in value up to two million dollars in cities from Louisville to Jacksonville.

From the beginning the company has stressed three main concepts in client-builder relations: honesty, fairness, and professionalism. It has also emphasized moving projects along as quickly as possible, through experienced on-site management and constant communication.

To accomplish these goals, R. P. Industries utilizes the most modern management techniques. The Critical Path Method of scheduling, developed in the mid 1950s for the U.S. Navy's Polaris Missile Program and construction of E. I. Dupont de Nemours Company chemical plants, allows R. P. Industries to schedule all facets of a project by computer, make necessary changes quickly and accurately, and reduce normal construction times by up to twenty percent.

R. P. Industries also practices fast tracking and value engineering. Fast tracking is a technique that allows construction and design to proceed simultaneously, circumventing the more traditional method of completing the entire design before construction begins. Value engineering is a technique for evaluating different alternatives to provide the best balance between cost, reliability and performance. Unnecessary expenses are eliminated by reviewing the costs of several alternative construction solutions simultaneously.

Since Rowlette's departure from R. P. Industries, the company has become truly a family business, fulfilling a long-time dream of Joseph L. Parkes, Sr. His first son, Joe Parkes, Jr., joined the company in 1979. Gary Parkes came on board part-time in 1983 while completing his MBA at Vanderbilt University's Owen Graduate School of Management, and David Parkes entered the firm in 1986.

Today R. P. Industries employs 130 people, has construction projects in progress in most of the southeastern and midwestern states, and enjoys an annual project volume of $25 to $30 million.

This business biography provided by
R. P. Industries, Inc.

Saint Thomas Hospital

Saint Thomas Hospital has been an integral part of the Nashville community since 1898, when the city's Catholic bishop, Thomas S. Byrne, persuaded the Daughters of Charity to open and operate a hospital here.

The Daughters opened a dispensary in the former home of Judge Jacob McGavock Dickinson on West Church Street. In 1902 they moved into a new facility constructed adjacent to the mansion. Ever since then, the hospital has been in an almost constant state of growth.

In an attempt to meet the community's health care needs, several wings were added to the 1902 facility until finally, in the mid 1960s, a decision was reached to relocate the hospital to an area that allowed for continued expansion. In 1974, Saint Thomas opened an ultra-modern 410-bed facility on twenty-eight acres off Harding Road, west of down-

town, and just eleven years later launched a comprehensive expansion project on that same site.

While still located downtown, Saint Thomas Hospital established a pioneering cardiac program. In 1967 Saint Thomas surgeons performed one of the first coronary artery bypass operations in Middle Tennessee, and in 1979 a Saint Thomas cardiologist performed the first balloon angioplasty in the Mid-South. In 1985 Saint Thomas made Tennessee history when a surgical team carried out the state's first heart transplant. Advancements in cardiac care continued, and in 1987 a Saint Thomas cardiologist performed Nashville's first valvuloplasty, a procedure that uses a tiny balloon to open valves in the heart. By then Saint Thomas had become a 571-bed adult acute-care teaching and referral hospital.

Today Saint Thomas Hospital operates the Tennessee Heart Institute to advance the diagnosis and treatment of heart disease. The Dan Rudy Cancer Center and the Sleep Disorders Center are also centers of excellence. And in a unique joint venture with Baptist Hospital, Saint Thomas Hospital helps oversee the 288-bed Middle Tennessee Medical Center in nearby Murfreesboro. The arrangement, made in 1986, marks the first effort by two not-for-profit hospitals to manage a similar facility.

Saint Thomas Hospital's commitment to education began in 1902 with the establishment of the Saint Thomas School of Nursing. During its 68-year existence, the school trained 1,508 nurses. The hospital's commitment to education continues today through affiliations with the Vanderbilt University School of Medicine for training physicians as well as several colleges and universities for allied health education. Saint Thomas also sponsors schools of medical technology and one of the few perfusion schools in the Southeast. In addition, the hospital operates the Laurence A. Grossman Medical Learning Center for continuing medical education for physicians and other health professionals through seminars, courses, and teleconferences.

In 1986, the Daughters of Charity National Health System was established, uniting Saint Thomas Hospital with the other Daughters of Charity institutions into the largest not-for-profit health care system in the United States.

From a staff of five in 1898, Saint Thomas Hospital now employs 2,700 people and is the fifteenth largest employer in Nashville. Well known for its care of critically ill patients, it is one of the most advanced and sophisticated diagnostic, treatment, and rehabilitation centers in the state.

Saint Thomas Hospital's modern facility on Harding Road.

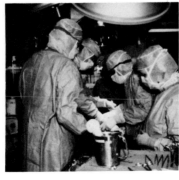

Saint Thomas Hospital surgical team performing the state's first heart transplant in 1985.

This business biography provided by
Saint Thomas Hospital.

Southern Colortype Company

Southern Colortype built this head-quarters building at 2927 Sidco Drive in 1955. Photography by J. C. Jones

Reid T. Groomes and his wife, Leila Mae Groomes, founded Southern Colortype Company in 1928 in the back of a leased building at 142 Eighth Avenue North. They started small with only four employees, and Reid T. Groomes, a skilled printer, performed many pressroom jobs for himself, while Leila Mae Groomes kept the company books and managed office operations.

Product mix in the early days consisted largely of commercial printing for a variety of accounts and specialty die cutting for other printing firms locally. Increasingly, however, the firm specialized in developing and producing labels for the local garment industry, and this soon became a mainstay.

By 1941 business had increased to such an extent that the founders purchased land and built a printing plant at 1519 Demonbreun Street. By this time the workforce had doubled to eight, and additional letterpress equipment had to be purchased to meet the growing demands of the garment industry. Overalls were the garment makers' large volume item, and Southern Colortype added a local artist to the staff and began designing and producing overall labels for both local manufacturers and those in several surrounding states. These labels included large pocket labels, string tags, and even composition leather-like patches.

In 1955 the company built a new plant at 2927 Sidco Drive. By this time, the number of employees had grown to fifteen, new and larger presses had been brought on line, and the product mix had become more extensive and varied. The garment

Reid T. and Leila Mae Groomes, shown here, founded Southern Colortype Company in 1928. Kenneth L. Groomes, their son, owns the company today. Photograph by J. C. Jones

industry remained an important customer, but the company was now producing point-of-sales labeling and packaging for hosiery mills, toy manufacturers, and makers of wire products and bath carpets and accessories.

In 1960 Reid T. and Leila Groomes retired, and their sons Reid B. and Kenneth L. took over the business. The following year they decided to add to the product line a large range of flexible film packaging. The installation of four-color and later six-color flexographic presses enabled the firm to print and manufacture shirt bags, ladies' hosiery envelopes, blanket bags, and many other items.

Southern Colortype Company was incorporated in 1962 with the entire stock issue owned in equal amounts by the two sons of the founders, Reid B. Groomes and Kenneth L. Groomes.

Reid B. attended to administrative and accounting duties and Kenneth L. to sales and production.

John C. Groomes, son of Reid B., joined the firm in June, 1965 as part of the sales department and remained until December 30, 1986. Lee Anne Groomes, daughter of Kenneth L., also came with the company in February, 1982 and now serves as Vice President, Sales and Production.

Reid B. Groomes retired in June, 1984, and the company is now entirely owned by Kenneth L. Groomes, producing sales in the millions with a workforce of sixty persons. As it has for nearly sixty years, the firm still follows its founders' philosophy to provide "exceptional quality and performance beyond the accepted norm." This business biography provided by Southern Colortype Company.

Southern Library Bindery Company

The Southern Library Bindery Company is the only certified library bindery in Tennessee and one of only about fifty in the entire country. The bulk of its business is binding theses, dissertations, and periodicals for college, university, and government libraries, and it binds more than 100,000 volumes each year. It also restores rare and other valued books, at the rate of about 1,000 annually.

Ethel Paul (later Ethel Paul Reavis), Ethel Birdsong, Emma Watts, and Sam Elliott founded Southern Library Bindery in February 1934. Located temporarily in the Presbyterian Building on Fourth Avenue North, the firm operated initially with equipment borrowed from Baird-Ward Printing Company. Within a year, however, the bindery moved to a new site at 429 Commerce Street.

Eventually all the original stockholders except Mrs. Reavis left the bindery, and in 1951 it was purchased by a local book bindery, which retained it only a year before selling it to Ernest M. Allen III. Allen incorporated the company and retained the services of Mrs. Reavis, who stayed on until 1972, when she retired.

In the meantime, in 1959 Allen moved the company to a new building where the bindery is presently located, 2952 Sidco Drive. Allen died in 1975, and four years later Catherine Allen Brown purchased

Catherine Allen Brown and Norman J. Brown, current owners of Southern Library Bindery, with a computerized hot foil stamping machine.

Mrs. Ethel Paul Reavis, one of the founders of Southern Library Bindery, with a Ludlow typesetting machine, which was used for many years to hot foil stamp the bindings of books.

the company from the First American Bank Trust Department.

Today, the bindery's specialty is custom leather binding; however, the company's expertise expands much further than that. They also bind new documents and periodicals, rebind older books and other materials, and restore heirloom books. Most of the restoration work is done on family Bibles and other books of sentimental value.

Automation came more slowly to the binding industry than to others. Until relatively recently binderies relied upon the Ludlow typesetting machine to hot foil stamp the bindings of books. Now, however, the Southern Library Bindery Company stamps customized library bindings with a computerized stamping machine, which represents the most innovative change in the binding industry in the last twenty years.

Another relatively recent development in the binding industry is its ability to provide services to the general public at affordable prices. In addition to serving institutional customers, the thirty employees of Southern Library Bindery now proudly serve many individuals in Middle Tennessee and throughout the Mid South.

This business biography provided by
Southern Library Bindery Company.

Sovran Bank/Central South

Opened as One Commerce Place just as Nashville was entering the 1980s, this pair of triangular towers included a new hotel and headquarters for Commerce Union Bank. From here Sovan Bank now operates a regional hub with responsibility for banking interests in the Central South.

The Sovran Bank logo.

The story of Sovran Bank/Central South is the story of two financial partners: Nashville's Commerce Union Corporation and Norfolk-based Sovran Financial Corporation. Sharing customer-driven, quality-oriented business philosophies, the two corporations merged in 1987 to form one of the largest financial organizations in the Southeast. The combined organizations have 13,800 employees, more than 600 offices in 12 states and assets totaling $21 billion.

Both Sovran and Commerce Union have long histories. Sovran, which takes its name from an alternate spelling of sovereign, implying stability and leadership, was established in 1984 through the merger of the Virginia National Bank of Norfolk and the First & Merchants National Bank of Richmond.

Both of those Virginia banks were formed in the 1860s and enjoyed distinguished records of financial service. Both also grew tremendously following the mid 1950s, and their merger was the largest ever in Virginia.

Commerce Union was established in 1923 through the leadership of Edward Potter, Jr., who combined Nashville's Farmers and Merchants Bank with four other area banks, located in Springfield, Lawrenceburg, Sparta and Lebanon. The new bank grew steadily during its early years and came through the Great Depression stronger than ever.

In 1936 Potter introduced consumer credit by creating an automobile loan department, and the following year the bank became a member of the Federal Reserve System. In 1940 Commerce Union added a municipal bond department, which it retained until 1948, and during World War II, the bank kept books for the government's rationing system and cooperated with United States Army officials by filling payrolls for soldiers on maneuvers in Middle Tennessee.

During the postwar years Commerce Union continued to expand, and by 1956 it was the largest state bank in Tennessee. In 1961 Potter, who was then both chairman of the board and president, gave up the latter position, and William F. Earthman, Jr., was elected to succeed him.

In 1972, just four years after Potter's death, Commerce Union organized and became the lead bank of Tennessee Valley Bancorp, a holding company made up of fifteen affiliated banks and related institutions, plus twenty-eight branch banks.

At the same time that Commerce Union was growing in Tennessee, the parent banks of Sovran Financial Corporation were growing in Virginia. Eventually the same forces that brought them together led Sovran to merge with other southeastern banks and then with Commerce Union. Sovran chairman C. A. Cutchins III and Commerce Union chairman Denny Bottoroff forged the new partnership with a determination to continue building customer relationships and providing superior service in their respective dynamic markets.

Today James A. Rainey is chairman and Owen G. Shell is president and chief executive officer of Sovran Financial Corporation/Central South, which operates as a regional hub for Sovran west of the Appalachians. As the lead bank in the hub, Sovran Bank/Central South carries on the service traditions that Middle Tennesseans have always associated with Commerce Union.

This business biography provided by Sovran Bank/Central South.

The United Methodist Publishing House

In the early 1900s Southern Methodist Publishing House employees used trucks such as this one to transport Methodist publications.

This building, which stood near the northeast corner of Nashville's old Public Square, housed the Southern Methodist Publishing House from 1854 to 1872.

The origins of today's United Methodist Publishing House can be traced back to 1789, when Methodist preacher John Dickins was named Book Steward of the Methodist Book Concern in Philadelphia to publish religious material. During its first three decades the Book Concern was a relatively modest operation that had its publications printed on a contractual basis. Matters changed greatly after 1820, though, when Nathan Bangs took charge of the Book Concern. Under his leadership, it became a genuine publishing house, with a bindery, print shop, and increased range and scope of publications.

Bangs launched periodicals and newspapers, the most important of which was the *Christian Advocate*. This paper became so popular that regional editions were published. One was produced in Nashville in the 1830s, and it established a foothold for Methodist publishing in the city.

During the 1850s and afterwards, Nashville emerged as a major center of Methodist publishing. In 1844 the Methodist Episcopal Church (MEC) split over the issue of slavery, and after a lengthy legal battle, the U.S. Supreme Court awarded ownership of the church's southern operations, including the Nashville depository, to the southern branch. In the aftermath of this court decision, the Southern Methodist Publishing House was established in Nashville in 1854 to publish and distribute materials for the MEC, South. It was one of the first major publishing firms established in the South and it helped make Nashville a major center for religious publishing.

In 1939, after years of discussion, the three branches of American Methodism joined to form the Methodist Church. Because of the superior financial and organizational position of the southern publishing operations, the three groups decided to combine all publishing operations with those in Nashville. In 1968 the Methodist Church merged with the Evangelical United Brethren Church to become the United Methodist Church, and the publishing arm became known as The United Methodist Publishing House.

Today The United Methodist Publishing House, headquartered in Nashville, is that church's largest agency, with 1,400 employees working in 37 cities in 24 states. Under the direction and control of the church's General Board of Publication, the Publishing House is self-supporting and responsible for publishing, printing, and distributing materials for the United Methodist Church.

The Publishing House operates Abingdon Press, which publishes a wide range of books and multimedia resources; Graded Press, which publishes official Sunday School materials; Parthenon Press, which handles printing and manufacturing; and Cokesbury Bookstores, which includes 51 retail outlets and two mail-order centers in 24 states. Publishing House operations gross approximately $81 million annually and help support the ministerial pension funds of 73 annual conferences.

This business biography provided by United Methodist Publishing House.

WKDA and WKDF Radio

WKDA and WKDF Radio have been owned by the Dick Broadcasting Company of Nashville since 1976, and although they are now jointly owned and managed, they have quite different histories.

WKDA was founded in 1946 by Alvin Beaman, local automobile dealer and soft drink manufacturer, and Tom Baker, who managed it from penthouse studios in the old First American Bank Building at Fourth and Union. Programmed in a block format, it featured a mix of live music, news and heavy emphasis on sports, including play-by-play of the Nashville Vols baseball team.

Beginning in 1956 with the spread of the rock-and-roll craze and continuing until the early 1970s, the station was programmed Top 40. The station was sold three times in the late 1950s and early 1960s, eventually winding up under the ownership of Chatham, Inc., of Chicago in 1963. That same year the studios were moved to the twelfth floor of the Stahlman Building at 211 Union Street.

Throughout most of this period, from 1946 until

WKDA reception area at its former location on the twelfth floor of the Stahlman Building.

Radio KDF's reception area at its current headquarters at 506 Second Avenue South.

the late 1960s, WKDA dominated the Nashville market. Eventually, intense competition caused its ratings to fall, and the station switched to a country music format for the 1970s. The 1980s began for WKDA with a return to rock-and-roll, first progressive rock, and then finally, in 1984, to its current format of Golden Oldies, playing the same music that had made it so popular in its heyday.

WKDF, originally known as WNFO-FM, was started by the Hickory Broadcasting Company in 1962 and went on the air from studios in the 1808 West End Building. It featured diverse programming that in-

cluded MOR "Album Tracking," country, religious, and Hawaiian music. In 1964 Chatham, Inc., bought the station, dropped the Hawaiian music, and offered more sports programming, including Father Ryan High School football and the Dixie Flyers hockey.

In 1966 the call letters were changed to WKDA-FM and the studios were moved to the Stahlman Building, completing the merger with its new sister station. In late 1968, as WKDA-AM was losing its dominance in rock-and-roll, WKDA-FM began a gradual but important programming change by playing increasing amounts of heavy metal or underground rock music. The station went full-time underground in March 1970, then moved into a progressive rock format in August 1971. In 1972 the station increased its power to 100,000 watts, and in 1975 began programming with its current format, Album Oriented Rock. Shortly after Dick Broadcasting Company acquired the stations in 1976, the call letters were changed from WKDA-FM to WKDF, and in 1978 the studios for both stations were moved to their current location at 506 Second Avenue South.

Once again locally owned, both stations have earned recognition for their community involvement, especially for supporting agencies such as the United Way and promoting special fundraising events. Carl P. Mayfield, the morning air personality, has attracted considerable attention for his summer concerts, which have raised over $200,000 for local charities and for his Christmas fundraisers that provide gifts for needy children.

This buisness biography provided by WKDA and WKDF.

Acknowledgments

In gathering material for this book we received invaluable assistance and encouragement from many individuals, both in Nashville and elsewhere. We are especially grateful to Mary Glenn Hearne, Leonard Tidwell, and Elsie Kolar of the Nashville Room, Public Library of Metropolitan Nashville-Davidson County; Marilyn Bell, Kathy Joyner, and Lesley Pritikan of the Tennessee State Library and Archives; Danny R. Hatcher and Robert K. Oermann of the Country Music Foundation; Sandra Roberts, Jimmy Ellis, and Joe Rudis of *The Tennessean*; Ann Vines Reynolds of the Historical Commission of Metropolitan Nashville-Davidson County; Odelle Thomas of the Nashville Area Chamber of Commerce; Kay Beasley of the Vanderbilt University Photographic Archive; Nancy Malan of the National Archives and Records Service; ALicia D. Stamm of the Historic American Buildings Survey; and Monroe H. Fabian of the National Portrait Gallery.

We are also indebted to George Carpenter of the Nashville Symphony Association; Johnny DeGeorge of the Nashville Association of Musicians; Peter La Paglia of the Tennessee State Museum; Wesley M. Paine of Fort Nashborough; William G. Hiles and Sue Ann Cunningham of George Peabody College; Beth M. Howse of the Fisk University Library; Millie McGehee of The Ladies Hermitage Association; Marice Wolfe of Vanderbilt University Library Special Collections; Mack Wayne Craig of the Association for the Preservation of Tennessee Antiquities; Frederick Strobel of Seigenthaler Associates;

Joe Zinn and Ed Temple of Tennessee State University; Cliff Sargent of Watkins Institute; Fred C. Sternenberg and Gwinn Jolley of AVCO Aerostructures Division; Fred Harvey of Harveys Department Stores; Marlene Thomas of Nashville Gas Company; David Ward of Henderson, Kelly, and Ward, Inc.; Larry Brinton and Jack Gunter of the *Nashville Banner*; John Van Mol of National Life and Accident Insurance Company; Carl Magnone of RCA Records; Bart Walker of WAMB Radio; Leah Hall and Patricia Hogan of the American Association for State and Local history; and the following persons who provided photographs from personal or family collections: Deborah Cooney, Catherine T. Avery, Mildred Stahlman, Don L. Goad, Richard Weesner, Paul Schumann, Joe B. Sills, Polly Wiley, and Andy Corn.

We wish in addition to thank Gerald George, Patricia A. Hall and James B. Gardner, who read portions of the manuscript and provided helpful suggestions for its improvement; Gayle Adams, who typed and helped edit the final draft; and Donna Reiss Friedman, who served cheerfully as copy editor.

For assistance with the revised edition, we are grateful to Laura Rehnert of the Nashville Room, Public Library of Metropolitan Nashville-Davidson County, and to Steve Neighbors and Pamela Pendergrass of Historic Nashville Incorporated.

George Rollie Adams
Ralph Jerry Christian

Selected Bibliography

Art Album of the Tennessee Centennial and International Exposition. Nashville: Marshall and Bruce Company, Publishers, 1898.

Art Work of Nashville, Tennessee. Chicago: W. H. Parish Publishing Company, 1894.

Broadcast News, 1 (November 12, 1932). Special issue on WSM, 1925-32.

Brumbaugh, Thomas B., Strayhorn, Martha I., and Gore, Gary G. *Architecture of Middle Tennessee: The Historic American Buildings Survey.* Nashville: Vanderbilt University Press, 1974.

Bucy, Carole S. *Your Metropolitan Government: A Handbook about Nashville and Davidson County, Tennessee.* Nashville: League of Women Voters of Nashville, 1986.

Burran, James A. "The WPA in Nashville, 1935-1943." *Tennessee Historical Quarterly,* 34 (Fall 1975), 293-306.

Burt, Jesse C. *The Historic 'Tennessee Line': The Nashville and Chattanooga Railroad Company, 1845-1873.* Nashville: Jandeco Press, 1976.

_____. *Nashville: Its Life and Times.* Nashville: Tennessee Book Company, 1959.

_____, and Ferguson, Robert B. *Indians of the Southeast: Then and Now.* Nashville: Abingdon Press, 1973.

Carty, James W., Jr. *Nashville as a World Religious Center.* Nashville: Cullom and Cherton Company, 1958.

Centennial Album of Tennessee. Nashville: J. Prousnitzer and Company, 1896.

Clayton, W. W. *The History of Davidson County, Tennessee,* 1880. Reprint. Nashville: Charles Elder, 1971.

Conklin, Paul. *Gone with the Ivy: A Biography of Vanderbilt University.* Knoxville: University of Tennessee Press, 1985.

Connelly, John Lawrence. *North Nashville and Germantown: Yesterday and Today.* Nashville: The North High Association, 1982.

Connelly, Thomas L. *Army of the Heartland: The Army of Tennessee. 1861-1862.* Baton Rouge: Louisiana State University Press, 1967.

_____. *Autumn of Glory: The Army of Tennessee, 1862-1865.* Baton Rouge: Louisiana State University Press, 1971.

_____. "The Vanderbilt Agrarians: Time and Place in Southern Tradition." *Tennessee Historical Quarterly,* 22 (March 1963), 22-37.

Cooney, Deborah, ed. *Speaking of Union Station: An Oral History of a Nashville Landmark.* Nashville: Union Station Oral History Project, 1977.

Crabb, Alfred Leland. *Nashville: Personality of a City.* Indianapolis: The Bobbs-Merrill Company, 1960.

Creighton, Wilbur Foster. *Building of Nashville.* Nashville: Wilbur F. Creighton, Jr., 1969.

Crutchfield, James A. *Early Times in the Cumberland Valley From Its Beginnings to 1800.* Nashville: Williams Press, 1977.

_____, comp. *Footprints Across the Pages of Tennessee History.* Nashville: Williams Press, 1976.

_____. *Tennesseans at War: Volunteers and Patriots in Defense of Liberty.* Nashville: Rutledge Hill Press, 1987.

Dekle, Clayton B. "The Tennessee State Capitol." *Tennessee Historical Quarterly,* 25 (Fall 1966), 213-38.

Douglas, Byrd. *Steamboatin' on the Cumberland.* Nashville: Tennessee Book Company, 1961.

Doyle, Don H. *Nashville in the New South, 1880-1930.* Knoxville: University of Tennessee Press, 1985.

_____. *Nashville Since the 1920s.* Knoxville: University of Tennessee Press, 1985.

_____. "Saving Yesterday's City: Nashville's Waterfront." *Tennessee Historical Quarterly,* 35 (Winter 1976), 353-64.

Durham, Walter T. "Kasper Mansker: Cumberland Frontiersman." *Tennessee Historical Quarterly,* 30 (Summer, 1971), 154-77.

_____. *Nashville: The Occupied City, the First Seventeen Months, February 16, 1862-June 30, 1863.* Nashville: Tennessee His-

torical Society, 1985.

_____. *Reluctant Partners: Nashville and the Union, July 1, 1863-June 30, 1865.* Nashville: Tennessee Historical Society, 1987.

Dykeman, Wilma. *Tennessee: A Bicentennial History.* New York: W. W. Norton and Company, 1975.

Egerton, John. *Nashville: The Faces of Two Centuries, 1780-1980.* Nashville: PlusMedia Incorporated, 1979.

Farringer, John L. "History of Nashville-Davidson County Hospitals." *Journal of the Tennessee Medical Association,* 67 (April 1974), 295-305.

The 400: American Society Journal of Travel, 7 (April 1897). Special Tennessee Centennial number.

Fox, David. "Nashville 1973-1983: The Decade That Was." *Nashville,* 11 (June 1983), 41-44, 80-81.

Frank, Fedora Small. *Beginnings on Market Street: Nashville and Her Jewry, 1861-1901.* Nashville: Jewish Community of Nashville and Middle Tennessee, 1976.

Gilmore, Rose L., ed. *Davidson County Women in the World War, 1914-1919.* Nashville: Foster and Parkes Company, 1923.

Goodstein, Anita S. "Leadership on the Nashville Frontier, 1780-1800." *Tennessee Historical Quarterly,* 35 (Summer 1976), 175-98.

Graham, Eleanor, ed. *Nashville: A Short History and Selected Buildings.* Nashville: Historical Commission of Metropolitan Nashville-Davidson County,Tennessee, 1974.

Harper's Weekly.

Harris, Pat. "Nashville's Mammouth Baptist Sunday School Board." *Nashville,* 6, (December 1978), 38-41, 90-91.

Hawkins, Brett W. *Nashville Metro: The Politics of City-County Consolidation.* Nashville: Vanderbilt University Press, 1966.

The Historic Hermitage Properties. Hermitage, Tennessee. The Ladies Hermitage Association, 1973.

Hoobler, James A. *Cities Under the Gun: Images of Occupied Nashville and Chattanooga.* Nashville: Rutledge Hill Press, 1986.

Horn, Stanley F. *The Decisive Battle of Nashville.* Baton Rouge: Louisiana State University Press, 1956.

Howell, Sarah McCanless. "The Editorials of Arthur S. Colyar, Nashville Prophet of the New South." *Tennessee Historical Quarterly,* 27 (Fall 1968). 262-77.

Jacobs, Dillard, comp. *Early Industrial Sites of Middle Tennessee: An Inventory.* Nashville: Nashville Section, American Society of Mechanical Engineers, 1978.

Johnson, Leland R. Engineers on the Twin Rivers: A History of the Nashville District, Corps of Engineers, United States Army. Nashville: U.S. Army Engineer District, 1978.

Kaser, David. "Nashville's Women of Pleasure in 1860." *Tennessee Historical Quarterly,* 23 (December 1964), 379-82.

Kelley, Sarah Foster. *West Nashville: Its People and Environs.* Nashville: Sarah F. Kelley, 1987.

Kirby, Kip. "The Battle of the Nashville Airwaves." *Nashville,* 6 (March 1979), 28-31, 128-30.

Kornell, Gary L. "Reconstruction in Nashville, 1867-69." *Tennessee Historical Quarterly,* 30 (Fall 1971), 277-87.

Lamon, Lester C. *Blacks in Tennessee, 1791-1970.* Knoxville: University of Tennessee Press, 1981.

Lequire, Louise, and Dunning, Natilee. "Swensson's Design for the Future." *Nashville,* 8 (April 1980), 39-41, 113-17.

Lewis, Thomas M. N., and Kneberg, Madeline. *Tribes That Slumber: Indians of the Tennessee Region.* Knoxville: University of Tennessee Press, 1958.

Lindsley, John Berrien. *Military Annals of Tennessee.* Nashville: J. M. Lindsley and Company, 1886.

Little, Vance. *Historic Brentwood.* Brentwood: J. M. Publications, 1985.

Lossing, Benson J. *The Pictorial Field Book of the Civil War in the United States of America.* Hartford: T. Belknap, circa 1874.

McBride, Robert M., ed. *More Landmarks of Tennessee History.* Nashville: Tennessee Historical Society and Tennessee Historical Commission, 1969.

———. "'Northern, Military, Corrupt, and Transitory,' Augustus E. Alden, Nashville's Carpetbagger Mayor." *Tennessee Historical Quarterly*, 37 (Spring 1978), 63-67.

McFerrin, John Berry. *Caldwell and Company: A Southern Financial Empire*. 1939. Reprint. Nashville: Vanderbilt University Press, 1969.

McGraw, Robert A. *The Vanderbilt Campus: A Pictorial History*. Nashville: Vanderbilt University Press, 1978.

McGee, Gentry R. *A History of Tennessee: From 1663 to 1900*. New York: American Book Company, 1899.

McRaven, Henry. *Nashville: "Athens of the South."* Chapel Hill, North Carolina: Scheer and Jarvis, 1949.

Maiden, Lewis Smith. *Highlights of the Nashville Theater*. New York: Vantage Press, 1979.

Malone, Bill T. *Country Music, U.S.A.: A Fifty-year History*. Austin: University of Texas Press for the American Folklore Society, 1968.

Millard, Bob. "The Nashville Network." *Nashville*, 10 (January 1983), 54-56.

Morrow, Sara Sprott. "Adolphus Heiman's Legacy to Nashville." *Tennessee Historical Quarterly*, 33 (Spring 1974), 3-21.

———. "A Brief History of Theater in Nashville, 1807-1970." *Tennessee Historical Quarterly*, 30 (Summer 1971), 178-89.

———. "The Church of the Holy Trinity; English Countryside Tranquility in Downtown Nashville." *Tennessee Historical Quarterly*, 32 (Winter 1975), 333-49.

Nashville. Nashville: Newspaper Printing Corporation, 1979.

Nashville Business Journal.

Nashville: A Family Town. A series of lectures presented at the Public Library of Metropolitan Nashville-Davidson County. Nashville: The Public Library of Metropolitan Nashville-Davidson County, 1978.

The Nashville Banner.

Nashville City Directories: Nashville: Various publishers. Issued annually.

Nashville in the 20th Century. Nashville: Chamber of Commerce, 1900-01.

Norman, Jack. *The Nashville I Knew*. Nashville: Rutledge Hill Press, 1984.

Parks, Robert Jones. "Grasping at the Coattails of Progress: City Planning in Nashville, Tennessee, 1932-1962." M. A. thesis. Vanderbilt University, 1971.

Parrish, Dolores, ed. *Nashville: Conserving a Heritage*. Nashville: Historical Commission of Metropolitan Nashville-Davidson County, 1977.

Plaisance, Aloysius F., and Schelver, Leo F. "Federal Military Hospitals in Nashville, May and June, 1863." *Tennessee Historical Quarterly*, 29, (Summer 1970), 166-75.

Powers, Ken. "The International Connection: Nashville Firms Find New Profits Abroad." *Advantage, the Nashville Business Magazine*, 2 (August 1979), 70-77, 80-83.

———. "Made in Nashville." *Advantage, the Nashville Business Magazine*, 2 (July 1979), 36-43, 62-67.

Rabinowitz, Howard N. *Race Relations in the Urban South, 1865-1890*. New York: Oxford University Press, 1978.

Raulston, J. Leonard, and Livingood, James W. *Sequatchie: A Story of the Southern Cumberlands*. Knoxville: University of Tennessee Press, 1974.

Remini, Robert V. *Andrew Jackson and the Course of American Empire, 1767-1821*. New York: Harper and Row, Publishers, 1977.

Reynolds, Ann Vines. "Nashville's Custom House." *Tennessee Historical Quarterly*, 37 (Fall 1978), 263-77.

Richardson, Joe M. "Fisk University: The First Critical Years." *Tennessee Historical Quarterly*, 29, (Spring 1970), 24-41.

Riley, Mark B. "Edgefield: A Study of an Early Nashville Suburb." *Tennessee Historical Quarterly*, 37 (Summer 1978), 133-54.

Rose, Miriam. "Minting Music." *Nashville*, 13 (June 1986), 32-35, 61.

Seven Early Churches of Nashville: A series of lectures presented at the Public Library of Metropolitan Nashville-Davidson County. Nashville: Elder's Bookstore, 1972.

Sherman, Joe. *A Thousand Voices: The Story of Nashville's Union Station*. Nashville: Rutledge Hill Press, 1987.

Stamper, Powell. *The National Life Story: A History of the National Life and Accident Insurance Company of Nashville, Tennessee*. New York: Appleton-Century-Crofts, 1968.

Stealey, John Edmund. "French Lick and the Cumberland Compact." *Tennessee Historical Quarterly*, 22 (December 1963), 322-34.

Stribling, Dees. "Discovering 'Midtown Nashville.'" *Advantage, the Nashville Business Magazine*, 9 (January 1986), 57-60.

———. "Nashville Braces for a Room Boom." *Advantage, the Nashville Business Magazine*, 9 (February 1986), 47-53, 60.

———. "The Nashville Housing Market: A Study in Evolution." *Advantage, the Nashville Business Magazine*, 9 (April 1986), 41-56.

———. "Roaring Ahead in the Airport Market." *Advantage, the Nashville Business Magazine*, 9 (July 1986), 82-84, 89-90.

———. "The Second South Side Office Boom." *Advantage, the Nashville Business Magazine*, 9 (March 1986), 94-96, 100, 102, 104.

Summerville, James. *Educating Black Doctors: A History of Meharry Medical College*. University, Alabama: University of Alabama Press, 1983.

Tennessee, Old and New: Sesquicentennial Edition, 1796-1946. Nashville: The Tennessee Historical Commission and the Tennessee Historical Society, 1946.

The Tennessean.

Thomas, Patrick. "Behind the Boards: The Business Side of the Music Industry." *Advantage, the Nashville Business Magazine*, 1 (October 1978), 53-64.

Thorton, Lee Ann. *Victorian Memories. . .A Study of Second Ave. N*. Nashville: Historic Nashville, Inc., 1977.

Tindall, George Brown. *The Emergence of the New South, 1913-1945*. Baton Rouge: Louisiana State University Press, 1967.

Tipton, C. Robert. "The Fisk Jubilee Singers." *Tennessee Historical Quarterly*, 29 (Spring 1970), 42-48.

Van Deusen, Glyndon G. The Jacksonian Era, 1828-1848. New York: Harper and Brothers, 1959.

Waller, William, ed. *Nashville, 1900-1901*. Nashville: Vanderbilt University Press, 1972.

———. ed. *Nashville in the 1890s*. Nashville: Vanderbilt University Press, 1970.

Ward, John W. *Andrew Jackson, Symbol for an Age*. New York: Oxford University Press, 1955.

Weaver, Blanche Henry Clark. "Shifting Residential Patterns of Nashville." *Tennessee Historical Quarterly*, 18 (March 1959), 20-34.

Wellford, Harry W. "Dr. Thomas Walker, His Celebrated Impact on Early Tennessee." *Tennessee Historical Quarterly*, 34 (Summer 1975), 130-44.

Wells, Ann Harwell. "Lafayette in Nashville, 1825." *Tennessee Historical Quarterly*, 34 (Spring 1975), 19-31.

Windrow, John E., ed. *Peabody and Alfred Leland Crabb: The Story of Peabody as Reflected in Selected Writings of Alfred Leland Crabb*. Nashville: Williams Press, 1977.

Wolfe, Charles K. *Tennessee Strings: The Story of Country Music in Tennessee*. Knoxville: University of Tennessee Press, 1977.

Wooldridge, John. *History of Nashville: Tennessee*. 1890. Reprint. Nashville: Charles Elder, 1970.

Woolverton, John F. "Philip Lindsley and the Cause of Education in the Old Southwest." *Tennessee Historical Quarterly*, 19 (March 1960), 3-22.

Zibart, Carl F. *Yesterday's Nashville*. Miami: E. A. Seemann Publishing, 1976.

Index